OPTICAL POETRY: The Life and Work of Oskar Fischinger

breaking into several parallel configurations. At the lecture, Diebold encouraged Oskar to shoot these graphs on to film so that the time element could be built in – and suggested that they would become abstract Visual Music, their own work of art, quite independent from the Shakespeare model that inspired them. Early in 1922, Oskar prepared another dynamics graph for an expressionist play by Fritz von Unruh, *Ein Geschlecht* [Generations]. Since the new play was not familiar, Oskar wrote in some of the text beneath the drawings, so we can follow more exactly the relationship between the text and images that Oskar posited.

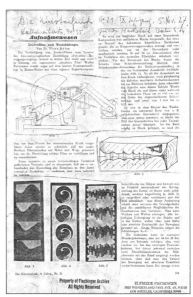

Wax Experiments newspaper article.

Oskar began working seriously on plans for creating an abstract film. He carefully avoided the possibility of a drawn or painted film, since Ruttmann was already doing that so well (his *Lichtspiel Opus 2* premièred in Frankfurt, January 1922). Oskar experimented at home with coloured liquids, trying different oils and chemical components that might co-exist in parallel swirls, that might be controlled into predictable configurations [a brief sample of this footage appears in Oskar's later *Wax Experiments* film]. These experiments took place in the family bathtub, and Oskar's older sister Maria, who kept house for the family, endured daily agony trying to erase the traces of Oskar's latest test. He also began experimenting with wax, clay and other maleable substances which might be manipulated in three-dimensional shapes. Maria fell afoul of these too, when, while cleaning, she inadvertently moved a tray of wax figures next to a window, where the sun melted them. While scraping away this melted mass of variegated wax, Oskar conceived the idea for an animation machine that would bring him his first artistic success.

The "Wax Machine" synchronized the blade of a guillotine cutting-machine (the kind used to make ultra-thin slices of ham or cheese in a deli), with the shutter of a movie-camera. Every time the machine made a slice, the camera would shoot one frame of the fresh surface exposed by the latest cut. The resulting film showed a time-lapse cross-section moving through the wax block which, according to whatever configurations had been modelled into the wax, might depict representational or abstract movements. Rudolf Schneider explained it thus in his article "Formspiel durch Kino" [*Frankfurter Zeitung*, 12 July 1926, reprinted in the Berlin trade paper *Film-Kurier* 15 July 1926]: If you began slicing away a hard-boiled egg starting at one end, you would see at first a white circle getting larger, then a yellow dot in its centre would begin to grow larger and larger until only a thin white line remained around the circumference of the large yellow circle, then the yellow circle would begin to shrink again, and the white circle to increase, until the yellow became a dot again and disappeared, leaving the pure white circle which in turn would grow smaller. Thus if the filmmaker wanted to design an

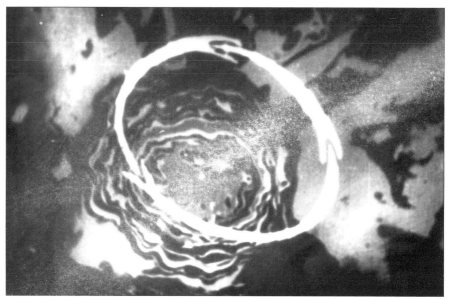

Above: *The Wax Slicing Machine.*

Right: *Image from* Wax Experiments *with triple ouroboros.*

interaction of two circles similar to this, he would mould an egg-like configuration into a block of wax, feed this block into the Wax Machine, and the finished film sequence would be shot in a few minutes – much quicker than rendering hundreds of sequential images on paper.

Fischinger wrote to Ruttmann at his Munich studio asking if he might be interested in purchasing or licensing such a Wax Machine for use in his abstract animation. Ruttmann invited Fischinger to come to discuss the matter with him, and Fischinger went to Munich (probably in June 1922) to go over the technical drawings. Ruttmann was encouraging, although he wanted certain improvements in Oskar's designs. Meanwhile, Oskar, still employed at Pokorny and Wittekind, had on his own time invented some other technical machinery which he was able to sell to a Dutch company for a considerable amount of money. When he received his Engineer's diploma in August 1922, he resigned from Pokorny and moved to Munich to begin his film career. He left behind at least one broken heart. Oskar kept a letter from an anonymous person, addressed to "Dear Ossie", lamenting how dull Frankfurt would be without Ossie's wit and charm and warmth, begging him to come back soon. But he would never return to Frankfurt.

In November 1922, Ruttmann paid Oskar for the license to commercially exploit the Wax Machine, and with this money Oskar started to construct the first sales model. During the three months it took him to construct the machine, Ruttmann moved to Berlin, where he was about to begin special-effects work on Lotte Reiniger's feature-length silhouette animation film, *Die Geschichte des Prinzen Achmed* [The Adventures of Prince Ahmed]. In February 1923, Oskar wrote to

Diebold in Frankfurt that at last the first Wax Machine was nearly ready, and he hoped it would live up to all their expectations. Oskar delivered the machine to Ruttmann in Berlin, and Ruttmann used it immediately to create the Sorcerer's magic conjuring of the flying horse in the opening sequence of *Prinz Achmed*. He had intended to use it much more widely in that film, but he reported to Oskar that it did not run as smoothly as he had expected – the slices would only be sharp and clean if the wax block remained very cold, and the hot film lights tended to heat it up before the shooting was done. Oskar insisted that if the proper mixture of wax and kaolin clay were used in the preparation of the block, melting or warping should not be a problem. Ruttmann insisted that the slices simply were not accurate enough for character animation, gave up using the machine, and asked Oskar to come to take it away.

Oskar and Karl at the animation stand, Munich.

Meanwhile, Oskar himself had considerable success in producing intricate, organic abstract imagery with the Machine. While no whole *Wax* film by Oskar survives with titles that guarantee its integrity, a beautiful sequence about 10 minutes in length shows the development of concentric layers of crescent undulations which suggest flowers opening and closing their petals in a slow, voluptuous rhythm of almost hypnotic intensity. Other portions use quick cutting between opposing directional movements, and some layered combination of wax imagery with drawn or cut-out animations – in one particular scene, three simple drawn lines turn into three snakes which bite each other's tails, like a triad of the alchemical ouroboros. Wax imagery also found its way into Oskar's silhouette animations and his multiple-projector performances in the later 1920s, so he himself may have cut apart earlier films to re-use the footage in later works.

In March 1924, Oskar signed a contract to produce representational movie cartoons for an American-born quick-sketch artist and entrepreneur, Louis Seel, who had been making cartoon shorts under the series title *Münchener Bilderbogen* [Munich Album, a famous "comic strip" of the 19th century] for several years. These sophisticated, satirical animated films poked fun at current fads and fashions – and about half of them were only approved for adult audiences. Oskar worked on six Seel films, including two *commedia dell'arte* love farces centred around Pierrette. Oskar's younger brother Karl came to Munich in 1924 and roomed with Oskar during this period; he remembered Oskar working on a short cartoon of the *Gulliver's Travels* type, with trick effects combining tiny people with a giant man.

Only one of Oskar's *Münchener Bilderbogen* films is known to survive, and that in a copy which Oskar cut apart in order to remove English-language titles [Seel maintained an office in New York for American distribution] in order to replace them with German-language

Above right: Pierrette's Room *with villain*.

Below right: *Oskar's villain from* Pierrette.

Below: Studie Nr. 8.

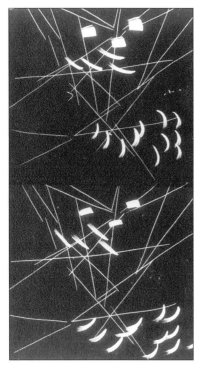

OPTICAL POETRY: The Life and Work of Oskar Fischinger

(or French or Italian) titles so that he could sell the film in Europe. Unfortunately, Oskar never made the replacement titles and he never reassembled the film sequences in their proper order, so the story line and sequence remains unclear (if, indeed, the footage is actually complete). This *Pierrette I* is obviously a farce in which, for some unknown reason, the heroine is persuaded by three suitors to allow her jewels to be stolen by a friend; however, an actual jewel thief coincidentally (?) visits the house at the appointed time and really steals the jewels. Pierrette is furious with her three suitors and throws them out ... Oskar's original scenario for *Pierrette I*, which exists on Louis Seel letterhead stationery, offers no clue to the final product, for Oskar planned a flowing, symbolic scene that could be shot with the Wax Machine and modelled wax figures, featuring characters that, for example, transform into a butterfly and a rose, and back to themselves. The existing film is partly rotoscoped [traced frame by frame from live-action footage], with elaborate backgrounds based on the expressionistic/art déco settings notorious from Wiene's popular live-action features *Cabinet of Dr. Caligari* and *Genuine*. Karl remembered that some dozen young women, art students, worked in the studio drawing and inking the images, and doing the rotoscope copying on machines that Oskar had built, using a sewing-machine treadle to advance the frame of live-action film that was being copied. A few touches in the film, especially a close-up of the villain-thief's grinning face, are in typical Oskar Fischinger graphic style.

Oskar worked with Seel until late 1926, when the company dissolved for financial reasons, largely due to the devastating effects of the inflation/depression, which sent women to the market with wheelbarrows full of money to buy a few vegetables or a loaf of bread. Simultaneously, Oskar had invented a type of motor that used natural gas as fuel, and became involved with a business partner, Güttler, who not only lost his own personal fortune but also charged substantial debts to Oskar – which plagued him with lawsuits and collection agents all during 1926 and 1927.

Despite these distractions and difficulties, Oskar managed to make the years 1925–1927 among his most adventurous and artistically successful for his own abstract filmmaking. He continued to experiment with different technical means for producing imagery, including cutouts, drawings, rotating moiré patterns, and layering combinations of images through optical superimpositions – the short film *Spirals*, for example, contains most of these techniques.

The Hungarian composer Alexander Laszlo had been fascinated with the possibility of extending his own compositions into the realm of visual music, and wrote in 1924 (published 1925) a theoretical text on *Farblichtmusik* [Colour-Light-Music], including his plans for a colour organ which would project colours as he played his piano compositions.

Title card from Fieber multiple projection show.

Laszlo's first attempts at colour-light concerts used painted abstract slides and moving coloured spotlights for visuals, but critics found them unsatisfactory, not as fluid as the music. Laszlo then contracted Oskar to prepare about 20 minutes of film material that could be integrated, along with the painted slides, into the amorphous coloured stage lights during his concerts. Laszlo toured Germany in 1926 giving Farblichtmusik concerts, but now the reviews tended to criticize the quality of his old-fashioned romantic music compared to the modern filmic effects, so he withdrew Fischinger's film component from his performances. Fischinger, however, prepared his own multiple-projection shows (including some of the imagery from the Laszlo shows) with three side-by-side images cast with three 35mm projectors, slides to frame the triptych, and at climactic moments, two additional projectors which overlapped the basic triptych with further colour effects. As Ruttmann had, Oskar used all three systems for colourizing (tinting, toning and hand-colouring) to give a wider variety of colours. Several journalists report seeing these shows in Oskar's studio, and in a letter Oskar says Erich Korngold was composing a musical score for *Fieber I, II, III* [Fever]. Another show, *Vakuum*, was accompanied by a percussion ensemble. Letters also mention the likelihood of a theatrical show in Berlin, and Laszlo remembered seeing a public performance in Munich accompanied by a percussion group which, Laszlo said scornfully, were hardly making music but rather trying to create enough ruckus to drown out the roaring and klunking from seven projectors.

One of these multiple-projector pieces has survived, with the title *R-1, ein Formspiel* [R-1, a Form-play], which may be the final version, since Rudolf Schneider, while praising *Fieber* in his article "Der 'Zeitkörper' im Film" [Bodies in Time] (*Nürnberger Zeitung*, 13 October 1926) suggests that "Formspiel" was a better term for Oskar's new type of artwork rather than Laszlo's "Farblichtmusik" or Oskar's own "Raumlichtkunst" [Space-light-art]. The "R" might, in fact, refer to "Raumlichtkunst", if not "regenbogen" [rainbow] referring to the elaborate colouring, or simply "Rolle" [reel].

R-1 constitutes one of Oskar's most brilliant achievements. Its primary imagery consists of serial re-arrangements of an alignment of "Stäbe" [staffs], a row of closely-parallel vertical bars, each of which can move up or down freely, thus creating patterns of motion across the screen – undulating waves, diagonal inclines, solos for individual staffs with their own eccentric rhythm, etc. Oskar's use of the word "Stäbe" suggests that each bar was actually a wooden lath mounted in a frame beneath the animation camera, so that Oskar could literally pull and push them up and down while shooting. In many places, the staffs are superimposed in multiples, which suggests animated organ pipes – perhaps a reminiscence of Oskar's early apprenticeship.

R-1 is elaborately edited, with some cuts only a few frames long, and a great deal of exciting alternation for energy. The two side panels, which are mirror images of each other, develop from the thin staff into clusters which form wide solid blocks that move almost like the square models in Oskar's later *Composition in Blue*, as if stairs with counter-movements were passing over them. The centre panel integrates the initial staffs with flashes of cosmic images – planets, spiral galaxies, explosions, atomic structures – that parallel abstract geometric versions

Above left: Dream *drawing: Snail graves.*

Above right: Dream *drawing: Factory tower.*

Left: Dream *drawing: glowing eyed man and the owl.*

Introduction: Gelnhausen, Frankfurt and Munich

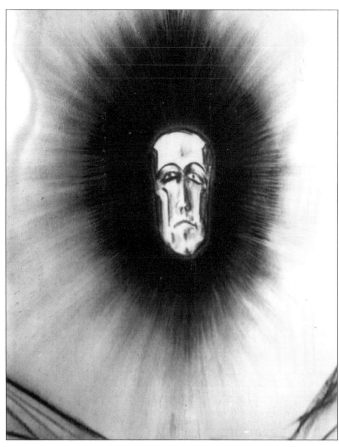

of themselves: circles, spirals, etc. Then increasingly organic forms establish analogies as well: the same stirrup-shaped crescent in flowing liquid currents [Stromlinien], in sliced wax imagery and in charcoal-drawn animation. As a finale, all of the staffs become coloured, with the two extra projectors making them even more variegated. In 1933, when Oskar first worked with the new GasparColor film, he experimented by trying to superimpose the actual tinted film-strips of these *R-1* staffs on to the three-colour separation composite. The effect is quite dazzling, and probably more precise and saturated than the 1927 original.

The *R-1* reels continued to be shown as silent single-projector films during the early 1930s at theatres such as Amsterdam's Uitkijk and Berlin's Kamera Unter den Linden, as well as accompanying lectures by Moholy Nagy (at the Bauhaus, etc.), Ruttmann, and Dr. Leonhard Fürst (at the Florence May Festival).

In his written scenarios for *R-1* and *R-2*, Oskar describes them with pantheistic terms, as if the universe were alive, and sun, wind and water were actors in his films – even though it is clear that he is assigning emotions to his abstract

Above:
Dream *drawing: the face.*

Right: *Untitled* Dream *drawing.*

OPTICAL POETRY: *The Life and Work of Oskar Fischinger*

Dream *drawing: rabbit moon.*

Dream *drawing: pornographic sunset.*

forms: "A gentler tremor of excitement begins to run through the points ... until single staffs break loose wildly. The tempo rises furiously in a steep ascent and attains such wild strength that it takes your breath away. Now the violent storm rages in all its power and beauty ..." (Munich, 29 March 1927). In one letter he uses the Sanskrit term "Atman" parallel to the German word "Atem" [breath], indicating that he was familiar with Hindu mysticism, so the "cosmic" analogies in the *R-1* film were not accidental. It is possible, by the way, that Ruttmann introduced Oskar to Asian mysticism, since in 1923 and 1924, just when Oskar was trying to sell his wax machine to Ruttmann, Ruttmann was making special effects for a Paul Wegener feature *Lebende Buddhas* [Living Buddhas] about the esoteric practices of Tibetan lamas.

Among Oskar's most fascinating personal documents from this Munich period are materials relating to a set of three dreams from 20, 22 and 23 October 1926. Oskar typed a narrative for each dream, and also made some dozen charcoal sketches to illustrate them – which, fortunately, he photographed on to glass-plate negatives, so they have survived. The first of the dreams, "Schneckengräber" [Snail Graves] begins with the image of a snail weeping beside a grave in the snail cemetery, and progresses through war recruiting, a hospital, a storage room where Oskar's cousin Wilhelm Michel works, to a factory where Oskar holds up a twig that turns into a snake that joins its head and tail (recalling the ouroboros of the *Wax Experiments*). The second dream concerns a sad encounter with Alexander Laszlo, and the third travels from a library (where Oskar must work finding books) to the railroad yards where he drops his camera on the tracks from a bridge and must try to rescue it before a train comes. Some of the dream drawings do not correspond to specific incidents in these three dreams, so perhaps other written manuscripts were lost, or other dreams were merely illustrated and not described verbally. In any case, the sketches – a conversation between a glowing-eyed man and a cat and an owl, a factory tower that becomes an erect serpent, a monster peering up over an urban landscape, a gaunt dour face hanging above the horizon in a dark aureole, a landscape with a sunrise and clouds forming the body of a woman in an erotic pose – have a dynamic vigour that make one regret that Oskar did not make more representational, surrealistic films.

One of his masterpieces from the Munich period is in fact a silhouette animation film with nightmarish atmosphere and transformations, *Seelische Konstruktionen* [Spiritual Constructions]. Lotte Reiniger's silhouette feature *Prince Ahmed* screened in May 1926 to rave reviews. This film that Ruttmann worked on (using Oskar's Wax Machine) must have inspired Oskar to make his own silhouette animation. He obviously made numerous tests to find the right technique. A photo of Oskar in his Munich studio shows pinned to the wall behind him a finished charcoal drawing of a bearded man's head which appears in *Spiritual Constructions* filmed in single frames as the image was being drawn. Several short pieces survive in other techniques – *Irene Tanzt* [Irene Dances] is made with traditional cut paper, *Die Boxer* [the Boxers] from three-dimensional modelled clay figures (including, coincidentally two waterboys that prefigure Mickey Mouse and Donald Duck). In his article "Bei Fischinger in München" (*Film-Kurier*, 15 January 1927), Walter Jerven mentions seeing another silhouette film (now apparently lost) entitled *Der Vortrag* [The Lecture], in which, before the astonished eyes of the audience, the speaker transforms into whatever he is talking about.

Seelische Konstruktionen builds a simple situation – two men get drunk in a bar, fight, and stumble home to bed – into an epic of expressionistic metamorphosis: when one man kicks, his leg becomes longer and thicker, when he is choked he shrinks to a thin line and wilts. During the voyage home, both men hallucinate obstacles that become vivid antagonists. Oskar employed "shock tactics" to emphasize this disorientation of the men: one or two frames of a different scene interrupt the flow sometimes; when someone sits down or touches a door to open it Oskar scratched directly on to the film little lines like an explosion from the point of contact; several times the background changes suddenly while the action continues smoothly.

In order to accomplish these many smooth transformations and deformations, Oskar needed a technique more supple than cut paper. He made a flat layer of clay [possibly the same wax/clay mixture used

Noah's Ark *special effect*.

Noah's Ark *animals special effect*.

for the wax slicing] across the surface of a glass plate beneath the animation camera; the clay was just thick enough to be opaque, so Oskar could model the figures and then alter them by cutting away, adding on or manipulating the shape while shooting. Backgrounds could be sup-

OPTICAL POETRY: *The Life and Work of Oskar Fischinger*

plied by paper graphics lying on a lower level beneath the clay glass, or, since the silhouettes made very dense images on the film, by superimposing another filmed image which would simply be blacked out wherever the silhouettes were. [One test fragment superimposes silhouette drunkards over a live-action shot of Nymphenburg Palace, which was not far from Oskar's studio at Neustätterstrasse 4. in Munich]. In a few scenes, at the height of the drunken men's confusion, Oskar used some of his sliced wax patterns as a moving background that suggests the kind of viscous vagueness of severe drunkenness.

In addition to this spectacular surreal film, Fischinger also used his silhouette technique to make special effects of scenes of Noah's Ark for a feature, *Sintflut*, released in 1927. He modelled out of kaolin two gigantic idols gloating over the tiny Earth, and a surviving still photo shows what excellent representational skills Oskar commanded. Another still shows the animals entering the Ark, all silhouettes, in a stylized pattern: the Ark in a circle in the centre with six pathways leading toward it, two upper diagonals for birds, two horizontal for land animals, and two lower diagonals for tortoises, lobsters, snakes and such. Apparently the feature was not a success [perhaps another casualty of the hideous inflation], and Oskar was not paid fully for his work.

During his last year in Munich, Oskar fell into such financial difficulty that he borrowed money from both the Fischingers and Michels back in Gelnhausen. He also borrowed money from his landlady, Emmy Scharf, as well as falling behind on the rent. Emmy Scharf was much older than Oskar but fancied him, and offered to cancel his debt to her if he would marry her. Oskar did not relish that idea. In desperation, hounded by bill collectors – most of them for his former business partner Güttler – Oskar resolved to sneak out of Munich and quietly resettle in Berlin. On 1 June 1927, Oskar took a back-pack with a few

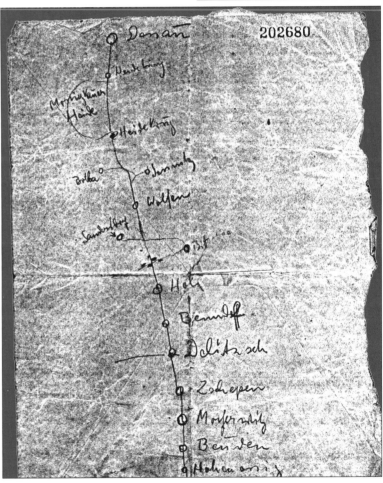

Above: *Emmy Scharf.*

Right: *Map of walking from Munich to Berlin.*

crucial film prints and his camera, and set out walking some 350 miles to Berlin.

Hoping no one would catch up with him, or find out where he went, Oskar took mostly country roads through fields, pastures, little villages with unpaved streets and one inn "Zur Post" [where the post carriage stops]. Oskar shot single frames of the things he saw, and the resulting film, *München-Berlin Wanderung* [Walking from Munich to Berlin], compresses three-and-a-half weeks into three-and-a-half minutes. The film demonstrates a sharp contrast between the almost mystical serenity of nature (clouds surging over a sunset, leaves of grass on a horizon line caressing the sky) with the giddy transitoriness of human activity (hops pickers scurrying over their vines, the flow of the sheep herd, the furious paddling of boatmen on a placid river). Between these two equivocate human tokens longing for immortality: a roadside cross, a couple in elaborate elegant peasant costume who calmly stand quite changeless, and various men, women and children who pose for a portrait then also squirm with shyness, boasting or mischief. In a written note about the film, Oskar says: "I saw many beautiful landscapes, met friendly people, farmers and workers, and here and there Gypsies. I got along well with all of them, and we had good conversations. There is a lot less difference between people than is commonly supposed. I must say that people are the same everywhere. There are some differences, of course, but these stem primarily from character and temperament, and those same variations occur everywhere."

1

Berlin

irst thing when he arrived in Berlin, Oskar borrowed 1,000 marks from his Uncle Albert Fischinger in Gelnhausen, so that he could build an animation stand, buy a projector and other equipment necessary to continue filmmaking. At first he rented studio space at Friedrichstrasse 15, until he found in March 1929 a six-room space in which he could both live and use his animation equipment, at Friedrichstrasse 238, Aufgang D, IV. Stock, [D block, 4th floor] where he would keep his studio until he left Berlin in 1936. Friedrichstrasse had been the centre of the German film industry since Oskar Meester built his studio there in 1900. By the 1920s, it was a highly-competitive honeycomb of offices and studios, lining the old tenement buildings over a dozen blocks with agents, distributors, small labs, screening rooms, and the whole range of technicians (carpenters, electricians, seamstresses, designers, title craftsmen, etc.) who derived a good deal of their income from film-related jobs. It was also a centre for prostitution, especially the boy hustlers who walked from the Passage at Unter den Linden down to the Adonis Lounge near the Hallesches Tor, as so vividly recounted in John Mackay's 1926 novel *Der Pupenjunge* [Little Farts] and Curt Morek's 1930 *Führer durch das lasterhafte Berlin* [Guidebook to the Vice-zones of Berlin]. Unemployed actors, musicians and technicians roamed the street beside cocaine dealers, beggars, prostitutes and thieves.

For some time Oskar kept his typewriter, rewinds and other equipment attached to chains and ropes so that as a bailiff climbed the four floors to attach his possessions, he could lower his work tools out the window to avoid having them impounded. But Oskar did have better luck in Berlin. Within a few months he was making special effects for UFA films, including a dragonfly sequence for the documentary "Kulturfilm" *Schöpferin Natur* [Mother Nature, The Creator] (which opened in December 1927), and some battle effects for *Der Weltkrieg. 2.Teil*

Berlin studio.

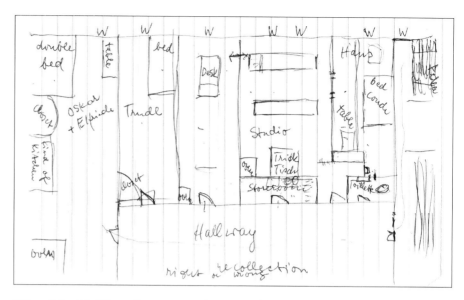

[The World War, Part 2], a feature documentary which opened in February 1928. He also made for an SPD (Socialist) party film *Dein Schickslal* [Your Destiny] directed by Ernö Metzner (released March 1928) a number of sequences, including a satirical scene in which the heads of various Russian and German political figures (Trotsky and Sinowjew, Ruth Fischer and Scholem) ride around on two rival merry-go-rounds proclaiming "We lead you!" as they revolve; then, when the Communist leaders enter their office building, the sign instructs them to check in their heads along with their hats at the garderobe, and subsequently a headless Communist is seen leading blindfolded followers "like the Breughel painting". Oskar's effects for a September 1928 feature *Der Unüberwindliche* [The Invincible] involve a hero and heroine named Silvio and Spaventa, so possibly it was a *commedia dell'arte* episode like *Pierrette*. He also worked on a project about building a tunnel from Europe to America, and did several other commercial jobs, including an ad for Dr. Spieker's yoghurt.

At the same time, he tirelessly sent out letters to producers and distributors trying to sell a series of silhouette comedies, seemingly without any luck. A few of the proposed scenarios clearly refer to the film we have as *Seelische Konstruktionen*, with the "torklender Mensch" [staggering person] in an unstable environment. Others propose extensions of *Die Boxer* and *Irene Tanzt* into full 7-minute cartoons – indeed, he may have sent around those test pieces as samples of his new, fluid silhouette technique.

A number of the scenarios describe elaborate new ideas: a January 1928 treatment, *Die Marsmenchen*, [Mars Men] proposes that two creatures from Mars (who can shift their shape at will and are lighter

than water so that they can walk over the surface of ponds) come to explore Earth, visit the African jungle and the Orient, are captured by sailors and sold as monkeys, etc. A second, longer treatment extends this idea into a serial: Raidon has been banished from Mars because he advocated social reforms, and flees to Earth where he also attempts to fight against human greed, deceit and fraud, eventually mobilizing the forces of Good to take over Earth, but later he is overthrown by a revolution of Evil people, and flees back to Mars. This epic moral fable, somewhere between Milton's *Paradise Lost* and *Superman*, had a personal meaning for Oskar, who originally dreamed of this name as his own in a hazy context that seemed to imply that Oskar/Raidon in fact came from another planet. In July 1929, Oskar filmed a series of charcoal drawings as he made them, taking a single frame each time he added a detail – and signed each one "O.F. Raidon". The most spectacular of these half-minute films shows a man whose brain projects out through his eyes a complete range of modern technology: autos, airplanes, boats, typewriters, sextants, etc., etc. Oskar entitled it "Der Unternehmer aus Verstandeskraft" [He who Accomplishes through Mental Power"]. Was this Raidon?

Although no one seems to have bought any of Oskar's many proposals, he continued to send out new scenarios for sound cartoons throughout 1929, including a *Kasperle und Mutzl der gestiefelte Kater* (Little Kasper and Mutzl Puss-in-Boots, who is actually the bewitched Professor Katzengold). In August 1929, *Irene Tanzt* becomes *Der*

Stepptänzer [The Tap-Dancer], tightly synchronized to music, who, as he dances, gradually loses one arm, then the other, then one leg, then the second leg, and finally his head – but all the parts continue to dance on their own! And in July 1929, Oskar wrote to the noted humourist Joachim Ringelnatz asking him to write a spoken commentary which would be used as a soundtrack for *Seelische Konstruktionen*[Spiritual Constructions], but Ringelnatz wanted a cash advance, which Oskar could not afford. Despite remaining silent, however, *Spiritual Constructions* continued to be screened, like *R-1*, at the circuit of film societies (League of Independent Film) in "art house" theatres around Europe which regularly showed Oskar's and other avant-garde films. In September 1932, for example, Oskar wrote for the return of a *Seelische Konstruktionen* print from Holland, as it was needed for a screening in Munich, which would present several of his silent films. The Dutch reported that Oskar's silhouette film was a favourite with their audiences – and a fragment of the opening sequence still survives in the Netherlands Film Museum.

Despite this flurry of activity, however, Oskar still had a hard time financially in Berlin at first. He contracted with the firm of Ludwig Brager to finance the production of silhouette films, but after a few months, when no commercial return was forthcoming, on 1 December 1927 Oskar ended up repaying Brager his investment, nearly 1,000 marks, as well as 200 marks that Brager would have owed to Oskar's cousin Wilhelm Michel. All of this aside from the repayment of Munich debts in order to regain equipment and films from his former landlady! [In fact, Oskar was never successful in regaining such items as the wax-slicing machine, which presumably perished in Munich ...].

Oskar first managed to get on an even financial basis when he was hired in July 1928 by UFA studios to work full-time producing special effects for Fritz Lang's science-fiction feature *Frau im Mond* [Woman in the Moon]. Oskar worked at UFA until June 1929, when he accidentally broke his ankle at the studios, and was hospitalized for a month. A year's steady wages, 500 marks per month, finally stabilized Oskar's finances somewhat.

Lang wished to make the launching of a rocket ship to the moon as scientifically accurate as possible, so he hired as advisors Prof. Hermann Oberth and Prof. Willy Ley, both of whom were engaged in rocket research and testing (and both of whom would continue until actual rockets were launched over a decade later, Oberth in Germany and Ley in exile in the US). Oskar was assigned to work with them, and following their advice, he prepared the launch of the rocket (using a blow-torch inside a model rocket to create the exhaust), starscapes, and visualizations of the Moon from an approaching rocketship as well as the distant Earth, seen from the Moon's surface, slowly rising over the moon's horizon – and Oskar's image looks uncannily like one of the famous NASA photos from the actual 1969 Moon landing! In addition to these special scientific shots, Oskar also made the skywriting of the word "start" just before the rocket launch, the weightless champagne bubbles during flight, and the word "Gold" echoing across the caverns of the Moon when the mad professor (quite unscientifically) discovers that precious metal in abundance.

Oskar may, in his year's employ, have done other special effects, but it is hard to tell exactly which. The Russian cameraman Konstantin Tschetwerikoff also worked on the effects crew, specializing in models, including the vast rocket installation as seen from above by the skywriting pilot, and the main launch pad with its pools of water to absorb the heat of the blast-off. There are a number of other clever tricks, such as the weightless cabin boy suspended in mid-air [a dozen years later Tschetwerikoff would create similar floating effects for the man-in-the-moon and Hans Albers riding a cannonball in *Münchhausen*]. *Frau* was only Tschetwerikoff's fourth film, but the previous three included *Metropolis* and *Der Weltkrieg. 2.Teil* [The World War, Part 2], so he may well have collaborated with Oskar before. Lang wasted days of time, according to Oskar, lavishing attention on a scene like the weightlessness of the cage with the test mouse in it, so it is also difficult to judge now how long it might have taken to shoot a given effect to Lang's satisfaction.

Frau im Mond came in well over budget, and met a cool reception. While the "science" part seems astonishing, the "fiction" script by Lang's wife Thea von Harbou is idiotically banal and absolutely contrary to all scientific principles: the tepid love triangle and the stereotype mad professor wander around the Moon's surface without any protective suit or breathing gear, and find plentiful gold in an area of volcanic hot-springs and water-drip caverns. This aesthetic schizophrenia is mirrored by the sound problem: after more than a year of shooting, by the time the film was released October 1929, talking sound films were the new sensation, and Lang's faux-modernistic epic must have seemed old-fashioned to audiences who had seen Walther Ruttmann's brilliant *Melodie der Welt* [Melody of the World], an intricate, dynamic, fast-paced feature-length documentary that juxtaposes similar cultural habits from countries around the world, with a superb orchestral score by Wolfgang Zeller and many synchronized sound effects – or the jazzy American musicals for that matter.

While working for UFA, Oskar had a little love affair with Elfriede Benitz, who was also working at the studio. Her husband, the famous cinematographer Albert Benitz, was then shooting on location for an extended period (he shot many mountain adventure films) at that time. This was only one of many dalliances for Oskar. Although bald by this time, he exercised and kept in good shape, and was quite charming and seductive in personality. Dr. Diebold, Oskar's mentor in other, artistic matters, also introduced him to the joys of a "cruising" game – following girls down the street, wagering from their behinds what their fronts looked like. Diebold, indeed, was most attracted to shapely buttocks, and Oskar described one of his own girlfriends, Martha, as having a divine rump like a Belgian packhorse. Martha visited Oskar numerous times in his studio on Friedrichstrasse, and let Oskar film her nude.

Oskar's UFA contract had extension clauses, so he might have stayed employed by the studios for a longer time, but his month in the hospital caused him to take a fresh direction with his personal abstract filmmaking. While languishing in bed, he asked to have his drawing board and charcoal brought to him so he could sketch out ideas, such as *Der Unternehmer* described earlier. He realized that this same technique of charcoal on paper would allow him to draw an entire film himself, unlike the systems used in commercial animation studios like Seel's, which required a staff of ink-and-paint people to fill in shapes on paper or cels. He set to work immediately drawing out thin lines moving in clusters and configurations, working to perfect the choreography and pattern and design of timing for an overall composition of this type. Now that Walter Ruttmann had abandoned abstract animation for his finely-filmed and superbly-edited documentaries, Oskar felt free for the first time to explore the arena of small shapes performing elaborate movements.

His impetus to pursue abstract filmmaking was undoubtedly encouraged by Dr. Diebold. Oskar wrote to his parents 25 July 1929 (shortly after getting out the hospital) that he had been visiting Diebold – and in the same sentence Oskar suggests that Friedrich Holländer would be writing the music for his new film, so perhaps Diebold was instrumental in introducing Oskar to the successful theatrical composer. Or perhaps Oskar merely hoped to use a Holländer song, like the Spoliansky "Auf Wiedersehen" ["Goodbye"], which he would use as the music for his *Studie Nr. 4*.

Oskar's only commercial work during the coming year were brief special effects for two features: some representations of atoms, molecules and electricity for a documentary *Das Hohelied der Kraft* [The Hymn of Energy] released in June 1930, and "dancing stars and moon" for the operetta film *Die Försterchristl* [Christl the Forester's Daughter] which Oskar shot in November 1930 (the film premièred in February 1931). The rest of the time he devoted to experimenting with his new series of hand-drawn charcoal-on-paper films. A number of short fragments on film and animation paper attest to his experiments. In one of these, for example, the drawn lines seem trapped inside the film frame (or rather the screen), and when they try to escape, they merely hit the edges and bounce back, deflected at an angle like billiard balls, though they remain thin lines at all times; this same effect does not occur in any of the finished *Studie*, so Oskar must not have liked it and purposely discarded it – or saved it for use with some "comic" music that never turned up.

Studie Nr. 1 only survives in a copy without a beginning title other than a note "Begleitet auf der Wurlitzer Orgel von Hans Albert Mattausch und Gert Thomas" [Accompanied on the organ by Mattausch and Thomas] who were the house accompanists at Kamera Unter den Linden art cinema in Berlin. Unfortunately no indication of the date, the nature of the music (original, classical or popular), or indeed whether both of the musicians played the same organ at the same time, survives. *Studie Nr. 2* received its censorship approval in August 1930, but may have been finished some time before that, since normally a film was assigned a censorship number only when it was actually going to be screened publicly. *Studie Nr. 2* is listed on its censorship record as *Tanzende Linien* [Dancing Lines], so it may be that a set of 600 drawings with the title *Ein Spiel in Linien* [A Play with Lines] and an "ende" title might represent the actual head and tail section of *Studie Nr. 1*, since the brief but complex motions of the lines in that paper fragment would fit very well as a climax to the style and structure of the film fragment.

Studie Nr. 2, *Studie Nr. 3*, *Studie Nr. 4* and *Studie Nr. 5* are all four synchronized very tightly to popular music released on Electrola records, and a surviving end title on one copy of *Studie Nr. 2* is obviously designed as an advertisement for the record, saying that you have heard "Vaya Veronika" on Electrola record No. 1663, available now at music stores. In a letter to the Electrola Company dated 20 August 1930, Oskar boasts that his *Studie 2, 3, 4 and 5* have been running for some four weeks at Kamera Unter den Linden, and at least 15,000 people have been introduced to their recordings by this artful movie advertising [foreshadowing MTV!].

Not only were the *Studie* popular with audiences at art theatres like the Kamera, but also they received a kind of critical acclaim that provided inspiration for Oskar. Dr. Georg Anschütz, a Psychology Professor at Hamburg who specialized in Music, Art and Synaesthesia, arranged a successful Kongreß für Farbe-Ton-Forschung [Congress for Colour-Music Research] in 1927. The second Kongreß took place from 1–5 October 1930 also in Hamburg. Among some two dozen lectures figured one by Walter Behm, "Über die Abstrakte *Filmstudie Nr. 5* von Oskar Fischinger (Synästhetischer Film)" [Concerning the Abstract Film *Studie Nr. 5* by O.F. (Synaesthetic Film)]. Oskar also prepared a short speech to introduce the screening of his new film, which was a sensational success, repeated several times during the Kongreß – deservedly so, since its supple choreography of the foxtrot transcends usual ballroom dancing into a sublime fantasy worthy of Busby Berkeley. The programme also included live performances on various colour-organs by Ludwig Hirschfeld-Mack, Zdenek Pesánek and Baron Anatol Vietinghoff-Scheel. Hans Stoltenberg, who had drawn abstract images directly on the film surface in 1911, and published a theoretical book *Reine Farbkunst in Raum und Zeit* [Pure Colour Art in Space and Time] in 1920, also delivered a lecture. The Berlin dance critic Fritz Böhme, who had lectured on "The Unity of Light, Music and Dance on the Stage", proclaimed Oskar's film as "The Dance of the Future", and he would write numerous articles in praise of Oskar's work over the coming decade. At last Oskar had found a supportive community of like-minded people.

One of these people, Josef Voltz, became close friends with Oskar, and just a few days after the Kongreß, on 10 October 1930, moved into Friedrichstrasse 238. Voltz had been a dancer, but had turned to film production as an option for his mature years, after he could no longer dance. He had written an essay on the "Psychophysiological Basis of Film and Sound-Film Production" [Psychophysiologische Grundlagen der Film-und-Tonfilmproduktion], which brought him to Hamburg for the Kongreß. Oskar and Josef signed a contract for the co-production of artistic and worthwhile films [künstlerisch und wertvollen] which would be released under Oskar's name. Voltz lived at 238 for only a few months, but kept in touch with Oskar for about a year longer, though none of their film ideas were realized.

Oskar's next film, *Studie Nr. 6*, is the most brilliant of the black-and-white *Studie*, the film in which his peak technical virtuosity perfectly

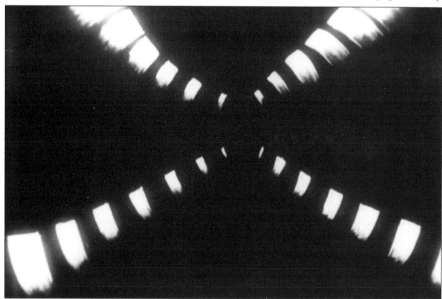

Studie Nr. 6.

expresses the kind of ideas that obsessed him. At this time, he subscribed to a Buddhist magazine, and had constructed an electric Tibetan prayer wheel, which would cast his supplications heavenwards 24 hours a day whether he was home or not. His contacts with the scientists Oberth and Ley had complemented his own passion for hermetic, mystical systems, resulting in a syncretistic speculation about "relativity" that reconciled the sensational new quantum mechanics of Heisenberg and Einstein's relativity with the traditional theories of Theosophy, Anthroposophy, Vedanta, and other oriental religions. *Studie Nr. 6* uses thick supple shaded figures that remain constantly in flight, bending and warping as they seem to change direction (or dimension), and collecting in configurations that could be a mandala exuding vibrations, then an eye momentarily, then a target for an imploding crescent. One sequence, which Oskar referred to as "splitting the atom", shows a figure disintegrate into a complex multiplication of interreactive dots. All of this takes place in 2 minutes, with such energy and smooth bravado that the spectator must smile and sigh with delight – which also corresponds to a pet theory of Oskar's: someone will automatically receive the message of an abstract image sub-consciously, without being able to put it into words, but if the image is experienced in pleasure and wonder, the understanding will be impressive and precious, whereas if the image agitates and disturbs, the ideas inherent in the piece will always seem unpleasant to the viewer and will gladly be forgotten. Like a fine piece of music, *Studie Nr. 6* can be seen again and again [even silently] with increasing pleasure, and always a new revelation about some nuance or interaction of cosmic and spiritual matter.

Although Electrola may have agreed to allow Oskar to use their discs in theatrical engagements as a sort of advertising [50 years before MTV], when it came to having the recordings transferred to optical soundtracks, the question of composer copyright had to be handled directly. Oskar fell foul of this problem immediately, with *Studie Nr. 6*, which received a censorship number November 1930, but could not be distributed because the composer Jacinto Guerrero [who was enjoying lucrative success in Spain with his zarzuelas, and coincidentally was an activist agitating for international composers' royalty rights] wanted too much money for the rights to use his fandango "Los Verderones" [Greenfinches]. Oskar's film was already so tightly synchronized with that music that he simply shelved the film, pending a distributor who wanted the film so much that they would pay the music fee. In 1931, Oskar asked his composer friend Paul Hindemith [they looked very much alike, and would play practical jokes pretending to be each other] if some of his students at the Hochschule für Musik [College of Music] might compose original scores for the film. Hindemith screened the film several times for his class, and he himself composed a score as well as

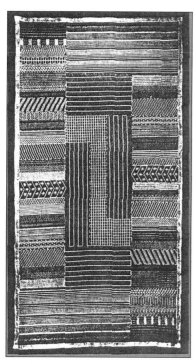

Elfriede's prize winning design, 1931.

several of his students, including the later-famous Oskar Sala and Harald Genzmer. These scores were recorded on discs, and stored in the archive of the Musikhochschule, where they may have been lost in bombings at the end of World War II. In 1931, both Hindemith and his prize students Sala and Genzmer had been experimenting with a new electronic music instrument, the Trautonium [developed 1928–1930 by Dr. Friedrich Trautwein], with which Oskar also got acquainted. Whether any of the students chose to use the Trautonium as part of their score for *Studie Nr. 6* is not known, but it certainly would have emphasized the futuristic aerodynamics of the imagery.

In each of the successive *Studie* Oskar chose a slightly different optical issue, so that each film has a character of its own, and all 16 together form a true serial arrangement with each other. For *Studie Nr. 7*, Oskar, following Brahms' "Hungarian Dance No. 5", divides the imagery into two contrasting sections: a sharp and vigorous furiant seen as razor-thin planes moving along perspective lines through a deep space toward the viewer, and a set of slow interludes in which languorous soft shapes sinuously curl around each other, almost like jugendstil [Art Nouveau] organic intertwining. The hard-edged, efficient geometrics of the first section, with their astonishing illusion of depth (even though they are simple charcoal drawings on paper, all from Oskar's hand), gain considerable force from the contrast with the moments of lush, almost-erotic softness. This particular film proved so impressive that four filmmakers at least (Norman McLaren, Alexandre Alexeieff, Claire Parker and Len Lye) were encouraged to pursue a career in abstract musical animation after seeing it.

In 1931, *Studie Nr. 5* was purchased by Universal for distribution in America as a novelty short in regular cinemas, and *Studie Nr. 7* was booked to run as the short with the prestige feature *Ariane* [remade later by Billy Wilder as *Love in the Afternoon*], in which Elisabeth Bergner as a young music student has an affair with an older man (Rudolf Forster) whom she meets at a concert. *Ariane* opened on 20 February 1931 at the Capitol Theater in Berlin and proved a big hit which played for weeks at first-run cinemas, and *Studie Nr. 7*, really the ideal (and sensational) short, kept being screened with it.

While *Studie Nr. 7* was still playing at the Capitol, Uncle Albert's daughter, Elfriede, also came to Berlin. She was a student at the Kunstgewerbeschule [College of Applied Arts] in Offenbach [now the Hochschule für Gestaltung, College of Design], and one of her intricate abstract designs for a "Tülldurchzug" [diaphanous tulle] had won a prize, part of which was a trip to Berlin where all the prize-winning designs were exhibited. Her design was also published in the November 1931 issue of *Stickereien und Spitzen* [Embroidery and Lace] (Jrg. XXXII, Heft 2). Since she was to be in Berlin for a long weekend, her

father asked her to visit Oskar and find out if he was making good use of all the money he borrowed from Uncle Albert. Luckily, Oskar could take Elfriede to the glamorous Capitol to see packed crowds cheer and stomp with glee after the screening of *Studie Nr. 7*. Elisabeth Bergner also happened to be her favourite movie star, as she bore a strong resemblance to the actress both in features and personality. After the screening, Oskar took Elfriede on a little tour around Berlin in one of the double-decker busses, sitting on the open-air top level for a better view – but also because it was rather cold, Oskar put his arm around Elfriede to keep her warm. She thought it might mean he was in love with her. She dawdled and delayed until it was too late for her to get back to her school group, hoping something romantic might happen between her and Oskar – but he behaved like a perfect gentleman, and she was given her own private room in the Friedrichstrasse studio. Nevertheless, needless to say, she was very impressed indeed, recognizing Oskar's special genius: she gave a glowing report of his success to her parents. She had fallen in love immediately with Oskar's wit and charm, and vowed to herself to return to Berlin as soon as possible, to stay in Berlin, to stay with Oskar, to share his bohemian artist's life.

Oskar was not so attached to Elfriede at first. Since his family had moved to Frankfurt, then Oskar himself had moved on to Munich and Berlin, he had not known her well, and met her last 10 years before (when she was 9 and he was 19) at a party in Gelnhausen, when he wrote

Right: *Elfriede and school chums.*

Below: *Elfriede and Trudl.*

a page in her scrapbook – a little parable about a lonely crane. She was an eldest child, with a younger brother Robert (who would eventually inherit the Fischinger drugstore), a sister Maria (who would operate a camera store in Heidelberg) and a younger brother Werner (who would open a drugstore in Karlsruhe). Elfriede was to a certain degree spoiled and pampered at home. She loved parties and made many of her own clothes and costumes, quite elaborate, in daring new styles. Attending the prestigious Applied Arts College in Offenbach, where she studied not only fashion design (textiles, weaving, knitting, dyeing) but also typography and drawing with celebrity artists Rudolph Koch and Fritz Kredel, was a considerable coup. Temperamentally she was the exact opposite of Oskar. High-strung, high energy, she could hardly sit still for very long, and talked continually, often switching subject-matter in the middle of a sentence, and frequently interrupting other people who were talking. She loved to read, but rarely finished a whole book, often skipping around to find parts that caught her interest, or jumping prematurely to the ending just to find out what the conclusion was. While Oskar's branch of the Fischingers, undoubtedly due to mother Michel, were susceptible to various illnesses and weaknesses including diabetes, Elfriede's branch of the family was naturally more robust. She loved dancing and sports and games, and was very popular among her schoolmates. She joined a group of "Wandervogel" rather like Girl Scouts, which promoted exercise, hiking and camping out, and Elfriede learned to play the lute with them – and was able to perform in an amateur production of Weber's operetta *Preciosa* as a lute-playing

OPTICAL POETRY: The Life and Work of Oskar Fischinger

gypsy. She also practiced the Loheland dance technique which promoted interpretive dancing in the open air, across fresh meadows. At the end of World War I, Gelnhausen had been occupied by French troops, and that experience may have been traumatic for her, as she retained certain habits of a 10-year-old – for example, to her last days she would seek confirmation or approval with the phrase "Was I a good girl?" spoken in a girlish tone. But her great energy allowed her to work very hard. Her best friend from Gelnhausen, Gertrude (Trudl) Gudjons, also attended the Offenbach college, so they would take the train each day from Gelnhausen to Offenbach and back together. When I first interviewed Elfriede and Trudl, I asked what they remembered most about Offenbach. Elfriede immediately said, "Oh, we had such fun, making fabulous costumes for the annual Zinnober costume ball, and the other parties, and the pranks we used to play – getting six into one toilet stall and all showing our feet just to fluster one of the teachers when they came in ...". Trudl replied, "I remember being hungry – I always brought a huge lunch from home, mother wouldn't let me go without one, but when we got off the train in Offenbach we had to walk from the station across a square to the school, and the square was always crowded with people out of work, beggars, mothers in dirty clothing with babies – I always ended up giving away all of my lunch to those poor people, then I was always hungry in classes." Elfriede seemed genuinely surprised, and blurted out "I don't remember anything like that at all". She probably really never noticed.

Oskar, by contrast, was moody and self-contained. He had a good

Elfriede and Lou Lindeman wearing sweaters designed by Elfriede, ca. 1929.

sense of humour and loved to tell and play jokes, but he would only do this in his spare time, at a party situation (when he would be charming and witty), or when comedy was relevant to his work. He would spend days and weeks concentrating on some planning or work and hardly speak or stop to eat. He loved discussions of ideas, on specific topics, but not small talk. He loved to read and research, and could spend whole days in a library studying quietly. He meditated, practiced yoga, and could sit absolutely still for hours while working. Although Elfriede loved jokes as well, she was fatally inept at telling them, always getting the essential details mixed up – and she was extraordinarily gullible, always falling for any teasing tricks or deceptions. It would seem that she would be a very unlikely partner for him.

During her first brief visit in Berlin, Elfriede chanced upon many of Oskar's peculiarities. She happened to be there (and Oskar was out on business) when Martha dropped in. Elfriede realized Martha must be a girlfriend, and invited her in warmly, made tea and cakes for the increasingly nervous girl, and chatted endlessly about Oskar, until he came home, and Martha fled, never to return to Friederichstrasse again. Similarly she recognized Josef Voltz as a homosexual, and thought he was a bad influence on Oskar. She did her best to drive Josef away – successfully, for he left shortly after Elfriede's visit. Oskar told her he would be hiring his younger brother Hans to work for him, and Elfriede did her best to disparage Hans, noting that he had a temper, smoked too much, etc. In fact she was jealous that Hans had attended a real Art Academy in Frankfurt, while she was only in a trade-tech school. Back in Gelnhausen, she sang Oskar's praises to everyone, and immediately began scheming how to get back to Berlin. She was obliged, however, to finish school and then serve an apprenticeship, running a Durer House [a state-subsidized shop where homemade handicrafts and folk art could be sold] in Fulda until the fall of 1932. She did manage to "drop in" on Oskar several times when she could arrange to get someone to take over her duties for a week. Once she dropped in and removed all the old textile wallpaper from Oskar's apartment (because the cloth harboured insect pests, she said) and repainted the entire house. Oskar wrote despondently to Uncle Albert, "Please don't let Elfriede come to Berlin again, because we can't get any work done when she's around ..." But she did return often for a few days or a week, and her training with intricate repetitive knitting and embroidery made her very good at filling in Oskar's hundreds of animation drawings with charcoal and paint. She was, however, quite shy with mechanical equipment, and never learned to be comfortable with cameras, splicers, re-winds or other film paraphernalia. She never shot animation, but her friend Trudl was quite expert with all that.

The commercial success of *Studie Nr. 5* and *Studie Nr. 7*, along with the enduring popularity of all the *Studie* at the film clubs and art cinemas on the circuit of the League of Independent Films created an immediate demand for more *Studie*. Oskar did send for his brother Hans, who was 9 years younger than Oskar. Hans left for Berlin on 3 March 1931. Oskar had begun two different studies, one to the "Sorcerer's Apprentice" of Paul Dukas, and one to the ballet music from Verdi's *Aida*. Because of the popularity of *Studie Nr. 7*, Oskar was tempted to begin another of Brahms' "Hungarian Dances". He put Hans to work on the *Aida*, filling in with charcoal the outlines that Oskar had already drawn, thus learning something about design and timing for animation. Hans learned quickly, but he disliked working with charcoal, which was messy and imprecise, from his point of view. At his art college, Hans had practiced drawing and painting with inks and poster colour [Tusche und Tempera], so he felt more comfortable with that technique. Oskar had drawn sharp outlines with the edge of a charcoal stick, then smudged it with his finger to create lighter shading or sometimes "trails" behind quickly-moving crescent shapes to make their movement seem even smoother. Hans wanted to codify a grey scale, numbering mixed bottles of Tusche so that a precise shade of grey could be assigned to a particular

Studie Nr. 8, *atom splitting.*

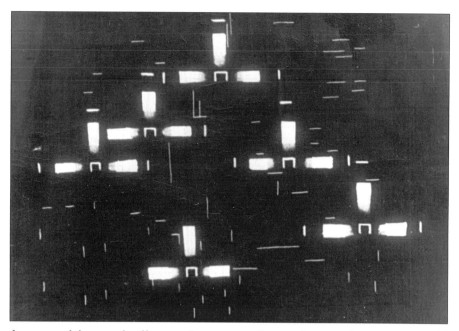

form, and by gradually moving up or down the numbers, one could make a given shape fade in or fade out; also one could differentiate shapes that were performing contrary actions simultaneously by making some consistently greyer than others. Hans carried on with his techniques and Oskar continued with his own simple, direct charcoal.

Oskar again experienced difficulties with music rights concerning *Aida*. Although he had inquired and received permission from the German representative of Ricordi (the Italian publisher who handled rights to Verdi's estate), he belatedly discovered that the rights to *Aida* were sold country by country, since a local agent could monitor the performances of the opera, so even though Oskar was using merely an orchestral excerpt for his film, he had acquired only the permit for Germany, and would have to negotiate additional fees for any other country! The German fee was already rather high, so Oskar held back on finishing the *Aida*, which became *Studie Nr. 10*, and assigned Hans to work full time on Brahms' "Hungarian Dance No. 6", which became *Studie Nr. 9*.

Oskar marked out the synchronization, which he always determined [thanks to his engineering training] by scratching an "X" across a phonograph record, then calculating the exact time a certain sound occurred by using a slide-rule to compensate for the diminishing size of the grooves toward the centre of the disc! Oskar also designed the main shapes and general choreography, but Hans was entirely responsible for the actual drawings and animation. The combination of their two talents makes *Studie Nr. 9* particularly exciting. Hans rendered the lines astonishingly thin, while the circles and arches arising have a stream-lined moderne/Bauhaus look that seems to make their movements more elegant. The precision of the "atom splitting" sequence sparkles and dazzles, very differently from Oskar's own hand-drawn "atom splitting" in *Studie Nr. 6* and *Studie Nr. 8*, which derive a fascination from their very irregularity that makes them seem organic, natural, even "real".

Meanwhile Oskar suffered another blow concerning the music rights to "L'apprenti sorcier" [The Sorcerer's Apprentice] for his *Studie Nr. 8*. The composer, Paul Dukas, was still alive, and his publisher demanded a sizeable fee for the composition. Oskar had chosen a particular recording (he fastidiously sought bright, crisp, energetic performances) which occupied two sides of a disc. He had bought the rights to the first side of the recording, and largely animated his images for it, under the assumption that he would get enough money to purchase the second side soon. But the worldwide financial situation daily drifted closer to absolute disaster, and Oskar never managed to acquire the rest of Dukas' music. With an advance on film rental from the Uitkijk Theater in Amsterdam, Oskar bought the rights to the last two bars of the music so that it would have some kind of finale.

Studie Nr. 8 is the most complex composition in Oskar's series of black-and-white musical studies. At times as many as 30 separate figures are being animated in a single frame. Perhaps following Goethe's parable of *Der Zauberlehrling* [The Sorcerer's Apprentice], Oskar seems to stress the mutability of matter, contrasting incredibly soft gestures (such as a cluster of crescents swirling around, brushing together) with bright explosive trajectories of hard-edge rectangles – and mediating between them shapes that warp and stretch and contract in unstable mutation. The "atom splitting" in this context takes on new meaning – the real dangers feared from the possible explosive power of nuclear fission, which Oskar was well aware of, as he haunted the university libraries and lectures on the new physics which fascinated him.

Studie Nr. 9 and *Studie Nr. 8* both received their censorship approval in September 1931, and in November 1931 *Studie 5, 7, 8* and *9*, received the Prädikat [government rating] of "künstlerisch" [artistically valu-able], which meant a tax-rebate inducement for regular cinemas to screen them. A poll of German film critics in the newspaper *Der Deutsche* awarded Fischinger's *Studie* the critics' choice for 1931. As a result of rave press notices, orders for the *Studie* began to pour in from countries all over the world, not only Europe, but also Japan, Syria, Palestine, Egypt and Uruguay. In February 1932, Joris Ivens took Oskar's films to Moscow and Leningrad, where they also enjoyed great popular success. Specialty art cinemas like The Uitkijk in Amsterdam guaranteed to screen a new *Studie* every month, or as often as new ones could arrive. Oskar hired a secretary and two other women from Berlin who could fill in with charcoal and ink the shapes outlined by Oskar and Hans as animators, and he even allowed Elfriede to come to work for a few weeks. A 3-minute film required about 5,000 individual paper drawings, since Oskar never filmed a given drawing twice as commercial studios do, because he wanted the movement to be as smooth as possible.

While Hans completed *Studie Nr. 10* to the *Aida* ballet music, Oskar began working on a film that may have been intentionally silent. *Liebesspiel* [Love Games] in its simple perfection proves that the black-and-white *Studie* are visual artworks in their own right, separate from the accompanying music. Oskar never intended to "illustrate" music; he only used music [which is, of course, abstract sound art] as a parallel to make it easier for audiences to accept his radical visual abstract kinetic art. When one hears music, no one asks what it is supposed to represent, but many people scorned abstract painting because it didn't look like recognizable objects. Oskar dealt with both sound and image so well that it truly became Visual Music.

Liebesspiel has a classic dramatic structure, though the "story" is "acted" by simple geometric shapes. A comet-like figure swirls toward the screen as if it had come from afar, turns and circles back into the obscure distance. It returns and is joined by a second, similar "comet", then a third – and once when two pass each other, they momentarily create a sudden "black hole" negative area where they overlap [painted in tempera though all the rest of the film is pure charcoal]. Suddenly a crescent appears and performs the same choreography, and three such crescents swallow up the comets in an exquisite flurry of jugendstil tendrils that wind into perfect little circles with a dot in the centre. Then the lead comet pursues the lead crescent in a sinuous path until the crescent engulfs the comet, swells into a perfect circle, then splits into a roseate mandala that twists and dissolves into nine pairs of crescents and comets. The analogy with yang/yin lingam/yoni theories of the balance of active/passive from oriental philosophies elevates these "love games" to a cosmic revelation, while the graceful "rondo" musicality impresses with the serene inevitability of its harmonics. In a projection of the actual film in a dark auditorium, the viewer also experiences an astonishing "light cone" effect: the pure white beams of light show up in the auditorium space like search-lights, and create deep-space patterns as they swirl around – an effect quite lost in video. The surviving film materials (a film print and the charcoal-on-paper drawings) have no title on them, and the title "Liebesspiel" was supplied by Elfriede Fischinger in 1970. She had not seen the film before, but said she recognized what Oskar meant by it. There is no record of a *Liebesspiel* (or whatever else it may have been titled) having been screened, so perhaps audiences were not, after all, interested in seeing a silent film at that time. Since no trace of *Studie Nr. 4* survives, however, perhaps

Liebesspiel is actually *Studie 4* – and the repetitive motions of the circling shapes might well correspond to the repeated "Goodbyes" in the lyrics to the waltz which accompanied *Studie 4*. [No copy of the precise record has been found, so an exact synch check cannot be made.] The charcoal drawings continue beyond the film materials, with similar swirling motion performed by more squared sharp shapes. This might also correspond to another verse of the musical song. The brief tempera effect, however, would appear to date the production after *Studie 4*. Oskar's *Studie 13* from 1934, synchronized with Beethoven's *Coriolan* overture, also remains unfinished, and the repetitive swirling melody of its missing section might also correspond to the lithe swirls of "Liebesspiel".

Oskar worked on *Studie Nr. 11* (see illustrations on pages 68 and 69), synchronized with a minuet from Mozart's "Divertimento in D, K.334", while Hans created virtually on his own *Studie Nr. 12*, to "Der Lichter-tanz der Bräute" [The Candle Dance of the Kashmiri Brides] from the obscure opera *Feramors* [sometimes called *Lalla Rookh*] by Anton Rubinstein. This sensuous exotic music provides the perfect raison d'être for the thin, sinuous, streamlined shapes of Hans, and he uses the grey scale to develop layers of primary and secondary dancers. The screen area remains overtly a plane, and even the bold, thick bars that accompany the final climactic chords rise up aggressively from the bottom of the frame, but still seem as flat as the wiggles of thin lines. The overall effect is impressively graceful and vigorous and decorative.

Oskar's style in the Mozart could not be more different. To find the appropriate choreography, Oskar analysed rococo architectural motifs, refined them down to their inner geometric structures (literally "abstracting" them), and then using the ribbon-like curves that resulted as trajectories over which his simple geometric shapes would travel. Some of these shapes are the familiar "comets" and others rectangular planes that can fold and bend and ripple. The curving trajectories take them toward and away from the viewer in a sensation of deep architectural space, and the ripples seem to flow along perspectives, sometimes "turning corners". The effect is ravishingly elegant, and provides a living proof to Schelling's Romantic adage, in his statement to Goethe, that Architecture is frozen Music.

Oskar's work on *Studie Nr. 11* was interrupted at least twice by commercial assignments. In March 1932, Oskar received a commission for a preview trailer to the new Gitta Alpar film *Gitta entdekt ihr Herz* [Gitta finds her heart], which would première on 5 April 1932. Oskar was given the soundtrack for Gitta's final spectacular coloratura aria, "Was kann so schön sein wie Deine Liebe?" [What could be as lovely as your love?] and he created an abstract interpretation of the last minute, which ended with a question mark. When Oskar's trailer played during the last weeks of March, the voice of Alpar was so well known then, that everyone would guess that a new Gitta film would be opening soon at this cinema. Oskar's visualization of the love lyrics is similar to *Liebesspiel*, with a pair of figures gliding around together until they implode and explode again in a dazzling vortex of little replicants. It is, however, rendered in a style closer to Hans', using inks and poster-colour to control grey scale, and the figures themselves are leaner. After the run of *Gitta entdekt ihr Herz*, Oskar was allowed to distribute the film, along with his other works, under the name *Koloraturen* [Coloratura].

Oskar also did special effects involving skywriting for a musical with Martha Eggerth and Hermann Thimig (script by Billy Wilder) *Das Blaue vom Himmel* [The Blue of Heaven]. At the film's climactic moment, the hero must tell the heroine he loves her by writing the message in the heavens above her: "Ich liebe Dich, Anni" [I love you, Annie]. Oskar, who had done skywriting in *Frau im Mond* was the first asked to do these sequences, but he wanted too much money, so the producer tried several other special effects people, none of whom could render a satisfactory, realistic-looking image, including a friend, Radelmesser, who lived just downstairs from Oskar, and who tried rendering the writing with salt on black velvet. Finally the producer was forced to return to Oskar and pay his fee. Oskar repeated his technique from *Frau im Mond*: on a lower level of glass he laid a drawing of blue sky with a few clouds, on a second level of glass he wrote the words using a mixture of glycerine and white chalk, and on the top level he moved with tweezers a tiny model airplane only a few centimetres long; the subtle difference in focus made the writing and sky look more realistic. Furthermore, Oskar was paid to re-do the trick several times in other languages – "Te amo, Anita", etc. – as the film was sold in foreign countries. Oskar's success with such difficult effects earned him the nickname "The Wizard of Friedrichstrasse".

Oskar also did a representational logo for Merkur film company in Prague, which probably showed Jupiter and Mercury throwing a thunderbolt, prefiguring an image in Disney's *Fantasia*. This plethora of work allowed others to be engaged at the Fischinger studio, including Elfriede's best friend from the Offenbach Kunstgewerbeschule, Trudl Gudjons (later Mende). When Elfriede made one of her lightning trips to Berlin, as she was cleaning up the rooms to do the laundry, she found a magazine of naked women stuffed under Hans' mattress. Later that day Hans told her that he found her very sexy and wouldn't mind having an affair. Elfriede, still nursing an unrequited love for Oskar, felt rather insulted, and went back to Gelnhausen again without telling Oskar.

Oskar did prize Elfriede's graphic skills, however. He made a portable animation setup for her (basically registration pins glued to a clear glass

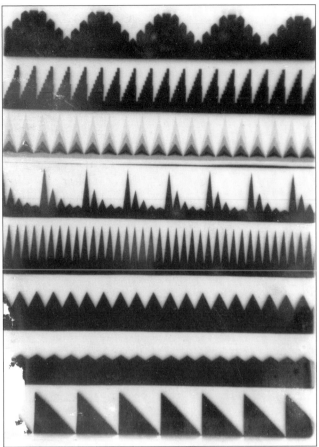

plate the size of the animation papers, so that tracing and comparison of adjacent sheets could easily be accomplished with any light behind the glass) and prepared the musical synchronization specifications for a recording of a harpsichord rondo by French baroque composer Louis Daquin, *The Cuckoo*. Elfriede carried her animation glass with her to Gelnhausen and Fulda, and even on the train back and forth to Berlin. She designed and eventually completed the animation drawings for this film, which would have been one of the series of black-and-white *Studie*. *The Cuckoo* is an intrigu-

Both images: Ornament Sound.

ing and challenging subject, with a busy buzzy ostinato in the bass, and a repetitive imitation of the plaintive cry of the cuckoo bird in the treble. Did Elfriede design it as background and foreground layers of imagery, or as upper and lower activities on the same image? And were her shapes like the supple forms of Oskar's or the streamlined contours of Hans' – or indeed like the intricate intertwinings in her textile designs? Unfortunately, we may never know. By the time Elfriede had finished the animation, the Nazis were already in power and had forbidden abstract art, so her drawings were never shot on to film. She did package the *Cuckoo* drawings and stored them along with all the other *Studie* in Gelnhausen, but none of them were found among the materials brought back to Hollywood in 1961. Were they destroyed when Gelnhausen was bombed?

Meanwhile, *Studie Nr. 12* premièred at Kamera Unter den Linden on 31 May 1932, and Dr. Bernhard Diebold gave an introductory lecture. We can guess what he said by referring to the text of a radio broadcast he delivered on 16 June 1932 from Frankfurt, entitled "Die Zukunft

der Micky-Maus" [The Future of Mickey Mouse], in which he suggests that animation is the way to real art through cinema, because in animation the total creation of image makes possible "living painting", "musographics", "eye-music", "optical poetry" and "ornament dance", of which the popular Disney character no less than the absolute films of Fischinger is a pioneer. Lotte Eisner's sensitive review in *Film-Kurier* 1 June 1932 praises the personal style of Hans as a complement to Oskar's, and says that together they give the concept of "Absolute Film" a new resonance.

At this same time Oskar was also distracted by another line of thought. Since the Farb-Ton-Kongreß, he had been intrigued by the possibility of fundamental correlations between sounds and visual images, and he had been corresponding with some scholars doing research in this area. The "new music" of the Trautonium had further fascinated him. In spring 1932 he made his conceptual breakthrough, realizing that the kind of "ornaments", abstract designs that he used in his films, were not substantially different from the sort of patterns that were generated by sounds on the optical soundtrack. But what kind of sounds were inherent in the different primary geometric shapes? What noises or "new music" might be created by irregular or stylized patterns? Did different leaf formations, for example, bear distinct tonal patterns? Did the shape of a birch or elm leaf make different sounds, not only when the wind whistled around them but under the camera eye? Did the chosen or most-common type of ornamentation of a given culture correspond to the musical scales or harmonics or folk songs particular

to that culture? Elfriede claimed that she inspired Oskar's thoughts about this because once when he was lying down in a darkened room she dropped a key in the adjacent room; he recognized the sound as that specifically of a key, not a coin or a spoon or some other metal object – so might the form of the key correspond to a distinctive sound? Whether that is true or not, Oskar became obsessed with such questions and abandoned his other work (including *Studie Nr. 11*) in order to prepare and shoot hundreds of trial soundtrack images. He had to file open the soundtrack-area on the aperture of one camera in order to shoot drawings directly on to the soundtrack. By studying pre-recorded soundtracks, he quickly mastered the calligraphy of the conventional European music, drawing out "Fuchs, Du hast die Gans gestohlen" [a nursery rhyme, "Fox, You Stole the Goose"] and other simple melodies. Unconventional ornamentation proved more problematic. The filmic frame-line caused difficulties, unless the particular size of an ornament happened to overlap perfectly on the next ornament in the adjacent frame area. Duration of tone, modulations in volume, attack and decay of sound, and such things were key factors in western music, yet the Trautonium could glide over long intervals without any perceptible notes or scale modulations. What kinds of dynamics could validly be imposed on ornaments? It quickly became a massive undertaking – and not an easy one: when he picked up his first reels of *Ornament Ton* [Ornament Sound] from the laboratory, and had them play the film on their test projector, the technicians were horrified by the weird sounds, and feared that any further such reels of noise might damage their equipment!

In an attempt to get help and financial backing for these extended experiments, Oskar published a statement in the press, gave a demonstration in the Haus der Ingenieure [the Society of Engineers] and applied for a grant from the Kaiser Wilhelm Gedächtnis Stiftung [Emperor William Memorial Foundation]. No financial backing was forthcoming, although the announcement of Oskar's experiments in the press caused the greatest rash of publicity he would ever experience: articles were syndicated during July and August 1932 in hundreds of newspapers, as far afield as Japan. Two statements by Oskar, "Klingende Ornamente" or "Tönende Ornamente" [Sounding Ornaments] and "Der Absolute Tonfilm" [The Absolute Sound-film] continued to be published well into 1933, along with press photos that showed Hans and Oskar standing beside long rolls of butcher paper with triangles painted on them – although these "scrolls", which might have reproduced conventional music, hardly lay at the heart of Oskar's investigations, and in fact Hans, Oskar and the hired young women had quickly painted them just for the purpose of having a flashy object for press photos – and possibly to deceive anyone who would try to mimic Oskar's work for his own profit. Some newspaper critics also mentioned (or confused Oskar with) the Munich animator, Rudolph Pfenninger, who had codified a system for "writing" conventional music with prepared hand-drawn templates. Pfenninger had worked for Tobis in the early 1920s when they tried an experimental sound-on-film process at a special Berlin theatre [which proved unsuccessful largely because the loudspeakers could not amplify the sound well enough]. One of Pfenninger's tasks had been repairing and enhancing the sound by drawing directly on the soundtrack. In the early 1930s Pfenninger produced several animated films with "drawn sound" music tracks that merely reproduced conventional melodies. But Oskar's interest and goal was quite different: he wanted to find new sounds, new music that could only derive from the forms of ornaments – something quite distinct from any conventional music.

Oskar never managed to finish his experimentations, nor to create any satisfactory, artistic *Ornament Ton* reel. He did send sample reels of his experiments to be played at the London Film Society, with a Moholy-Nagy lecture at the Bauhaus, and a few other places, but they remained fragments of experimentation. Oskar would only find a fruitful conclusion to the *Ornament Ton* experiment in the late 1930s, when he spoke about his theories to John Cage and Edgard Varèse, who were inspired by Oskar's ideas to integrate a broader range of natural "noise" and silence into their musical compositions.

Oskar's *Studie Nr. 11* was not finished by October 1932 when he had a retrospective of his complete abstract films at Munich's Marmorhaus Cinema, with enthusiastic capacity audiences for several screenings.

2

The Nazi Terror

skar was still working on *Studie Nr. 11* early in 1933 when the National Socialist German Workers Party [the Nazis] seized power through the ruse of burning the Reichstag [the capitol building]. All Friedrichstrasse ground to a halt. Elfriede happened to be in Berlin at the time of the Nazi takeover. The next morning she went downstairs to buy some rolls for breakfast, and was struck by an eerie emptiness and silence. Overnight the beggars and gypsies, prostitutes and drug dealers had all disappeared. Elfriede's parents demanded that she return to the relative safety of Gelnhausen immediately. Many Jews and homosexuals fled in the next few weeks, emigrated before the Nazi policies had a chance to catch up with them. International uncertainty and boycott closed off money exchange. Oskar's always tenuous business seemed cut off, and he began to dismiss his various employees; Hans left to live with his older brother and sister, Joseph and Maria, who now ran a restaurant in Alzenau, a resort town in the forests not too far from Gelnhausen.

Oskar's own position seemed questionable. Quite aside from his identification with abstract art, which was frowned upon by the Nazis, Oskar's past associations would have compromised him. Oskar had worked for the SPD (Socialist Democratic Party), one of whose leaders (and also co-chairman of Magnus Hirschfeld's Scientific Humanitarian Committee) Kurt Hiller, had his home looted on 7 March 1933, and was arrested on 23 March. Oskar had happily collaborated with many now-banned Jewish and "half-Jewish" artists (including Fritz Lang, Billy Wilder, Mischa Spoliansky and Gitta Alpar) whom he would not repudiate. Temperamentally, Oskar's strong mystical bent (from utopianism to superstition) and his cool scientific expertise made him impractically honest and direct in speaking out, confident in the justice with which he spoke.

At the beginning of 1933, Dr. Leonhard Fürst, a philosopher of musical aesthetics and great film enthusiast, was promoting Oskar's films in his articles in the prestigious music journal *Melos*. Oskar was enchanted with Fürst's commentaries and they became close friends. They discovered that they shared a passion for backpacking as well as Visual Music, and Fürst encouraged Oskar to attempt a live-action musical piece like Ruttmann's *In der Nacht* [to Schumann's "In the Night"], synchronizing nature scenes with symphonic music, from Bach and Telemann to Martinu and Schönberg. Oskar agreed, but only if Loni Fürst himself would agree to collaborate with him, and they looked forward to romantic strolls through forests and mountains, camera in hand.

Loni was scheduled to deliver a keynote address at the International Music Congress (part of the Florence May Festival) on 2 May 1933, where his topic again would be film music. Among his film examples were two of Oskar's *Studie* and a reel of *Ornament Sound*, along with Rudolf Pfenninger's *Tönende Handschrift* [Sounding Handwriting]. Oskar procured him a print of Sergei Eisenstein's *Romance Sentimentale*, too, and Loni also showed clips from various features, including Fanck's *Stürme über dem Mont Blanc* [Storm Over Mont Blanc], with music by Paul Dessau and electronic effects on the Trautonium – and three films that would be shortly banned: Erik Charrel's *Der Kongreß tanzt* [The Congress Dances], Reinhold Schünzel's *Das schöne Abenteuer* [The Lovely Adventure], and Robert Siodmak's *Stürme der Leidenschaft* [Storms of Passion]. The Florence lecture was a huge success, and Loni travelled on to Geneva and Paris to follow up on contacts from the festival. He wrote to Oskar on 19 May from Paris, bubbling with excitement over the prospect of their forthcoming "Tippeltour für unsere neuen Studien" [drinking-tour for our new Studie], but he questions, "ob nicht Herr Göbbels oder Herr Völger einen Kulturfilm nach üblichem Schema mit fadem Text erwarten" [Whether Mr. Goebbels or Mr. Völger expect a documentary along the conventional lines, with a boring narration].

Meanwhile, back in Berlin, conditions were even worse than Loni suspected. Oskar was supposed to have joined him on the trip to Florence, and on 20 April he wrote from Nürnberg asking Oskar to let him know which train he was taking so that Loni could join him. But the world was crashing in around Oskar. The Bauhaus had been closed, and curators of Modern Art fired. Oskar barely knew where money would come from to pay expenses during the next months, and he was forced to fire the last of his employees, Miss Sperling, who very competently acted as secretary, accountant and booking agent. He could hardly afford a trip to Italy. On the very day of Loni's lecture in Florence, the German academies were "purged" of such "radicals" as

Paul Tillich, Thomas Mann, Georg Kaiser, Franz Werfel and Magnus Hirschfeld. When Hirschfeld's Institut für Sexualwissenschaft [Institute for Sexual Science] was looted on 6 May 1933 (while Goebbels ostentatiously attended the première of the largely Jewish film *Ein Lied geht um die Welt* [A Song Goes Round the World], starring tenor Joseph Schmidt, to signal that anti-Semitism was not the chief issue ...) and Hirschfeld's library was ceremoniously burned on 10 May [the famous "bookburning" footage always used in documentaries], the news filtered down to Oskar that his friend Kurt Hiller was already in prison.

On 15 May Oskar received an official notice that Goebbels' Reichsministerium für Volksaufklärung und Propaganda [Ministry for Public Enlightenment and Propaganda] had established a "Zentralstelle für geistigen Aktivismus" [Headquarters for Mental Activity] dedicated to "die schöpferischen Kräfte der Nation an die produktive kuturelle Betätigung heranzubringen" [to bring the creative strength of the nation to bear on productive cultural activity] – which required that two free passes to all performances must be given to Nazi censors. Oskar was also scheduled for regular obligatory interviews at this office, and would be reminded if he had not reported enough artistic activity – although a censorship number for *Studie Nr. 11* was denied, which made the continuance of Oskar's normal work (including the completion of two other *Studien* that Hans had begun, to more Brahms Hungarian dances) futile and dangerous. So Loni's satirical remarks about Goebbels in his 19 May letter carried more truth than he expected.

On 19 June, Oskar wrote to Loni apologizing for not being able to pay the 8 marks due German customs on the return of the Florence film prints, and he begged him to return to Berlin soon. "Money has practically disappeared from Berlin." Oskar wrote, "Business is at a stand-still. So I still haven't been able to get to work on any of my projects yet – what a shame, and downright infuriating".

Erno Metzner, the director of the SPD documentary *Dein Schicksal*, for which Oskar had supplied satirical animations, was declared a race-defiler since, though a good catholic like Oskar, Metzner had married the beautiful Chinese actress Grace Chiang. They fled to France where they worked on G.W. Pabst's feature *High and Low*, then continued their emigration to England (1934–1936) and America, where Metzner only found work on a few films during 17 years.

In July, Oskar got a commission to do rather dull animation of graphs and maps for a documentary *Eine Viertelstunde Großstadt-statistik* [A Quarter-Hour of City Statistics]. Although the job did not pay all that much, Oskar hired an assistant, Peter Sachs, a young Jewish man who had been employed by George Pal before Pal fled to Holland. Sachs himself was trying to save up enough money to flee the country, and welcomed even such a boring work. With his salary from Oskar, he did manage to emigrate to London where he taught at art colleges for many years.

Bela and Imre Gaspar, Hungarian brothers, had invented a system which would allow three-colour separation [yellow, cyan, magenta] images to be shot on three successive frames of a single black-and-white film-strip, then reconstituted on to a full-spectrum colour release print which was actually coated on both sides with three separate emulsions, one for each of the component colours. Oskar helped them by engineering the camera mechanism to take the three successive frames while the filters changed. Although the release prints projected a full spectrum of vivid true colours, the exposure time necessary, almost a half-minute for each colour filter, precluded the use of GasparColor for live-action filming of fast moving subjects, but worked well with animation. The Gaspar brothers were eager to produce a spectacular three-colour movie by Christmas time, so Oskar got to make Europe's first full-spectrum colour film.

By the beginning of October, Oskar had completed several satisfactory colour tests, among them a striking version of the hand-tinted Stäbe [Staffs] from the end section of his 1927 multiple-projector *R-1 ein Formspiel* – now superimposing the staffs with great precision in brilliant, saturated colours. Oskar synchronized this footage with a popular concert aria by Tosti, "Ideale", which ends with the repeated supplication, "Return! Return to the Ideal!"

This test film was shown only once, on 4 October 1933, at the third Farbe-Ton-Kongreß in Hamburg. Loni Fürst gave a lecture on "Das Formproblem im Film" (seemingly similar to the Florence lecture) that praised Oskar's abstractions over the efforts of live-action features – a conclusion echoed by the press notices that lauded the "wirklich herrlichen Farben" [truly magnificent colours] of Oskar's little film as opposed to the "braune Soße" [brown gravy] of a UFA live-action film *Herbst in Sans Souci* [Autumn at San Souci Palace].

The third Farbe-Ton-Kongreß was a much more modest event than the one before, with only a few foreign guests, notably the Swiss Musicalist painter Charles Blanc-Gatti demonstrating his colour organ, the Chromophonic Orchestra. Nine of Oskar's films were screened (including a reel of his early experiments, and a sample of the *Ornament Ton*) – all of which inspired Blanc-Gatti to begin making animated films later in the 1930s, including a charming film *Chromophonie* which simulates a performance on his colour organ.

Dr. Georg Anschütz took advantage of the occasion to assemble a secret meeting of sympathetic anti-Nazi people, including Oskar and Loni, Hans Stoltenberg, Fritz Böhme, Victor Schamoni, Hans Schuhmacher (from *Film-Kurier*, the leading film trade paper) and several others. In an impassioned speech, Anschütz outlined the dangers he foresaw for abstract art and colour-music under the Nazi regime, and insisted that a coordinated resistance could undermine the wishy-washy Nazi bluster. He urged all present to persist in mentioning and promoting abstract art, even if subterfuges were necessary, such as using different terms (like "ornamental") or swearing that it is the essence of Germanic art. He used the phrase "Maul halten, weiter dienen": by being cleverly reticent, one might be, in the long run, of greater service. He pointed out that scientist and artist alike at the Farbe-Ton-Kongreß had always agreed that abstract art and Visual Music have an automatic, implicit effect, a sub-conscious communication to the beholder of a joy, a calming satisfaction from release of tension, etc.; therefore, he insisted, no opportunity for exposing people to Visual Music should be neglected, even if it means working from the inside, publishing in official Nazi papers or working in their offices. Anschütz paid special tribute to Oskar as a creative genius, and charged everyone to help him continue to be productive despite all odds. Everyone was deeply moved by Anschütz's appeal and vowed to cooperate in a kind of guerilla warfare of journalism.

Fürst was particularly impressed, and his attachment to Oskar lent extra weight to his resolve. Loni realized that Oskar was particularly vulnerable because of his uncompromising honesty and his love for debate. At a business reception held by a carpenter, Sarkowski, whose business was downstairs from Oskar on Friedrichstrasse, Oskar recounted in detail a dream he had about the "Hitler Curve": how he was confident that Hitler's regime would topple soon, because he had dreamed that, like a graph, Hitler was on the rise now, but he would suddenly slump and disappear into nothingness. Oskar even drew the "curve" on the wall next to the telephone where Sarkowski left a pencil hanging on a string to write phone numbers with. Fortunately for Oskar, no one present was nationalistic or indiscreet enough to betray Oskar's foolhardy pronouncement. Knowing Oskar would need as much help as possible, Loni decided to try out the "double agent" strategy that Anschütz suggested. In the 30 November issue of one of the Nazi papers *Der Deutsche Aufbau*, Loni published an article which, tongue in cheek, quotes "Reichsminister Dr. Goebbels für die Reichskulturkammer dahin präzisiert hat, in Zukunft die *geistige Repräsentantin der gesamten Nation* zu werden" [Minister Dr. Goebbels has declared that the State Chamber of Culture will be in the future the intellectual representative of the whole nation", and concludes by slyly quoting an Italian fascist, "Massimo Bontempelli in einem herrlichen Aufsatz, betitelt *Kunst und Faschismus* wünscht: 'Die Kunst soll ein Wunder sein statt einer Langeweile, eine magische Tat statt der Erledigung einer Beamtentätigkeit'." [Massimo Bontempelli, in a magnificent statement entitled "Art and Fascism", desires that Art should be a wonder instead of a bore, a magical deed instead of the dutiful function of a civil servant.] The editor of the paper, Wolfgang Fischer, added a postscript noting that the French film *La Maternelle* (by the Jewish team Jacques Benoit-Levy and Marie Epstein) had played in Berlin to sold-out houses for weeks, precisely because it was a better film than the usual German feature: something he trusts that the Reichsfilmkammer will be improving soon – which must have secretly rankled Goebbels who had spent much of October and November trying to salvage the poor quality "Horst Wessel" movie, while the approved propaganda movie *Hitlerjunge Quex* had received its gala première 10 days before, to less than sell-out crowds.

Loni sent a copy of his article to Oskar with "Maul halten, weiter dienen" written across the top. But he knew that Oskar would never "hold his tongue", and in July 1934, when Fürst received an offer of a government job, he accepted with much trepidation. By 23 July 1934, he wrote "Mein lieber Fischinger, alter Kampfgenoße! Immer mehr komme ich zu der Erkenntnis, daß es für mich sinnlos, ja sogar schädlich ist, die paralytischen Transpirationen der deutschen Filmindustrie in abgequälten Feuilletons zu popularisieren" [My dear Fischinger, old comrade in the struggle, I recognize more and more that it is senseless, even harmful, for me to popularize the paralytic perspiration of the German film industry in worried newspapers]. On 20 May a critic of the *DAZ* had been publicly dishonoured and banned from future employment (and the paper forced to print an apology) for criticizing Goebbels, and on 17 June three writers had been executed when von Papen criticized Goebbels in a speech. In his new position, a Dramaturg for the Filmkammer, Fürst not only had access to privileged information, but was allowed to manage a newspaper, *Der Deutsche Film*, which, Hans Fischinger notes in a 3 April 1937 letter to Oskar, carried frequent mention of Oskar's films. Fürst's new job would also pay off in other ways for Oskar, who would be arrested three times during the coming years, and each time released with the inside machinations of Fürst, who could claim Oskar's talents would be useful to the film industry. By late 1937, however, Fürst's credibility with the toughening NSDAP (Nazi party) was wearing thin, and he was assigned to a "powerless" position in the government film offices, supervising the preparation of censored film copies – dubbing in new "correct" lines and re-mixing music to smooth over the cuts.

Meanwhile, Oskar worked frantically to finish the colour film *Kreise* [*Circles*] on time. In order to avoid trouble with music rights, he got Richard Ralfs and the orchestra of the Capitol cinema to record for him an arrangement of Wagner's "Venusberg" ballet from *Tannhäuser* which melted into the "Huldigungsmarsch" [Triumphal March] from Grieg's *Sigurd Jorsalfar*. Since Oskar had let all his salaried girls go, he begged

Elfriede and Trudl to come help fill in colours on the hundreds of drawings, and tend the camera for the long, precise exposures. They both came from Gelnhausen immediately, and with Elfriede painting and Trudl timing long hours of tedious triple exposures, the film was ready by Christmas. Although it consists of quintessentially abstract choreography of different kinds of circles – solid discs, concentric radiating circles, curved rainbow bands, etc. – Oskar was able to sneak it past the censorship office by licensing it to the Tolirag advertising agency, appending an end title reading "Alle Kreise erfaßt Tolirag" [Tolirag reaches all circles of society], and thus having it approved as an advertising film. Simultaneously, acting on advice from the Farbe-Ton-Kongreß, he sent out feelers to the Venice Film Festival to see if he could get a screening there in August 1934, and they replied enthusiastically. In theory, if Oskar could garner rave reviews in ally fascist Italy, German censors would be harder-pressed to refuse his films. *Kreise* [Circles] was also re-sold to other companies, such as Van Houten chocolate, with merely the last frames giving a new name to advertise any business. And Oskar prepared an entirely abstract version with no lettering at all over the ending moments.

Ernst Schimanek.

Meanwhile, Elfriede had returned to Oskar in Berlin with her own melodrama, as a desperate refugee. When she had gone back to Gelnhausen in March 1933, her parents were determined to make her settle down and take on a respectable role as wife, mother, and business-partner to someone involved in a substantial business. At that time they had a young apprentice, Ernst Schimanek from Vienna, visiting to study the successful Fischinger Drugstore before returning to Austria and a drugstore of his own. Elfriede's aunt and mother thought Elfriede and Ernst should make a perfect couple, and delighted in the prospect of an international chain of related drugstores. They purposely made every attempt to get Ernst and Elfriede alone together, sending them on joint errands and recreations. Finally in June, Elfriede, a little tipsy with new wine, made love with Ernst in the romantic forest near Gelnhausen. She became pregnant, but did not tell anyone. She liked Ernst, but certainly did not want to become the dutiful wife of a druggist, even a druggist in Vienna. She thought of secretly having an abortion, but she had done that before (after an escapade during one of the zinnober costume balls at her college in Offenbach ...) and did not want to go through it again. She thought seriously of suicide. When Oskar asked her to come to Berlin, it seemed a godsend. After a few weeks of concentrated work, trying to make herself indispensable, she told Oskar of her plight, and asked him if he would marry her, just to give the whole thing a stable end. Oskar said he had never wanted to marry, because his artwork took all of his time and energy – and what little money he made was never enough, certainly not enough to support a family. Elfriede wrote up a "pre-nuptial agreement" promising to be responsible for all the care and expenses of her child, promising never to bother nor hinder Oskar in his work. Oskar agreed. Elfriede was elated. They told Loni and Trudl, asking them to be best man and bride's maid at their wedding, which would be done quickly and quietly in Berlin without interference from Gelnhausen. Trudl agreed, and so did Loni, but Loni took Oskar aside and warned him that he thought it would be the greatest mistake of his life. Oskar explained about the "pre-nuptial agreement", but Loni did not believe that it could be practical or effective in the long run. Elfriede wanted the ceremony to be in a Catholic church, but she found immediately that the church looked quite negatively on the idea of first cousins getting married, and refused to proceed without getting approval from her priest back in Gelnhausen, as well as her and Oskar's parents. Undaunted, Elfriede opted for a civil ceremony. On 30 November 1933, Elfriede and Oskar were married in a civil service at the government offices in Berlin. Trudl was a bride's maid, and Loni was the Best Man – but he (who was ususally scrupulously punctual and well-groomed to the point of being a "dandy") arrived 20 minutes late, unshaven, rumpled and drunk, having given in to an all-night binge in despair at the thought of losing Oskar, and Oskar probably losing his creative vitality. The ceremony, though delayed, ran smoothly. A formal church wedding finally was approved and took place 31 January 1934 at St. Clemens church in Berlin – with Loni and Trudl again, but this time Elfriede's generous bouquet of flowers could not conceal that she was very pregnant indeed. A month later their son Karl was born. Oskar was thrilled, enchanted by the miracle of this little creature growing and changing, fascinated even by the diapers and moody tantrums of babyhood. Karl was always Oskar's son, and neither Oskar nor Elfriede ever spoke about Karl's genetic father either to Karl or to any of the other Fischinger children. Nor did Ernst Schimanek know that Elfriede had borne his child.

On 11 February 1934, just 5 days before a new tighter censorship law went into effect, Oskar received approval for another abstract film, *Ein Spiel in Farben* [A Play in Colours], which was a "colourized" version of the banned *Studie Nr. 11*, fronted as an advertising film for the AAFA Film company. Oskar did not like the results of adding colours and backgrounds to the minimal simplicity of his black-and-white film, especially the delicate Mozart, and he also disliked the two-colour (mostly orange and turquoise) process AAFA used – but this was the only way *Studie Nr. 11* could be legally seen in Germany. Although the Venice festival asked for it in February, Oskar did not after all send *Ein Spiel in Farben* for his programme at the August festival.

Advertising films became a lucrative venue for Oskar. In April 1934 he premièred a colour commercial for Muratti Cigarettes, which proved to be such a sensational success that it continued to run for more than a year (an extended censorship number had to be issued 1 June), partly because it capitalized on Olympic Games fever (tickets for the huge Berlin event went on sale 1 January 1935), showing the cigarettes parading into a stadium and performing little feats like ice-skating.

Muratti greift ein [Muratti gets in the act] is also a miracle of clever animation. After numerous tests with drawn cigarettes (some showing cigarettes parachuting down on to live-action Wilhelm Straße and walking through the Brandenburg Gate) and actual tobacco cigarettes, Oskar opted for a laborious process of creating small wooden sticks the same size and oval shape as Muratti cigarettes, covering them with genuine Muratti cigarette paper, then fixing a pin into the bottom of each. Elfriede and Trudl did most of this work creating

Trudl.

the "cigarettes". The "stage" was a metre-diameter table on ball-bearings, so that it could be moved small calibrated increments to give the impression that the cigarettes would be walking past the background, or that the camera was moving past the scene on a dolly. The glass top of the round table was covered with a layer of kaolin, then sprinkled with sawdust dyed to resemble tobacco [real tobacco warped under the hot lights, so Elfriede and Trudl, with their textile training, undertook the task of dyeing]. Each "cigarette" stood up by having its pin stuck down into the kaolin (the sawdust obscured the pinholes), and had to be pulled up and re-inserted for each new frame's exposure – and in many scenes dozens of individual cigarettes are moving at the same time. Oskar also calculated complex camera moves which give the impression that the camera descends on a boom down to the ground level where the "feet" of the cigarettes are passing close by – a manoeuvre which a live-action camera crew would be hard-pressed to pull off! While Oskar supervised from his chart of calculations, Elfriede would move the pins, and Trudl would carefully time and chart the three exposures for each frame of film. Again Oskar made a clever selection of music, well-chosen excerpts from Josef Bayer's ballet *Die Puppenfee* [The Doll-Fairy], which Richard Ralfs and the Capitol cinema orchestra recorded for him, that add just the right jolly, absurd touch to complement the extravagant cigarette epic.

The profits from this advertising film and the consequent commissions for a dozen more commercials allowed Oskar to hire a staff again, and begin concentrating on producing serious visual music films. He hoped to play on Goebbels' craving for good German-produced colour films, and use an advance groundswell of rave reviews to break through censorship and re-establish visual music as a viable German film genre – an open door for the return of modernist avant-garde sensibility in film.

This strategy did prove successful in getting Oskar's films approved for export to Venice. On 20 June 1934 he sent to the Reichsfilmkammer copies of enthusiastic requests from Attilio Fontana, the festival director, along with indications of how popular his films had been at previous screenings abroad, and careful hints as to how nice it would be if Germany were represented by a stunning colour film. Although he was officially reprimanded 21 June 1934 for having corresponded abroad without bureaucratic permission [the chilling letter began "Mir ist zu Ohren gekommen, daß die Ausstellungs-Leitung der Venediger Kunstausstellung sich an Sie direkt gewandt hat.": It has come to my ears that the management of exhibitions for the Venice Art Exhibit is in direct contact with you], nevertheless he received the export license on 28 June, in time for the films to be screened, to wild acclaim, at the festival.

Oskar's plans for new visual music films all went awry, however. In May and June (he wrote to Fürst on 20 June 1934) he went alone on the long-planned walking trip through the Swiss alps to film rivers and valleys that could be synchronized with music. When he tested out the footage in juxtaposition to Bach's *Brandenburg Concerto Nr. 3*, however, he realized how masterfully artistic was the camerawork of Walther Ruttmann's *In der Nacht*, and how informal or impressionistic was his own – not that his own really displeased him, but he feared that neither audiences nor censors would accept it as a "professional" film, though possibly the avant-garde Film Societies would appreciate it – but he would have no further easy access to the League of Independent Film, with the Nazis in vigilant control of imports and exports. The Reichsfilmkammer did reject three new projects in July: a colour animation of Berlioz's *Rakoczy March*, a black-and-white *Studie Nr. 13* (synchronized to Beethoven's *Coriolan* overture), and *Quadrate* [Squares]. Neither the Berlioz nor Beethoven were completed films, but *Quadrate*, one of Oskar's most daring experiments, was, and has been subsequently lost in its original form. *Quadrate* was designed specifically for the GasparColor process, which used a three-colour separation negative, and Oskar planned to alter the filters so that the same basic 300 animation paintings (tempera on paper) could be printed over and over again with different filter substitutions, so that the same colours would not appear until after about six minutes. Not only the looped repetition of the cluster of squares, but also the continual subtle changes in colour balance remarkably prefigure Josef Albers' serial "Homage to the Square". Unfortunately, only a badly-damaged fragment of this original version survives, and since the GasparColor process is no longer used, it could not be reconstructed easily, even though most of the original tempera paintings are intact. So this brilliant film must count as another of the casualties of the Nazi era.

When Oskar realized that his absolute films would be rejected by the Reichsfilmkammer as "contrary to the spirit of the times", he was temporarily depressed, but Dr. Johannes Eckhardt, manager of Kamera Unter den Linden, happened to remark that when the Kamera only received a scheduled print at the last moment, they applied for an "emergency permit", which then served *de facto* as a censorship number, unless someone bothered to revoke it, which did not often happen. On 16 August 1934 Kamera scheduled the wholly abstract version of *Kreise* for a one-night-only special screening. On 15 August Oskar obtained an emergency permit, and the absolute version of *Kreise* was officially approved for screening in Germany. Hans Schuhmacher arranged press support from *Film-Kurier*: on 18 August, an article about Venice, although containing only one sentence praising *Kreise*, bears the bold headline *Fischinger wieder erfolgreich* [Fischinger Successful Again]. Again on 2 October 1934 Schuhmacher printed a long, daring article with the simple headline *Fischinger*, which stresses Oskar's successes abroad and points out that absolute film is also universal and international, hence a good ambassador for Germany – which is why Oskar should be commissioned to make a Colour Symphony for the Olympics! An 18 October 1934 article headlined *Oskar Fischingers Farb-Ton-Spiel "Kreise"* conveys overwhelming raves from a Munich screening. For their New Year's Eve edition *Film-Kurier* created a veritable profile of the surviving avant-garde, by printing the wishes for the coming year of Oskar, Curt Oertel, Wilfried Basse, Lotte Reiniger and Frank Wysbar (alongside a few more traditional film industry people). Oskar said, "Ich wünsche 1935 das erste, große, abendfüllende Farb-Film-Werk – ein absolutes Farbwerk, das ganz aus Musik geboren, allen Menschen der Erdeverständlich ist – und ungeheure Devisen ins Land bringt! Das wünsche ich mit ganzer Kraft!" [I want to make in 1935 the first great feature-length colour film – an *absolute* colour work, born wholly out of music, *comprehensible to all the people on Earth* – which will bring huge amounts of foreign currency into our country! I wish this with all my might!]

A mild reprimand for this rampant enthusiasm appeared in the 10 January 1935 *Film-Kurier* in the form of a letter from Dr. Fritz Stege, the music critic of the Nazi "Völkischen Beobachter", titled *Filmkonzert statt Konzertfilm* [Film concerts instead of concert films], claiming among other somewhat confusing statements that "Das Volk hat einen Widerwillen gegen Begriffe wie 'Opus' und 'Sinfonie', hinter denen es Gelehrsamkeit und Kunstsnobismus wittert" [The people have an aversion to expressions like "opus" and "symphony", behind which they sniff erudition and art-snobbery.]

While this little battle for abstract film was being fought, the Fischinger studio continued to turn out commercials – for Meluka cigarettes, for Borg cigarettes (one half-minute fragment of a charming rhumba survives), for Muratti (to a Paul Linke march), for B-3 cigarettes, and one film that survives whole, a *Muratti Privat* commercial synchronized to Mozart music, in black-and-white, which in many places looks like one of the *Studie*, for the white cigarettes move in patterns against black velvet, like Oskar's drawn lines in the earlier absolute films. Charlie Engel, one of Oskar's hired staff, appears briefly puffing on a cigarette, and a line of cigarettes stroll out of his exhaled smoke.

Oskar also made a colour ad for Euthymol toothpaste in England. The Jewish Gaspar brothers had moved their company to London, and they arranged the deal for Oskar, who would shoot the film in Berlin, mail it to England to be processed, then get a copy of all the rough footage mailed back to Oskar in Berlin. Oskar would edit a sample version of the finished film and mail it back to London, where a professional negative cutter would assemble the final printing master, and the prints would be struck by Gaspar in London. The resulting film, called *Pink Guards on Parade*, was quite successful, with pink toothpaste squeezing out of tubes and rolling across a model landscape in charming patterns until they reach a palace (made of Euthymol boxes) where they climb a staircase toward a rising sun with the word "Euthymol" radiating from it. Oskar also shot some special effects for a musical feature about bosses and secretaries *Annette im Paradies*, and he created logos for two Berlin film companies, Europa and Rota [which consisted of the letters "R", "O", "T" and "A" racing from a vast distance towards the viewer, to the accompaniment of four trumpet blasts].

Meanwhile, Oskar and Elfriede had really become husband and wife. Although they were still temperamentally opposite – Elfriede high-energy and talkative, Oskar contemplative and more quiet – they adjusted well. Oskar went through a number of eccentric dietary changes (e.g. only eating raw foods for several months) but Elfriede adjusted and made whatever Oskar wanted, even if it meant cooking a whole different meal for Karl, Trudl or herself. She tried not to interrupt when Oskar was planning or working. And she recycled the energy she might have prefered to squander on dancing into making home improvements. Trudl had relatives in the neighbourhood of Danzig, which was an easy train ride away, so she often would be away for a few days or weeks. Oskar felt that the family would be better off farther from the city centre, in case of political riots, which Oskar assumed would come. They rented a new apartment on Rixdorferstrasse, on the outskirts of town, but an easy tram ride to the city centre. The Rixdorfer apartment was surrounded by some greenery, near tennis courts and strolling paths for leisurely walks – definitely an improvement from noisy Friederichstrasse. Above all, however, Oskar and Elfriede became compatible lovers. Oskar liked to play games with sex, pretending to be someone else, somewhere else, and Elfriede, with her costume-ball background, was more than willing to feign being an Inca princess or a Tartar warrior. All was not perfect on Rixdorferstrasse, however. The Nazis arranged that every building had an official Nazi party member in residence, nominally as a "manager" or "supervisor". Frau Schmidt, the

Elfriede on Rixdorferstrasse.

Nazi for the Rixdorfer apartments, was particularly zealous, and suspicious of Oskar and Elfriede as bohemian artists. When some Nazi celebrity was scheduled to drive past the Rixdorfer apartments on his way to central Berlin, Frau Schmidt insisted that every apartment in her building would fly the Nazi flag from their window. Oskar refused. She turned him in to the authorities and he was arrested. Through Loni Fürst's machinations (certifying Oskar as "valuable to the state" because of his ability to create special effects, possibly to "modify" newsreels), Oskar was fairly quickly released. Unfortunately Oskar had another run-in with the police soon after: near the Friedrichstrasse Studio, as he walked past the offices of the Volkische Beobachter [the official Nazi newspaper], which displayed its pages in glass cases along the side of the building, Oskar said "You don't really believe that bullshit, do you?" to someone who was indeed reading the propaganda. Within a minute Nazi guards arrested him, but once again, through Loni Fürst's intervention, Oskar was released fairly quickly. Loni warned him sternly that his influence could not protect Oskar much further, that Oskar must be more cautious, and even dissemble if he expected to survive. Oskar said simply, "I'm not sure I can. The truth just comes out."

All during the winter months of 1934/35, Oskar and Elfriede worked secretly nights and weekends, whenever the hired staff was away, on a new abstract colour film synchronized to the overture from Otto Nicolai's opera *Die Lustigen Weiber von Windsor* [The Merry Wives of Windsor], abridged and performed by Richard Ralfs and the Capitol orchestra. Using the same round turntable on which they had shot the colour Muratti film, they animated three-dimensional models about the same height as cigarettes: wooden cubes and cylinders, some painted, some Elfriede covered in cloth. The set seems at first to be a room, but then the floor begins to mirror the figures, cubes align to make a flat mosaic surface, then stagger themselves to create stairs. In this mutable universe, a cylinder can pound on the floor and create ripples, or a decorative flat circle can fly off into space. The serene beauty of coloured geometric shapes (a yellow rectangle gracefully dropping down into the frame) escalate into a zany enchantment of impossibilities that nonetheless seem inevitable. *Komposition in Blau* is the masterpiece of a totally mature, confident artist.

When the film was finished in April 1935, Oskar again set about arranging for a "sneak preview" in order to apply for an emergency censorship permit. He used the title *Lichtkonzert Nr. 1* [Light Concert No. 1] on the application, partly because he hoped to finish the Berlioz "Rakoczy March" as *Lichtkonzert Nr. 2*, and partly because he hoped to capitalize on Stege's Nazi demand for more "film concerts". Fritz Böhme in *DAZ* provided enthusiastic advance press notice in the form of a joint interview with Lotte Reiniger and Oskar Fischinger entitled "Beiprogramm ist keine Nebensache!" [Short subjects are no secondary thing!]. The emergency permit was granted on 10 May 1935.

These bureaucratic manoeuvres and newspaper articles may sound like simple matters, but no action could be undertaken without real fear during the Nazi era. The night before the sneak preview of *Komposition in Blau* at the Capitol, Elfriede could not find Oskar anywhere, and dinner was getting cold. When she switched on the lights in a dark room in order to see if Oskar had left any clue to where he had gone, she saw Oskar himself lying there rigidly.

"What's the matter, Oskar? What are you doing in the dark? It's dinner time." she said.

After a long hesitation, Oskar spoke in a subdued voice, "Nicolai died just a few months after the première of *Lustigen Weiber*. How soon will I be gone?"

The sneak première of *Komposition* itself was a smashing success, with the audience stamping their feet and crying out for "Fischinger!" Oskar, however, was hiding in the sound booth with Richard Ralfs, just in case the screening had been disrupted by Nazi agitators, or just in case he, as perpetrator of the film, would have been arrested.

The "subversive" efforts of the "avant-garde" continued. Fürst warned Oskar that new censorship laws restricting export of German films would go into effect in June, so on 23 May Oskar shipped a print of *Komposition in Blau* to Rome, without proper papers, so that the director of the Venice festival could see it and demand it.

No German distributor or theatre chain dared handle *Komposition in Blau* despite its success at the preview. The Waterloo Theater in Hamburg finally undertook an official announced première on 28 June 1935, as a short with *Chained*, starring Clark Gable and Joan Crawford [and, coincidentally, the same date the sex-crimes law, Paragraph 175, was enlarged to include such crimes as "having homosexual fantasies"]. Fürst undertook to pave the way with one of his most daring and witty escapades; "if they were going to get me," he said, "then I might as well go in style". Taking advantage of the vacation of the editor Hans-Walther Betz (soon to be co-author of the "Degenerate Film Catalogue" *Film-"Kunst" Film-Kohn Film-Korruption* [Film "Art", Film Cohen, Film Corruption]), Fürst managed to plant a whole page spread in the official Nazi film paper *Der Film* on 20 June 1935. Using a clever line drawing of a unicorn with a horn made of film, he posits a should-be-endangered species, "Das Zellhorn" [The celluloid unicorn], the stodgy distributor unwilling to take a chance on unusual films. Using *Komposition in Blau* as a specific example of a successful German film that has found no commercial outlet, he laments "daß die 'Experimentierer' im deutschen Film aussterben" [that the "experimenter" in German film will die out]. In a last brilliant touch, Fürst reproduced at the bottom of the column, almost as if it belonged to "das Zellhorn", a photo from a Czech newspaper in which their delegates to the recent film festival in Berlin are shown with the swastikas air-brushed out of the NS flags in the background; the caption reads "So groß ist die Angst?" [Are they *that* afraid?], and after a brief identification of the photo, concludes with the ineffably ambiguous phrase, "Kommentar überflüssig" [commentary superfluous].

The scheming worked. *Komposition in Blau* had been approved by an official Nazi newspaper, and they could not back down. For the Hamburg première, *Der Film* reprinted an Italian article "Filme ohne Schauspieler und Abenteuer" [Films without actors or plots] (thus shunting any blame on to their fascist neighbours to the south), although a notice about *Chained* [In goldenen Ketten] does conclude with the remark that *Komposition in Blau* is a "bedeutungsvolle Überraschung, und wir sind geneigt, sie als die größere zu bezeichnen" [a significant surprise, and we're tempted to declare it the greater film]. The author, "Ste.", admits that while it is hard to describe in words, it must be honoured as a pioneer work of the avangardist Fischinger. On the same page appears a letter from Werner Kark (a Hamburg film critic, friend of Anschütz, and later supporter of Hans Fischinger) protesting that censorship of feature films is getting too lax, because too many mediocre ones are being shown – clearly his ploy to enhance the value of Oskar's *Komposition*.

That same day, Fritz Böhme's *DAZ* article "Geschaute Musik" carefully avoids the term "abstract" while enunciating an impeccable critical context for Oskar's work, praising it as the logical epitome of a great ancient German tradition of "ornament art", including decorative motifs on clothing and books, architecture and landscaping. But now, Böhme points out, through filmic control of time, Fischinger is able to render ornament in dance choreography and create the full equivalent of the musical sphere in visual terms, of which colours are a key factor, representing nuances of musical tone colours. He also insists that Fischinger has an international reputation as significant as Lotte Reiniger or Walt Disney.

An anonymous front-page article in *Licht Bild Bühne* on 11 July, with the simple bold headline *Oskar Fischinger*, pleads for *Komposition in Blau* to be shown as an official German entry in the Venice film festival, and observes "Das Los des Propheten, der nichts in seinem Vaterlande gilt, hat auch Fischinger in seiner ganzen Schwere erfahren müssen" [The lot of the prophet, not to be honoured in his homeland, is something Fischinger, among all his other difficulties, must bear]. This article makes almost exactly the same points as Böhme's article, but freshly written, adding Carolingian illuminations, Dürer and Rembrandt to the list of Oskar's predecessors.

Licht Bild Bühne voiced similar sentiments a month later when *Komposition in Blau* did play at the Venice Film Festival, calling Oskar's film "wohl die größte Sensation" [by all odds the greatest sensation]. Chiding the German film industry for not using Oskar's talents, the article claims "Die amerikanische Filmindustrie hätte einen derartigen Könner zu populärem Ruf verholfen" [The American film industry would have helped someone of this kind of ability to reach popular fame].

Although clearly a popular favourite, *Komposition in Blau* did not win a prize in Venice (perhaps because Reichsfilmkammer President Fritz Scheuermann was on the jury), but Trencker's *Der verlorene Sohn* [The Prodigal Son] and Riefenstahl's *Triumph des Willens* [Triumph of the Will] did – and the best animated film award went to Walt Disney's *Band Concert* while the best colour award went to Rouben Mamoulian's *Becky Sharp*.

Elfriede had known since Christmas time that she was pregnant. On 22 July 1935 she gave birth to a son, who was christened Roland. Again Oskar was enchanted by the miracle of human life. But three months later, on 22 October, Roland died in a bizarre accident. Elfriede had laid him down to sleep on one of the large fluffy pillows common in Germany. The pillow was near a basin of water, and it gradually began to soak up the fluid until the baby was drowned or suffocated. Both Oskar and Elfriede were devastated. Trudl took charge of things, and Elfriede's mother came from Gelnhausen. But worst of all, Frau Schmidt, the Nazi organizer at Rixdorferstrasse, turned Elfriede in to the police for "the murder of an Aryan child", and she was brought to trial along with Oskar. Trudl and other friends testified to how much Elfriede loved Roland, and how preposterous it was to suppose she would have killed her baby, but the zealous Nazi prosecuter had dug up the details of Elfriede's abortion some six years before, during her school days [she had had at least one more abortion as well, probably Oskar's child, during the back-and-forth Gelnhausen/Berlin period, but fortunately that was not discovered or introduced into the trial]. And, fortunately, Loni Fürst was once again able to exert some behind-the-scenes political pressure in favour of Oskar and Elfriede, and after an agonizing week of insults and interrogations Elfriede was exonerated. They couldn't bear going back to Rixdorferstrasse, and began staying in the Friedrichstrasse studio again.

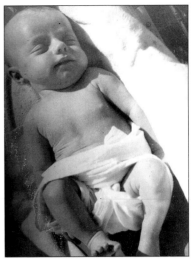

Roland Fischinger.

No German distributor dared to pick up *Komposition in Blau*, although the Waterloo Theatre played it again for two weeks in August (as a short with the Cukor/Hepburn *Little Women*) and generated another wave of rave reviews. Oskar and Elfriede had to handle the business end of *Komposition* from their Berlin studio, which the high cost of colour prints made specially difficult. Hans Fischinger was working in Alzenau on a colour organ which he had invented (it used hundreds of tiny light bulbs across a screen, almost like computer pixels) thinking that if the Nazi censors refused permission for abstract films, at least he could compose and play colour music live on this instrument; ironically he was denied a patent for this colour organ, and denied permission to acquire the parts to build it, so his "inner emigration" was also a failure. In any case, Hans helped with the distribution of *Komposition* in Frankfurt and the south, which included following the film around to theatres to make sure they did not damage the precious prints. Other friends helped out, as well. Fürst gave a special lecture "Film als Ausdrucksform" [Film as a means of Expression] to a convention of theatre owners, in which he recommended and showed Oskar's film – and *Film-Kurier* printed an abridged version of the lecture (11 November 1935). *Film-Kurier* also passed along to Oskar letters from readers enquiring about renting *Komposition*.

Despite the fact that this home-made distribution could barely keep the Fischinger family afloat, Oskar continued to paint images for his *Lichtkonzert Nr. 2*. Infuriated by the continuing decay of Nazi standards (the Nuremburg Laws of 12 September 1935 depriving Jews of citizen-

ship [which caused Mr. Burmester, one of the managers of Tolirag, to commit suicide because he had a Jewish wife], and the pogrom of 12 December 1935 which arrested 3440 Catholics and socialists), Oskar wrote on 19 December 1935 a (potentially suicidal) four-page letter to Goebbels demanding that Fischinger's work be treated with the respect it deserved, properly financed like other films, properly distributed like other films. Oskar made no attempt to hide the abstract nature of his films, and insisted that they were, in their very abstractness, the most noble kind of films possible.

Fortunately for Oskar, an MGM agent had taken a print of *Composition in Blue* and the colour *Muratti* ad to Hollywood for a test screening at a small art-cinema on Vine street, Filmarte Theater, where Ernst Lubitsch (a German emigrant, at that time head of production at Paramount) saw them – and saw a crowded audience stomp, shout and whistle, demanding a repeat of the two shorts. Impressed by the success of the Muratti ad and *Komposition in Blau*, Lubitsch had the German Paramount agent telephone Oskar. Elfriede and Oskar were sitting in an almost dark studio, still depressed. A voice with an American accent asked if this were *the* Fischinger who had made the *Composition in Blue*. Oskar replied, "Yes". The American voice continued: "Mr. Lubitsch would like to hire you to work for him in Hollywood. Would you be willing to leave Germany?" Oskar said "Yes" immediately. Paramount had already made some preliminary arrangements, and the bureaucratic mechanism began to help the Fischingers leave Germany. Paramount acquired the rights to distribute *Komposition* in Germany, and began showing it with their new releases, such as *Valiant is the Name for Carrie*,

Karl Nierendorf on board the boat to America [photo by Elfriede Fischinger].

long after Oskar had departed for America. Oskar himself was to leave immediately, but Elfriede would follow in a month, giving her a chance to pack up and store things they could not take with them.

The Fischingers – not only Oskar but also Karl and Elfriede, and Oskar's brother Otto and his wife Annie who lived near Bremen – were searched three times (including an intimate search of body cavities) on their way to the boat – when boarding the train to Bremerhaven, on board the train, and before going up the gangplank to the ship – to make sure that they were not taking any money or other things of value out of Germany – but their most valuable items, one copy of each of Oskar's sound films, had already been shipped covertly from Paramount offices Berlin to Paramount offices Hollywood, along with 42 paintings by Klee, Kandinsky, Feininger and other artists under attack as "degenerates", which the Berlin art dealer Karl Nierendorf (who fled Germany on the same boat as Elfriede Fischinger) would need to start up a new gallery in America.

Elfriede worked with Miss Sperling to pack all of the things in the Friedrichstrasse studio. Oskar had cautioned them not to throw *anything* away, because it might have some importance to him that wasn't immediately obvious. Faithfully they emptied the intact contents of drawers and shelves into boxes. All the cans of film, and loose pieces of

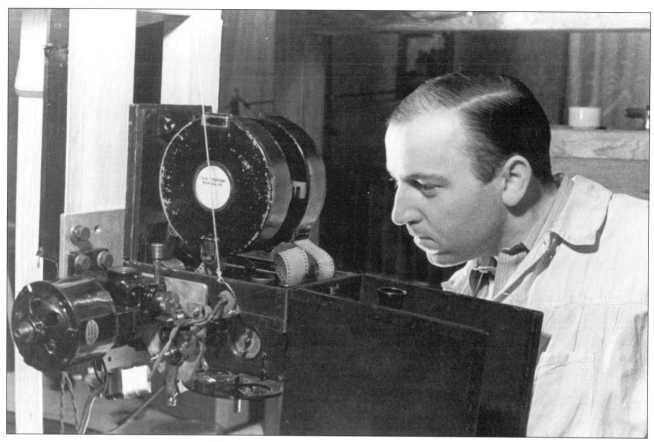

Hans Fischinger.

film were also boxed. All of the animation drawings for the *Studie* and other films were also packed up. And these entire contents of the Berlin studio were taken to Gelnhausen and placed in the large storage cellar of the Fischinger Drugstore, with the exception of a few boxes that would not fit in the cellar (which still had to be used to keep some extra stock for the store) and were wedged into the attic beneath the roof of the drugstore (Elfriede's parents and family lived on the upper floors above the drugstore, and also stored some items, such as an old sewing machine, in this attic).

On 4 March 1936, less than a month after Oskar left Germany, Ausstellung von "Kulturdokumenten" des Bolschewismus und jüdischer Zersetzungsarbeit: Entartete Kunst [An Exhibition of 'Culture Documents' of Communist and Jewish decadent work: Degenerate Art] opened at the Police Headquarters in Munich. Elfriede Fischinger, who had stayed behind to liquidate the contents of the Berlin Studio, as she boarded the train to leave Germany, bought a *Münchner Illustrierte Presse* to read, and found among the ads for Nivea and Palmolive, beside articles about Karin Branzell and Julius Patzak singing at the Opera, a two-page picture spread of *Kranke Kunst* [Sick Art] in which examples of Klee, Nolde, Dix and Lipschitz were derided. She was glad Oskar had already gone.

The resistance of the Visual Music avant garde lasted three more years in Germany. At the Farbe-Ton-Kongress Oct 1936 in Hamburg, the handful of devotees regrouped around Anschütz and, now that Oskar was gone, planned to support Hans Fischinger to prepare a new colour music film. In the two years it took Hans to complete his 7-minute *Tanz der Farben* [Dance of the Colours, synchronized to excerpts from Ponchielli's "Dance of the Hours"], Fürst continued to lecture and write; Victor Schamoni published a history of Visual Music, *Das Lichtspiel*, which pretended to be his 1926 dissertation, although it is full of information about Oskar's colour films; Hans Stoltenberg published an updated version of his *Reine Farbkunst*; and nostalgic, regretful mentions of Oskar appeared often in the trade papers. The Waterloo Theatre prepared a special film club screening series, Film Heute und Morgen [Film Today and Tomorrow], headed by Werner Kark, which began in October 1938, running such films as *Komposition in Blau*, the Sagan/Wysbar *Mädchen in Uniform*, Oertel's *Schimmelreiter*, and Wysbar's *Fährmann Maria*. Hans Fischinger's *Tanz der Farben* was planned for a première on 26 February 1939 as a short with Douglas Sirk's *Schlußakkord*. On 23 February Hans obtained a special emergency censorship number, as Oskar had done, with GasparColor's help. The screening was a smash hit, and *Tanz der Farben* continued to be shown for two weeks. Hans printed a statement "Der Mensch muß musikalisch sehen lernen" [People must learn to see musically] in several newspapers, and rave reviews made it into all the trades after a "sneak" press preview in Berlin. But the Reichsfilmkammer acted swiftly and effectively, apparently having learned its lesson with Oskar. On 14 March Tobis (now a government-owned company) purchased the rights to *Tanz der Farben*, but never screened it in Germany, thus tacitly suppressing it (although Tobis made back its investment by screening the film in Holland alone). On 29 March the Waterloo Theatre's film club was closed down. On 4 April *Licht Bild Bühne* printed a full-page article by "Georg Santé", celebrating Walter Ruttmann, "Bildsymphonie der Arbeit" [Picture-Symphony of Labour], which suppresses any

Newspaper headline.

reference to his abstract work, and identifies him an avantgardist who makes documentaries for the glory of the state. The last, futile rebuttal was Prof. Dr. Anschütz' full-page front-page headline *Von Pater Castel bis Hans Fischinger – Zur Geschichte des ungegenständlichen Tonfilms* [From Father Castel to Hans Fischinger – Toward a History of Non-Objective Sound Films]. But the avant garde film was dead in Nazi Germany. Hans Fischinger began another film, which journalist Erich Fornoff preserved in a few black-and-white photos and a few tests in 16mm. In April 1940 Hans was drafted into the army, sent to the Eastern Front, and disappeared without ever having finished it.

3

Hollywood

Oskar in America knew nothing of this. He arrived on a luxury ocean liner, was escorted to Hollywood on a first-class train by Paramount employees, and paid a salary of $250 per week (quite a substantial amount in Depression-era America), starting immediately upon his arrival on 26 February 1936, even though he had no work to do yet. He was given an office at the Paramount studios, and German-speaking secretaries to translate for him, as well as a tutor to learn English. Otto Werner, Ernst Lubitsch's own chauffeur, taught Oskar to drive. [Both the tutor and the chauffeur were as bald as Oskar, and the three had themselves photographed together as the bald graces.] Paul Kohner, his agent, told him that in Hollywood one must always *appear* prosperous in order to *seem* successful, which means "worth hiring". Kohner set Oskar up in a elegant apartment in "Normandy Village" on chic Sunset Boulevard, near Beverly Hills. The two-storey furnished apartment, including maid service, cost only $100 out of Oskar's $1,000 per month. As was fashionable then in Hollywood, the apartment complex had been created like a movie set, a perfect imitation of a 17th-century French village – all the apartments separate half-timbered buildings with a well and a spring winding down the centre of the court.

Those first few months in America, while he still had no particular assignment or deadline at Paramount, and Elfriede and their son Karl had not yet arrived from Germany (they came on 13 May), Oskar Fischinger actually enjoyed a worry-free comfortable leisure, for the first and last time. In addition to his lessons and sightseeing, he began to paint. He could not really do animation at Paramount: although he had an office and secretaries, supplies such as paper, cels, paints, or camera time could only be requisitioned with an account number for a specific studio project or production. But he bought watercolours and paper, oils and canvas panels, and painted at home.

Oskar had not formally painted before. At the crucial beginning of his career, Oskar had seen Ruttmann's ritual rejection of static oil painting as the artform of the past in favour of dynamic cinema as the artform of the future – and Oskar had seen some beautiful abstract paintings of Ruttmann's, large canvases with subtle, complex brush-strokes giving painterly texture to geometric and organic forms, so he knew how significant this rejection was for Ruttmann. Oskar kept three of Ruttmann's black-and-white Expressionistic graphics in his own collection. Oskar himself had adopted Ruttmann's stance, and refused to make static abstractions, only absolute moving images on film. But his films are composed of thousands of abstract paintings – about 1,500 for a minute of film time. In most cases, Oskar actually drew out all of

Left and right below:
Studie Nr. 11 *preliminary sketches.*

the images, but even in films such as *Wax Experiments* and *R-1*, which were not made with drawings, Oskar would have studied the imagery frame by frame in the process of shooting and editing. Thus, over a period of some 15 years and some 35 films, Oskar had repeatedly observed the fine gradations of balance and contrast between forms, while during the last three years he was sensitized to harmonies and tensions between colours. Oskar also drew habitually, and hundreds of sketches survive in his estate, many of which are not directly related to films, but rather constitute *quand même* conscious artworks on paper: at least a dozen black-and-white charcoal drawings from 1929 to 1931, for example, utilize the full area of the paper, which never occurs in the films since the camera needs blank borders to frame, and Oskar's stylistic choice for the films involved small generic abstract shapes performing elaborate choreography. Nor could these be "choreography" sketches: we know Oskar's thin-line notation for movement from the early Frankfurt "dynamics" of plays, and from a peculiar Munich scenario for a film *F.1* (about close encounters between a man, a woman, a snake, a tiger, and a Höllenhund [Hound of Hell]) with similar dynamics markings, as well as from the Berlin musical scores and synchronization graphs on which Oskar has notated movements with thin lines, and also the *Studie Nr. 11* sketches in which the crucial step between rococo architecture and the film image consists of thin lines tracing trajectories. By contrast, Oskar's formal drawings employ the whole range of shading, hatching and other painterly textures that render static areas and forms weighty, harmonic or characteristic. In 1931, while Elfriede was back in Gelnhausen, Oskar sent her a remarkable series of five "postcards" which are also intricate small graphic compositions, one of

Left and right below:
Studie Nr. 11 *preliminary sketches.*

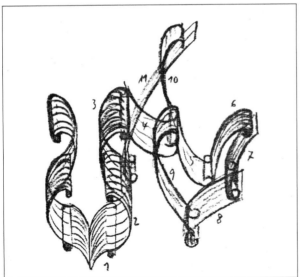

Christmas at Normandy Village, 1936, with Elfriede and Karl and paintings behind.

them rendered exquisitely with colour pencils, using a sensitive coordination of red/yellow/orange hues with subtle highlights in blue/green/brown.

Nor was Oskar ignorant of contemporary painting. He was an avid reader, and haunted libraries in Berlin, where he read Kandinsky's and Klee's texts. He visited the Bauhaus, probably in the company of Moholy-Nagy, who became a good friend in the early 1930s, when they shared many screenings with films and drawn-sound experiments. The gallery owner Karl Nierendorf also presented Oskar, as a going-away present in February 1936, with a copy of an elaborate Bauhaus book (including some colour lithographs by Kandinsky, Hirschfeld-Mack, Albers, etc.) which he had published in 1923. Nierendorf introduced Oskar to various painters, such as Lyonel Feininger, and arranged to take a print of *Komposition in Blau* to Paris to screen for Kandinsky, who reportedly loved it.

Nierendorf also took Oskar to visit painter Rudolf Bauer in his elaborate gallery/villa, Das Geistreich [Realm of the Spirit], in the elegant Charlottenburg district of Berlin, where Bauer, subsidized by the Solomon R. Guggenheim Foundation, could display a few fine non-objective paintings by Kandinsky and others, but chiefly Bauer's own canvases, which, paralleling Kandinsky's development, were busy expressionistic abstractions in the 1910s, but in the 1920s switched to clean-lined constructivist compositions, some in serial arrangements of triptychs and tetraptychons. Bauer gave Fischinger a copy of a text "Die kosmische Bewegung" [Cosmic Movement] which he had written in 1918 for an anthology published by Der Sturm – a text that seems a

precursor of Kandinsky's 1926 *Punkt und Linie zu Fläche* [Point and Line to Plane]. On the way home, Nierendorf and Oskar had a good laugh. Bauer was impossibly pompous. Oskar found Bauer's early Expressionistic paintings "schlamperei", ugly colours in cluttered shapes – exactly where Kandinsky created fascinating, complex and finally satisfying compositions, with a musical sense of harmony and dissonance. While some of Bauer's later constructivist canvases seemed much better, even occasionally beautiful or exciting, Oskar couldn't help but be reminded of his brother Hans' streamlined modern designs, which always risked being cold and mechanical.

The first paintings that Oskar made in America naturally involved a bit of experimentation. One set of canvases, four of which are now in the Guggenheim Museum in New York, have solid black backgrounds with a brightly-coloured cluster of circles and crescents floating in the centre – obviously related to the type of imagery one saw on the screen during some of Oskar's films, but not, perhaps, his most fascinating

Handmade postcard, 1931, sent by Oskar to Elfriede.

paintings. At that same time, however, he did create some astonishing paintings which work as paintings, such as a small, lush "Composition" in which layers of circles, mostly in hues of blue and gold, fill the entire canvas, overlapping but never crowded, each figure delicately shaded and textured with the tip of the brush. When Oskar did receive his first assignment from Paramount, he still continued to paint – in fact he did so for the rest of his life, whenever he had a free moment.

Oskar and Elfriede also spent a great deal of time exploring Los Angeles: the fantastic landscape of warm weather, ocean beaches; single streets like Sunset Boulevard running 30 miles from the train station to the sea; the Wilshire Boulevard "Miracle Mile" with its striking art-deco buildings in black and gold, pink, and aquamarine; the astonishing palatial theatres, both the luxurious modern palaces like the Wiltern and Pantages and the fantasy reconstructions of Egyptian temples, middle-eastern mosques and Mayan pyramids; restaurants shaped like hats and dogs and jungles, shops shaped like pianos and cameras, and private homes on one hand simulating a ramshackle witch's cottage or a palace at Versailles and on the other hand boldly embodying Frank Lloyd Wright's romantic concrete temples; the dazzling Farmer's market with a plethora of exotic and luscious foods – and oil wells pumping day and night behind them ... Frankfurt and Berlin had nothing like this. The Fischingers were also fascinated with the customs of the country, the many does and don'ts they were cautioned about. Oskar began to quip "You can't do that here – this is a free country!" Most touching of all, Gladys, the black woman hired as their Normandy Village maid, had never eaten in the same room with white people, and she was shocked and frightened when Elfriede insisted that she sit at the same table with her. Elfriede also asked her to bring her own baby daughter to play with Karl, and the two children became dear friends, Karl calling her "Chocolate Baby".

Oskar and Elfriede at first also did considerable socializing, mostly in the sizeable emigrant community, with whom Oskar could converse in German. The rival art dealers Galka Scheyer and Karl Nierendorf [who lived with the Fischingers in their Normandy Village apartment until he could establish a gallery and financial stability of his own] made sure that the Fischingers visited the Schoenbergs and Salka Viertel's salon where people as diverse as Thomas Mann, Bert Brecht, Lion Feuchtwanger and Franz Werfel might appear, side by side with a Greta Garbo or a Christopher Isherwood. But Oskar and Elfriede were actually somewhat out of place among these high literati – they were in fact people from a small town, and even their years in Berlin were not spent in intellectual circles, but rather among the narrower filmmaking community. Elfriede's education was specifically in textile design, and Oskar's avid self-education in endless library books followed his own

curiosity about scientific and mystical exploration. He would often remain completely quiet during long intellectual conversations, observing but not participating. And then his acute observations might fall suddenly like a bomb into the conversation. At one emigrant party where leftists predominated, Oskar shocked everyone present by interrupting with the assertion that Stalin was no better than Hitler – both of them bigoted ruthless murderers. No one wanted to believe then that Communism could be as bad as Nazism, though history would prove Oskar right. Karl Nierendorf was so angry he moved out of Normandy Village, but years later he apologized to Oskar.

Oskar and Elfriede were also ill-suited to the social life of the film milieu. Although a huge community of exile refugees and emigrés from many countries thrived in Hollywood, English was the chosen language for business and social occasions. Oskar spoke rarely and awkwardly. Elfriede, though her schooling had included English and she spoke relatively fluently, had little tact or the cautious social skills necessary for studio politics. She had the bad habit of interrupting people (even the most important) sometimes prefaced with unfortunate phrases like "that's nothing", to tell an anecdote about Gelnhausen or her student days in Offenbach. She also persisted in designing and making her own

Left: *Harald and Nanny Kirchstein with Karl Fischinger.*

Right: *Elfriede in Hollywood.*

clothes which had seemed fashionable and daring in Bauhaus Germany, but not here in chic glamour-prone Hollywood. Oskar gradually avoided taking Elfriede to social occasions, and insisted that she wear simple, plain black dresses. And they did indeed find a number of friends among the emigrants, but more among the plastic and musical artists, such as the architects and designers Rudolf M. Schindler and Richard Neutra – and Mrs. Neutra, who played the cello and sang lieder. Albert and Elfriede Benitz, with their daughter Cristl appeared one day at Normandy Village. Albert had taken advantage of an assignment to shoot footage in America for a Luis Trenker feature to defect, and hopefully stay in the United States. They had enough money to last them for a year or so, but the cinematog- raphers' union would not accept any more foreign refugees into membership, which meant that Albert could not work. When their money ran out, they were deported back to Germany in disgrace, and Albert lived out the war as one of Leni Riefenstahl's cameramen. While they stayed in Hollywood, the Fischingers helped them out as much as possible (though Oskar would soon have financial difficulties of his own). Elfriede Benitz had never disclosed her love affair with Oskar to Albert, so they were all four the best of friends in that special Noel-Coward 1930s way. The Benitz's fate loomed fearfully before the Fischingers for the next several years. By contrast, the musician Harald Kirchstein, whom Oskar had known as an arranger and conductor in Berlin, showed up in Hollywood as Henri René, and enjoyed a successful career, receiving a star on the Hollywood Walk of Fame (as the seemingly-French Henri René – no reference to his German origins). His star is on Vine Street between Hollywood and Sunset boulevards, and it is situated between the stars of Leopold Stokowski and Fritz Lang. Oskar Fischinger never received a star on the walk.

Paramount decided to include an animated episode at the beginning of their feature *Big Broadcast of 1937*, which was the latest in a series of anthology films with a thin comic plot that allowed many "guest stars", mostly known only as voices on radio, to perform before film cameras. *Big Broadcast of 1936* had included Richard Tauber and the Vienna Boys Choir side by side with Ethel Merman and Amos & Andy. *Big Broadcast of 1937* would again star George Burns and Gracie Allen along with Jack Benny and Martha Raye. The film would open with a trio of men singing "Heigh Ho, the radio, there's music in the air ..." which would dissolve into a radio broadcast tower that would become an element in Oskar's abstract composition, which would in turn dissolve into Martha Raye (a clumsy secretary at the radio station) dropping recordings as she trips on the stairs. For Oskar's animated segment, the studio composer Ralph Rainger (who also wrote Bob Hope's hit song "Thanks for the Memory" for *Big Broadcast of 1938*) composed a three-minute piece of orchestral jazz, "Radio Dynamics", somewhat in the vein of Gershwin. Seeing the vast resources of the studio, whose animation department had a staff of ink-and-paint people waiting to fill in designs on cels, Oskar created bold, intricate images reminiscent of *Composition in Blue*, which Lubitsch had admired and mentioned when hiring Oskar. Unfortunately, however, Lubitsch had vacated his position as Head of Production, and returned to directing, and Mitchell Leisen, the American director of *Big Broadcast*, was much less sympathetic to Oskar. When Oskar asked on 15 July for the cels to be shot in colour, he was informed that *Big Broadcast* was a black-and-white feature, and no colour film was included in its budget; "Radio Dynamics", although coloured on its cels, and shot on a three-colour separation negative, would be printed only in black-and-white.

Despite his English lessons, Oskar still felt handicapped in a quick conversation, so his protests had to take the form of memos typed by his secretaries, and the responses from the executives likewise had to be translated for him. Over the next three weeks, Oskar tried to explain that dark red and dark green both became black on black-and-white film, so many of the shapes and effects would simply be lost – but a black-and-white copy had to be struck before they believed him. Then he proposed on 7 August doing special effects of objects suggested in the lyrics of "Heigh Ho the Radio", which joked about commercial advertising on radio programmes. These images of autos, coffee, tooth-paste, cigarettes and such would be superimposed over Oskar's already extant abstract designs to give them extra vitality and detail in their muddy black-and-white version. This scheme was approved, but the absolute deadline for completion of all photography on *Big Broadcast of 1937* was set for 26 August, and Oskar failed to finish his assignment on schedule, although most of it was optically printed and edited. A mere six months after his arrival in Hollywood, Oskar's seven-year Paramount contract was terminated. Oskar's episode was not used at all in the film as released; an awkward cut connects the singing trio directly to an elab- orate wipe optical of the breaking recordings when Martha Raye falls.

Another episode in *Big Broadcast of 1937* involved Leopold Stok-owski conducting one of his arrangements of a Bach "Fugue". The treatment of him and the orchestra prefigures very closely the way he would be filmed for Walt Disney's *Fantasia* a few years later: we see Stokowski's silhouette, profile, and close-ups of his hands, while only certain areas of the orchestra are lit up at a given time, until the last climactic moments. Did this mode of visualizing the conductor and his orchestra originate with Stokowski himself, or with director Mitchell Leisen, or perhaps with Oskar Fischinger? While they were both at Paramount, Oskar had spoken to Stokowski about collaborating on films for which Stokowski would supply the music and Oskar the animation. In one letter Oskar suggests that the film begin with images of Stokowski's hands, which would guide the viewer's eyes off into infinite space ... .

One of Oskar's bilingual secretaries from Paramount, Ursula De-Swart, would remain a lifelong friend of Oskar's. Her husband, Jan De Swart, was a sculptor and artist, and Oskar liked his work very much – and the De Swarts followed Oskar's film screenings and painting shows as well.

Suddenly, in August 1936, Oskar was in a foreign country without any means of supporting himself and his family. Through the good efforts of Paul Kohner and William and Charlotte Dieterle (who would soon found the European Film Fund to aid refugees), on 30 December 1936, Oskar signed a contract with MGM to deliver an animated film which he would make privately on his own premises for them. It was to be a film of the style and quality of *Composition in Blue*. Out of the $11,000 he received for the film, Oskar rented a room across the street from the MGM Studios in Culver City and began to build the scaffolding necessary to animate *An Optical Poem*. He was able to get the MGM orchestra to record a sprightly rendition of Liszt's "Hungarian Rhapsody No. 2" for his soundtrack. By the time Oskar had figured in the salary of carpenters, building materials and supplies, film and processing costs [Oskar had to deliver a ready negative and release print to MGM], the budget only allowed him $50 per week for himself – and his rent at Normandy Village was still $100 per month. The Fischinger family only managed to get by with help from several friends, including the art dealer Galka Scheyer, who was something of a rival to Karl Nierendorf, since she specialized in Klee, Kandinsky, Jawlensky and Feininger – The Blue Four, as she called them. Galka lived only a few blocks away from Normandy Village – but they were very steep blocks up a mountainside. Elfriede would trudge over (or occasionally get rides) often and help her with cleaning, walking her dog Tuffy, or other chores as a slight way of repaying her kindness. The movie star Susannah Foster [best remembered for her starring role in the 1943 *Phantom of the Opera*] rented the lower half of Galka's building, and Elfriede also occasionally did some chores for her, for which she was nicely paid.

Meanwhile, on 23 January 1937, Stokowski wrote a letter of recommendation for Oskar, who had to travel to Mexico and wait for an immigration quota number in order to re-enter the United States for permanent residence, which fortunately turned out not to be difficult.

An Optical Poem grew directly out of the last scene in *Komposition in Blau*, in which a set of circles fly away from the background toward the viewer. Oskar now developed that same technique into an elaborate composition. The scaffolding in the room allowed extra-fine fishing line

to be suspended from above, and lights hung from numerous vantage points to create strong shadows that would emphasize depth. The geometric figures in the film – circles, triangles and rectangles – were cut from paper and painted in specific hues [Elfriede painted many of them "by numbers" at home in Normandy Village], then attached to a fine line that could be tied to one of the overhead cross beams. With a painted background behind, each of the paper figures would be moved a millimetre before another film-frame could be shot, then moved another millimetre, etc. Because the paper figures were suspended in air, they had to be steadied after each move to make sure they were completely still before the next exposure. Oskar used a broomstick with a chicken feather attached to the end as a "steadier". As in most of Oskar's films, complex choreography often required a dozen figures to move simultaneously, some in the same direction, but others at a different angle or direction, so each exposure was slow and had to be carefully monitored. The seven-minute music also required numerous changes of background and figures. All of this "technology" paid off, however, for the finished film is a masterpiece: the keen sensation of depth becomes a conceptual part of the action, with the circles that rotate around each other revealed as cosmic figures that could be either microscopic cels or stellar configurations.

Early in 1937, Galka Scheyer introduced a young composer, John

Oskar at MGM studio
[publicity still].

Cage, to Oskar, with the thought that possibly Cage could compose a more challenging, modern music for Oskar. John Cage invited Oskar to a concert of his percussion compositions on 10 March 1937. Oskar was excited by the possibility of making a film with "new music" but told Cage he should come to the studio and work for a few days on the current project, *An Optical Poem*, just to understand the process of animation, its potential and its incredibly slow, tedious pace. After a few days wielding the chicken feather, John made an error and gave up animating [see Cage's testimonial at the end of this book for the full details]. But during the long pauses while each new set-up was being arranged, Oskar told John about his *Ornament Ton* experiments, and his Buddhist-inspired belief that all things have a sound, even if we do not always listen or hear it, just as a stone has an inherent movement even if it is still. Cage credited Oskar with offering him the revelation that changed his whole perception of music and sound.

Oskar finished the film within the year, and as he dismantled the "set" for *An Optical Poem*, he sawed out one particular rectangle from an oil-painted background and thus created by selection a painting "An Optical Poem" which, with its cluster of golden circles, is one of his most delightful. MGM was enthusiastic about their short film. They prepared a thorough press campaign before the 5 March 1938 première, which included everything from the usual type of press photos (Oskar posed at a studio editing table and a moviola) accompanied by "interviews", to a bizarre item in "Screen Oddities" (a rival of Ripley's Believe It or Not) on 1 December 1937, which states that MGM is preparing a short film that shows the relation of sound and colour, with an illustration showing a Star of David on screen while musical notes float by. Louella Parsons gave the film a rave, and Ed Sullivan wrote that *An Optical Poem* was surefire for an Academy Award, which caused the ever-witty Oskar to quip, "Why give me an Oscar? – I *am* Oskar!"

Despite the critical acclaim for *An Optical Poem*, however, it did not become a real moneymaker nor a boxoffice favourite, though it did play throughout the year as a prestige short with "better" features that might have a classical music connection, or for prestige audiences, such as the first-class ocean-liner passengers. Oskar's contract contained options for further MGM shorts, but in April 1937 an oldtime business manager, Fred Quimby, was assigned to create an MGM internal animation unit

(which would become synonymous with Tom and Jerry within a few years), and Quimby did not think abstract shorts could do good business, so the options for Oskar's services were not exercised. Oskar became involved in a dispute over the accounting for *An Optical Poem* (due to supposed high administrative costs, Oskar received no profits from the film at all), and on the very day (8 March 1937) when Elfriede Fischinger was in hospital giving birth to a new son, Conrad, the *An Optical Poem* accountant threatened to smash Oskar with a typewriter that he raised above his head. Oskar began to defend himself, and he was arrested and jailed on "assault and battery" charges. Although Oskar was exonerated in court through the testimony of a witness, gossip about the "fight" and arrest may have contributed towards Fischinger's Hollywood reputation as an intractable person.

The Fischingers' finances were severely restricted again, but they moved discreetly to a cheaper bungalow without maid service in the same apartment complex, so that they could maintain their chic address for appearance's sake. Oskar continued to paint whenever he was not employed on a film, and by now he had a good collection of exciting canvases, including several daring but successful large works [the "Multiballs on Black" (now in the Milwaukee Art Center) with its hard-edged transparent circles in taut irregular tension; the "Experiment" (now in the Buck Collection, Laguna Niguel) with its sharp contrasts of large circles and broken lines, and light values confined to the upper part of the canvas while dark, almost-opaque values predominate on the lower half; and the splendid "Circles, Triangles and Squares" (now in the National Museum of American Art, Smithsonian Institution) with its fine layering of large geometric forms whose incompatible colours nonetheless blend]. Oskar also painted many smaller canvases, and Karl Nierendorf offered him a show at his New York gallery if he came east.

Dr. William Valentiner, a German refugee who had become Director of the Los Angeles County Museum, served as art advisor to Henry Ford, building his art collection in Detroit. Galka Scheyer urged Oskar to take advantage of knowing Valentiner by making a proposal for Henry Ford to finance a film. Oskar conceived the idea of making an abstract animation to Dvorak's "New World Symphony", which could be screened at the Ford Pavilion at the 1939 World Fair in New York. In April 1938, Oskar set out in his car, driving towards New York, stopping in Detroit to promote his proposal for the "New World Symphony". Unfortunately, Ford declined to fund the film, possibly because the nearly $40,000 budget was rather expensive for those depression years, and possibly because they doubted that a 45-minute animation film could really be finished in time for the Fair – or, indeed, perhaps they feared audiences would not sit through 45 minutes of abstract animation.

Oskar's reception in New York was much more encouraging. Not only did he have a one-man show of his paintings at Karl Nierendorf's gallery, but also a second show at the Phillip Boyer Gallery. Oskar's films were screened at the Fifth Avenue Playhouse in July 1938, with enthusiastic introduction and programme notes by film critic Herman Weinberg; Oskar was lionized by New York cinephiles, among them abstract filmmaker Mary Ellen Bute, who told him in her Texas drawl (which he barely understood) that at the beginning of her career as a filmmaker, his *Studie Nr. 5* had been a crucial inspiration to her. She urged Oskar to stay in the East and establish his art career there.

Katherine Dreier, an abstract painter who had encountered Man Ray and Marcel Duchamp in 1916 as part of New York Dada, had formed with Duchamp the Société Anonyme which began 1920 to promote and exhibit modern art in America, including traveling shows from Der Sturm and other European sources. Dreier acquired many paintings over the next two decades, and donated most of the best to Yale University in 1941 to form their core collection of modern art, still bearing the "Société Anonyme Collection" indentification. At Oskar's Nierendorf Gallery show, Dreier purchased a beautiful "Abstract Composition" of overlapping circles, in gouache and watercolour, dated 1936, which can be seen today at Yale.

Oskar also attracted the attention of another art patron: the Baroness Hilla Rebay von Ehrenwiesen, who would dominate his fate for the next decade. The Baroness Rebay was one of the grand eccentrics: ten years older than Oskar, she trained in classical painting and continued to do excellent portraits and representational graphics until the early 1930s. Her encounters with Hans Arp and Zurich Dada in 1916 made her aware of modern art, but her encounter with Rudolf Bauer at Der Sturm in 1917 changed her life, for she became infatuated or obsessed with him, and lived with him or supported him until 1925, when she went to Italy and then America, trying to make more money in order to fulfill Bauer's dream of establishing a gallery dedicated to abstract painting. In 1927, in New York, she became friends [some say lovers] with Solomon R. Guggenheim (then 66), whom she convinced to invest a sizeable part of his fortune in building a collection of abstract art which would later become the basis for a museum [as other millionaires, such as Mrs. John Rockefeller and Gertrude Vanderbilt Whitney, helped found the Museum of Modern Art and the Whitney Museum]. In 1928–29 Rebay toured Europe buying paintings for Guggenheim, and established Bauer as Guggenheim's resident agent to acquire more works. By 1 March 1936, the first public exhibition of Guggenheim's collection of "Non-Objective Art" took place in Charleston, South Carolina, and in 1937 the Solomon R. Guggenheim Foundation was established to promote education about and creation of non-objective art, as well as to build a permanent museum to house the Guggenheim collection. Hilla Rebay was named curator of the Foundation and collection/museum, which meant that she could offer grants, buy art-works, and validate artists by including them in her exhibitions. She did assemble a veritable treasure-house of abstract paintings, and in May 1939 opened the Museum of Non-Objective Painting, which in 1959 would move into the new Frank Lloyd Wright building as the Solomon R. Guggenheim Museum.

For Oskar, the Baroness seemed like a dream come true. This bountiful, German-speaking woman, enchanted by his films, autographed a copy of her latest catalogue "To the 'Great' Fischinger in friendship" ["dem 'grossen' Fischinger in Freundschaft, Hilla Rebay, 18 June 1938"]. The extra apostrophes around 'great" seem to imply that he is fat as much as wonderful ... She also encouraged him to abandon his family [no true artist, she said, could bother with a wife and children] and move to New York. She offered to help by letting him stay at her country estate in Connecticut [just a short train ride to New York] while she was away in Paris. Karl Nierendorf and Galka Scheyer both warned him that while Miss Rebay could be gracious and helpful, she could also be capricious and dangerous. But the thought of staying in her house, where her private collection hung – not only the many Bauers, but also Kandinskys, a Mondrian and a Seurat – was more than Oskar could resist. When he was recalled to Hollywood October 1938, and the Baroness returned to find that he had not moved to New York as she advised, she sent him a bill for staying at her house – a substantial bill equivalent to the rate of a luxury hotel.

The Baroness Hilla von Rebay.

Oskar would gladly have stayed in New York, but despite the excitement and glamour of his successful painting shows and the access to many other artists and museums, he did not really make any money, and could not send anything back to Los Angeles for Elfriede and the three children (another son, Richard was born in March 1938). When Galka Scheyer's resources grew too thin, she notified Irmgard von Cube, who was active with the European Film Fund, and she personally took charge of the Fischinger family's welfare. Irmgard was the wife of actor Erwin Kalser, and a successful screenwriter (including Robert Siodmak's *Abschied* [1930, Germany], Anatole Litvak's *Mayerling* [1936, France] and Hollywood films like the Robert Schumann biography *Song of Love* and *Johnny Belinda* for which she received an Academy Award nomination). Her kindness to the Fischingers at this crucial point made them life-long friends, and Elfriede and the Fischinger children ended up repaying Irmgard's kindness a dozen times over, caring for her son and her grandson for extended periods, as well a doing cleaning, gardening and other chores. When Irmgard died decades later, the Fischingers would inherit designer "Schindler" furniture and other interesting things from her.

The European Film Fund, headed by Paul Kohner and Charlotte Dieterle, found Oskar the job at Disney, and insisted that he take it or be deported as an indigent. Remembering Albert Benitz, Oskar was shocked and depressed. Already in Berlin he had contacted Stokowski about getting rights to use the Stokowski Bach arrangements; at Paramount in 1936 they had spoken and corresponded about collaborating on a feature-length animation film, at least as late as December 1936. In November 1937 Stokowski began collaborating with Disney on "The Sorcerer's Apprentice", and by September 1938, expanded the project into "The Concert Feature" which would be *Fantasia* two years later. Now Oskar arrived at the Disney Studio in November 1938 as a "Motion picture cartoon effects animator" for $68 per week (only a fourth of what he was paid at Paramount), to work on merely one episode, as a craftsman under someone else's direction. Whether it was true or not, Oskar believed that Stokowski had stolen Oskar's idea for a Concert Feature [which Oskar had published already in his 1935 New Year's wish] and sold it to Disney, without giving Oskar the credit, or even the major role as director/designer that he deserved. Oskar, of course, was not entirely correct in his assessment of Disney, who had been active with musical synchronization since the late 1920s, just as Oskar had. In dozens of *Silly Symphony* cartoons, Disney had explored all types of music, including classical selections – and Disney had worked out a production method (storyboard conferences, specialization of backgrounds, effects, etc.) which allowed him to make fine quality shorts and feature films.

Despite Oskar's justifiable and un-justifiable indignation, he threw himself whole-heartedly and good-naturedly into the project – after all, Disney's cartoon factory was the most sophisticated in the world, and perhaps Oskar could get a chance to make a complex and intricate work such as what he had tried at Paramount. Oskar brought prints of his films, which were screened every week for nine months for the entire Disney staff during lunch and breaks. Thus Oskar's influence at Disney was pervasive, spilling over on to other films like *Dumbo*, the South American features, and *Pinocchio*, for which Oskar actually animated the Blue Fairy's magic wand.

In the mimeographed transcript of the story meeting for 28 February 1939, Walt Disney says,

> "Everything that has been done in the past on this kind of stuff has been cubes and different shapes moving around to the music. It has been fascinating. From the experience we have had here with our crowd – they went crazy about it! If we can go a little further here, and get some clever designs, the thing will be a great hit. I would like to see it sort of near-abstract, as they call it – not pure. And new."

Perhaps because of the uneasy proximity of Oskar at these meetings, Walt exhibits a certain suspiciousness about abstraction, accompanied by a rather defensive attitude towards the prospective audience. On 24 January 1939, Disney says, "You should give something that the audience will recognize. I don't think the average audience will fully appreciate the abstract; but I may be all wrong ..." and Stokowski replies "Yes, they may be way ahead of us". Disney asks, "What will Bach-lovers think of this?", and Stokowski replies, "They will be against it, I think; but the public will love it", to which Walt confesses, "Well, the general idea here looks good to me. I only wonder if we're going a little too gypsy in the colour."

Disney's suspicion about the colour being too adventurous is typical of the way in which Oskar's designs were altered daily. Oskar kept trying for complex designs, typical of his work, that contain several simultaneous motions, different kinds of shapes in tension with each other, and a spectrum of hues that could interact in changing harmonic balances. Disney, however, on 5 June 1939, avows, "There's a theory I go on that an audience is always thrilled with something new, but fire too many new things at them and they become restless". Therefore Oskar's designs were simplified, so that only one thing at a time moved, and everything was altered a bit to make it resemble some natural form, from a violin to a tin roof to a cloudy sky. And Oskar's colours were tamed to suit the economics of inking-and-painting. On the other hand, Oskar's idea of showing the film's soundtrack to demonstrate how various noises and tones actually looked visually, strayed from the scientific black-and-white truth into a "gypsy"-coloured comedy routine in which, for example, the bassoon's timbre is represented by an intense red background before which flapping blue "tongues" splatter drops of spit.

Oskar himself summed up the situation in a letter to a friend: "I worked on this film for nine months; then through some 'behind the back' talks and intrigue (something very big at the Disney Studios) I was demoted to an entirely different department, and three months later I left Disney again, agreeing to call off the contract. The film 'Toccata and Fugue by Bach' is really not my work, though my work may be present at some points; rather it is the most inartistic product of a factory. Many people worked on it, and whenever I put out an idea or suggestion for this film, it was immediately cut to pieces and killed, or often it took two, three or more months until a suggestion took hold in the minds of some people connected with it who had their say. One thing I definitely found out: that no true work of art can be made with that procedure used in the Disney Studio."

Oskar's assertions about the unhealthy competitive committee work at Disney would seem to be borne out by the conference notes in which we see during nine months of work on the "story" incredible floundering, dreary

Oskar working at Disney Studios.

discussions and re-discussions of each scene, groping and pushing without any controlling factor besides making an entertaining film. [Oskar never spoke during these conferences because he still could not speak English well enough. He took the typed note home with him, and Elfriede helped translate and explain them to him each evening. To Disney's credit, however, *Fantasia* has some remarkable thematic strengths – the cycles of seasons parallelled with the cycle of "history" in the scientific, mythic and religious ages; excellent pacing between slow and fast, serious and funny, loud and soft, etc. – and passages of genuine beauty [most of these virtues conspicuously absent from the later *Fantasia 2000*]. However, many astonishing fine points seem to be marred by a parallel lapse of taste, kitsch, racist and sexist twist, and other banalities.

In fact some other true artists – Jules Engel, Sylvia Holland and Bianca

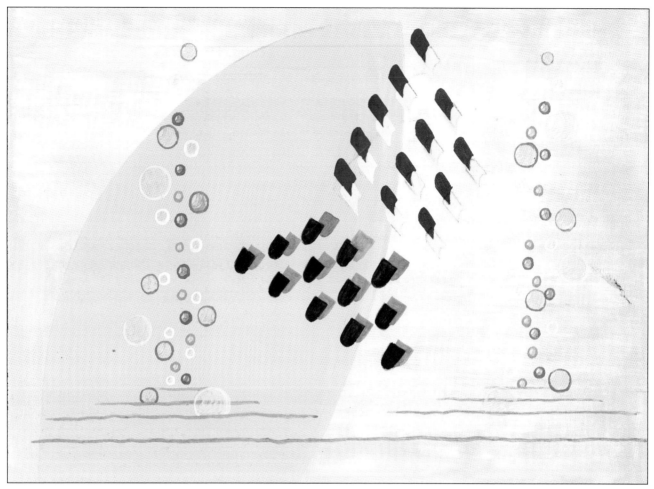

Oskar's original sketch in colour for wave sequence in Fantasia.

Majolie, to name a few – did manage to get their worthy artistic concepts into the final *Fantasia*. But Oskar may well not have known most of the other artists, since he worked in the special-effects section, with a stern supervisor, Sy Young, a small morose chinese man who had made a charming black-and-white animated version of Mendelssohn's "Spring Song" in the early 1930s, with conventional cartoon birds and bees. Young was experiencing marital difficulties (a domineering wife), and vented some of his distress on the innocent Oskar. The only other person in their room was a young apprentice, Les Novros, later a distinguished special-effects man, but then someone who rarely spoke.

Oskar's own surviving sketches show remarkable images that would have been thrilling on screen. One sequence preserved in a full range of material is Oskar's final work on the Bach episode, the scene in which large waves seem to be rolling right and left toward the spectator – after which point there is little true animation as opposed to pans across still art work, except for the standard falling fireworks and a curious image which Lee Blair identified as an out-take from *Snow White* in which a dwarf was carrying a diamond down the mine shaft. While the wave sequence is one of the more exciting, impressive moments in the Disney version, a comparison with Oskar's original sketches shows how much more powerful, subtle and imaginative the sequence might have been if Fischinger's intentions had been honoured. Oskar's original celadon "waves" are part of a complex composition that includes concentric rhomboids in browns, Chinese red, and graduated yellow-oranges, rising columns of circles, diagonal crescents, a graduated-shade oval, etc. The right/left waves are only a momentary manifestation of a radiating rounded triangle which fans through the frame. From Oskar's intricate, colour-keyed plans, the staff has chosen only the single wave movement, added clouds to the background as if it were sky, given purplish hues to the waves, which now have ribbing like a melon – or more precisely, like the motion breakdowns on Oskar's animation sketches.

Unfortunately, much of Oskar's work for *Fantasia* seems entirely lost. After looking at some of Oskar's sketches on 21 August 1939, Disney comments, "I think the contrast of black and white, and then a little colour coming in, would stand out" (something that nonetheless never reached the screen), and then, obviously watching some of Oskar's animation filmed, Walt says "Oskar has a pulsing effect in his test" – again a lost moment. Some dozen single drawings of Oskar's show polymorphous pastel clouds more subtle and intricate than anything in *Fantasia*, suggestive, indeed, of Jordan Belson's work of the 1970s.

Because he still spoke English haltingly, Fischinger rarely got a word into these fast, competitive conferences. The January 1939 issue of the magazine *Minicam* featured an article praising Oskar as the genius of visual music animation. He further became the butt of endless practical jokes contrived by his jealous co-workers. Some of them, apparently unable to deal maturely with the plight of a refugee artist, pinned a swastika to Oskar's office door 1 September 1939, the day the Nazis invaded Poland. Oskar applied for a release from his contract and after two months of red tape, terminated his employment at Disney on Halloween, 31 October 1939. In the terms of his severance contract, he specified that Disney could not use his name in relationship with *Fantasia*. He was confident that he would be more famous than Disney in the long run, and did not want Disney to be able to use his name to sell their "geschmacklos" [tasteless] product.

Two months earlier, on 4 August 1939, Elfriede had finally given birth to a girl, Barbara. Now they were a family of six, with no visible means of support.

4

Disney and Guggenheim

uring the agonizing months of work at Disney, Oskar assuaged his spirit by painting more, beginning one of his most characteristic, personal series: canvases covered with layers of grids made up of fine lines. In the exciting 1939 "Criss Cross", for example, the grids are primarily triangular in shape, some large triangles around 75 centimetres high, while others (created by a crossing of three other triangles) may be only six centimetres. The colours, rigorously confined to a narrow spectrum of yellow/orange/brown hues, barely differentiate some of the forms, creating a dynamic tension of angles, and implied (but unstable) perspectives. Each of the lines, including the fine hatching of the small grids, was painted free-hand by Oskar, whose long training with repetitive drawing for animation allowed him to draw perfect circles and straight lines without recourse to compass or ruler. The inevitable slight irregularity in these hand-made patterns adds to the equivocation between flatness and depth, and the maze of possible and impossible intersections. Above all, these incredibly intricate grid paintings constitute a meditation for Oskar himself, who would necessarily spend months patiently, delicately adding new layers of lines where those beneath had dried somewhat.

Just a few months after leaving Disney, Oskar had a small show of a few paintings at the Stendahl Gallery on Wilshire Boulevard, near the lovely Art Deco Bullocks Wilshire department store. A few months before, August 1939, Stendahl had displayed Picasso's "Guernica" so it was a very prestigious venue. Oskar showed some of his films at the gallery one evening, and the young John and James Whitney attended the screening. Neither of them had made abstract animated films at that time (although John had shot some live-action footage, close-ups of machinery in the style of *Ballet Mecanique*). The two young men found Oskar's use of "classical" music to be rather old fashioned, but they were still inspired to begin making absolute animations which they would synchronize with new and exotic sound.

One of the other artists at Disney, Jules Engel (who designed the choreography for the "Nutcracker" and "Dance of the Hours" sequences), was also an abstract painter, and they were able to share their art in a friendly way. Jules also saw Oskar's Stendahl show. In 1947, they would have a three-man painting show (together with Herb Klynn, who also worked at UPA with Jules) at the American Contemporary Gallery in Hollywood. Jules, after working several more years in the commercial animation field, would begin to make short abstract animation films, too, which now number more than 30. Jules was the founder of the Experimental Animation programme at California Institute of the Arts.

Other emigrants from Europe arrived regularly. Some, like Gitta Alpar, had virtually no career in America, and Oskar hardly had contact with her (she ended up living in the luxury resort town Palm Springs, more than 100 miles from Los Angeles). Alexander Laszlo settled in Los Angeles and became a regular composer of film and television scores. Curt Courant, who had worked with Oskar on Fritz Lang's *Woman in the Moon*, was (like Albert Benitz) refused for membership in the Hollywood Cameramen's union, so he could not work on any features shot in California, although he did several very prestigious foreign productions (Renoir's *La Bete Humaine*, Carne's *Le Jour se Leve*, Chaplin's *Monsieur Verdoux*). He also taught in the Film School of the University of California in Los Angeles for several years. Oskar visited him dutifully several times, but he found it a distinct chore. Courant lived quite stylishly in a very fancy house, and was clearly doing much better than Oskar, but both Curt and his wife seemed bitter, and Oskar could find little to say to them. By contrast, Man Ray was a total delight: despite the fact that he had been uprooted from his long-time residence in Paris, he made the best of his sojourn in Hollywood, cavorting with the elegant and posh Hollywood stars as well as the artists and experimental filmmakers like Oskar and Jules Engel. Man Ray came to Oskar's film screenings and they visited each others' studios often, exchanging anecdotes about techniques and inspirations.

Paul Hindemith, newly emigrated from Germany, also visited Oskar in Hollywood. In March 1939 he played as guest violist with the Los Angeles Philharmonic Orchestra, whose regular conductor then was Otto Klemperer. Backstage, after the performance, a lively crowd assembled, including the Dieterles, composers Ernst Toch and Arnold Schönberg, novelist Vicki Baum and her husband the conductor Richard Lert (who had produced Flotow's *Martha* at Hollywood Bowl in August 1938), Thomas Mann, Oskar and Elfriede Fischinger, and half a dozen more, all merrily chattering in German. Suddenly Klemperer cried out (also in German): "Are we, then, actually in Berlin, not in Hollywood?" Hindemith asked Oskar to introduce him to Disney, hoping that he might get some work at the studio as a composer. Oskar warned him that Stravinsky was less than happy with his fate at Disney's hands, that Disney was very obsessive and self-centred, and that if Hindemith once gave him a piece of music, any kind of distortion of it might happen. Nevertheless, Hindemith, with an unsure future, gave it a try. Later he wrote Oskar, "Of course, I should have believed you, but above all I should never have trusted anyone who dots his 'i's with a little circle".

Oskar himself dreamed of the possibility of doing a feature-length animation film using only the music of Hindemith, including some earlier works like the folk-song suite "Der Schwanendreher" and the symphonic arrangement of *Mathis der Mahler*, and a new piece, "Symphonic Metamorphosis on Themes of Carl Maria von Weber" on which Hindemith was then working. Oskar wrote to the Baroness Rebay asking if she could arrange financing for such a non-objective animation, which would benefit two German refugees. The Baroness denied that she had access to the amount of money – about $150,000 – necessary to make a feature, which Oskar knew was not true since, living at her house, he had seen the sort of prices paid for paintings and for Bauer's up-keep. Rebay encouraged him to plan a short film that would be a certain crowd-pleaser for American audiences, perhaps a patriotic American march, so that it could be distributed as a short in cinemas nationwide, resulting in sizeable profits as well as a prestige "track record" necessary to attract substantial film-industry funding. Rebay herself was a European in America, and conscious of the tense political situation in Europe, so she required Norman McLaren to make a *Stars and Stripes* film (not, however, using Sousa's music of that name) to prove his loyalty (as well as hers) to America. Similarly, Oskar was to make an abstract film actually based on Sousa's "Stars and Stripes Forever".

Oskar's agent Paul Kohner arranged for $1,000 backing for this project from Henry Koster (Koster-Pasternak Productions), and Oskar asked Rebay for an additional $2,000 necessary for the three-minute film. In January 1940, Oskar signed a contract with "Baronessa H. von Rebay" stating that in exchange for $2,000, he would give her one print of *Studie Nr. 8* and one print of *Komposition in Blau*, as well as two prints of the *An American March* when it was finished – which amounts to nearly $800 in film laboratory costs. Furthermore, he had to promise to repay the $2,000 from the profits of *An American March* and, as a guarantee, to "give possession" to the Baronessa of a copy of each of his other films! This means that Rebay advanced $2,000, for which she received 35mm prints of 12 of Oskar's older films, worth more than $2,000, as well as copies of *An American March* when it was ready. The prints were screened regularly at the Museum of Non-Objective Painting [with no royalties to Fischinger], and gradually wore out, so the question of returning them became a moot point. The supposed bounty of the Baroness, then, actually amounted to ruthless exploitation of an indigent artist. She now had his only copies of certain films; she could screen them, he could not.

Oskar definitely understood exactly how unfavourable this English-language contract was to him. A bi-lingual friend, lawyer Milton Wichner, and his partner Eva Mason, took care of Oskar's legal matters for years, accepting his paintings for fees, and they were able to explain to Oskar all the disadvantageous aspects of the deal. Galka Scheyer also warned him. But Oskar was simply desperate. He had been out of work for four months, with still $75-per-month rent to pay. All of them hoped that *An American March* would indeed prove so great a financial success that Oskar would be able to afford new prints of his older films, as well as easy production of new films.

The brittle, sadistic side of Hilla Rebay's personality became more evident the more Oskar dealt with her. She was hot-tempered and impetuous, egocentric and demanding. One moment she would be flattering and seductive (several people compared this to actress Elisabeth Bergner's flighty girlish energy), the next moment harsh and sharp. She must have been aware that her tenuous position was dependent on Solomon Guggenheim's goodwill, so she was jealous to the point of paranoia of other people and institutions that might challenge her supremacy in the field of non-objective art. The Museum of Modern Art in New York asked for Oskar's films late in 1939, but on 11 January 1940, on the eve of promising Oskar $2,000 for *An American March*, Rebay wrote to Oskar that if he let the Museum of Modern Art have any of his films "of course I will not help you". In the same letter appears an unexpectedly cruel, domineering tone: "As Mr. Bauer is here, his advice might be important to you ... Most of your films in the past were only partly good, and I don't know how much you have improved, but just the same, the advice of a master of non-objectivity would be of tremendous importance to you."

Rebay's relationship with Rudolf Bauer certainly created much of her increasing emotional distress during the 1940s. Since they met in 1917, he had treated her with callous contempt and used her flagrantly as a slave, but she continued to worship him. She was aesthetically dependent on him, having adopted his ideas and style into her own paintings and theoretical writings. She championed him in the June 1939 *Art of Tomorrow* catalogue of the Solomon R. Guggenheim Foundation collection as "the greatest of all painters ... whose every work of Non-objectivity is an accomplished masterpiece ...". Bauer's paintings also dominated the exhibitions and publications she made. Such lavish praise naturally elicits equally strong reactions of denial; so, for example, Karl Nierendorf wrote to Oskar on 26 February 1940 (the day before Oskar signed the *An American March* contract): "I have nothing to do with the Baroness, and I think it will be impossible for me to ever be on good terms with her, because her ideas about art are quite contrary to mine. She is still fighting against Kandinsky and considers Bauer to be the top of modern art."

Rebay managed to acquire almost the entire works of Bauer for herself and the Museum of Non-Objective Painting, which meant that one could only see his paintings in New York or through Guggenheim loan exhibits. After Guggenheim's death, when Rebay was ousted from control of the museum in 1952, the Bauer works were discreetly put in storage by new curators bent upon making the Guggenheim Museum a world-class museum. Bauer's works virtually disappeared from the art world's view and consciousness for twenty years, until the Guggenheim Museum tried to "de-accession" some in the early 1970s through galleries in New York and Germany, but by then, Bauer was forgotten by a whole generation of people for whom Abstract Expressionism, Pop Art, minimalism, assemblage, Fluxus and Happenings and "new technology" had created a "Post-Modern" crisis. While Bauer was definitely a follower of Kandinsky, some of his paintings still contain graceful and moving expressions – and specially because of how widely they were publicized in the 1930s and 40s, they had a certain influence, including perhaps scale of the canvases (many of his later canvases are eight and nine feet square) and the serial arrangements (he composed sets of three or four paintings with related imagery into "symphony" sets that must be hung side by side). For Oskar, who much preferred Mondrian to Bauer, it is hard to assess the influence, if any, of Bauer.

Oskar set to work on *An American March* instantly, drawing out the animated figures with pencil on paper, then hiring young women to ink and paint the images on to cels. He rented a studio room for the women to work in, upstairs from a Bank of America on Sunset Boulevard – a building which would become the famous Whiskey-a-Go-Go nightclub during the psychedelic 1960s.

Despite Rebay's derisive comments to Oskar in her correspondence, he wrote her pleasant, admiring letters regularly, which she required as part of the terms of her support. From his letter of 18 August 1940, we can tell that he was working on a second film as well:

"Mit den Aufnahmen des Films beginne ich jetzt. Die ersten Proben habe ich bereits gemacht. Die Arbeit wird sehr gut, und stellt etwas ganz Neues dar, auf Optisch Rythmischem Gebiet. Eine ganze Reihe neuer Erkentnisse habe ich gewonnen während meiner jetzigen Arbeit und diese Erkentnisse in diesem Film zum Ausdruck gebracht, angewendet und Wirksamkeit gegeben. Z.b. Farbmischungen,

Farbveränderungen in Rythmischem Wechsel, Farbfluktuationen an der Projectionsfläche die nur möglich sind durch den raschen Bildwechsel von 24 Bilder pro Secunde. Durch diesen Film werden, unter anderem, völlig neue Ausblicke eröffnet über das Gebiet der Farbwissenschaft. Die Statische ruhige Betrachtungsweise dieser Farbwissenschaft wird abgelöst durch eine Dynamische. Es entspricht dem Schritt von der Oberfläche zur Tiefe, die zu durchdringen ist. Der Witz liegt im schnellen Farbwechseln, in der Vibration der Farbe, woraus sich Rythmisches Leben ergiebt das dynamischen Steigerungen zugänglich ist. Der Psychologische Effekt ist durchaus Lustbetont. Über interessante Details der Zeitlich nacheinander-liegenden Farbmischungen im Gegensatz zu gleichseitig nebeneinander-liegenden Farbmischungen könnte man jetzt schon ein sehr interessantes Werk schreiben. Aber der Film muß zuerst fertig sein!"

[I am now starting to shoot the film. I have already done the first tests. It's going to be a very good work that presents something quite new in the field of optical rhythm. I have gained a whole series of new perceptions during this current work, and these perceptions will be expressed in this film: used and made effective. For example, colour mixture, colour mutation in rhythmic exchange of colour fluctuations on the motion-picture screen, such as is only possible because of the quick image-exchange rate of 24 frames per second. Through this film will be opened, among other things, a wholly new view of the field of colour science. The Static, the passive observations of former colour science, will be superseded by the Dynamic. This step corresponds to penetrating from the surface into the depths. The clever part lies in fast colour change, in the vibration of colours which results in rhythmic life that is accessible through dynamic, climactic gradation. The psychological effect throughout is pleasurable. Concerning the interesting particulars of the temporal intermittence of colour mix (one after another) in contrast to the spatial juxtaposition of colour mix (side by side at the same time), one could now write a very interesting piece. However, the film must be finished first!]

From laboratory receipts, and a curious framed set of three film-strips with written on it "Oskar Fischinger 8472 1/2 Sunset Blvd. Hollywood Cal. Sept. 17. 40. Korrespondierende Vibrationen aus neuer Produktion" [corresponding vibrations from the new film], we know that Oskar was shooting colour tests (at least) of the transparent paintings on English drawing silk and cels which would appear two years later in the finished film *Radio Dynamics*. Many of these brilliant transparencies never found themselves into a surviving film – such as one dated 1941 in which yellow and orange swirls are dripped on to a brown background, or another which contains triangular brown shapes on a yellow background including a small inset frame with a reproduction of the main painting including a small inset frame, like facing mirrors.

However, most of them are included in the stunning flicker and loop sequences of *Radio Dynamics*, where they appear in a dazzling barrage of single frames in sharp contrast to slow rhythmic waxing and waning of circles in adjacent sequences. Oskar's description of experiments with colour contrast in time and space also fits better with *Radio Dynamics*, since *An American March* is characterized by rich, smooth colour modulations, which fit the film's theme of America as a "melting pot".

Of all Oskar's films, *An American March* is most Disney-like. The forms are outlined, for example, as in traditional cartoons, and the primary "red, white and blue" of the flag give the general colour balance a cartoon feel. Most remarkable, however, is how much Oskar has worked to undermine the very flat characteristics of cartoons: he uses thick layers of cels to cause the inked-in edges of shapes to blur, and builds into the colours on successive cels a carefully balanced spectrum of shades and hues that enhances the sense of colours "melting" along with the shapes. And finally, Oskar's use of the flag in this abstract composition prefigures to a degree what Pop artists like Rivers and Johns would do with well-known representational shapes as modular vehicles for formalist experiment.

Despite the obvious care and serious thought Oskar expended on the production, when *An American March* was finally completed in time for Solomon Guggenheim's 80th birthday party, on 1 February 1941, Rebay felt obliged to send Oskar pages of sketches and notes criticizing the film's structure and colour balance, and claiming that if he used the flag at all, he should have introduced the star and the stripe separately as subjects for fugal development, which would then only appear together as a rousing climax that would form the complete flag for the first time. In the same letter, she asks with astonishing ignorance about the academy leader: "leider ist dazwischen eine lange leere Stelle mit Nummern fliegend – ist es blos ein Fragment?" [Unfortunately, between them was a long empty stretch with numbers flying by – is that just a fragment?].

She also tells Oskar that she hopes this Hindemith person doesn't compose too modernish music, because she really likes Bach. Apparently Oskar and Rebay still hoped that *An American March* would bring in enough income to finance the feature-length animation, but such would not be the case. Much to Oskar's chagrin, the rights to the Sousa music could not be obtained easily. Oskar had purposely chosen an older, authentic recording conducted by Sousa himself, and he applied for the rights as soon as the project was formulated, assuming that since there were many newer recordings, the rights would be granted fast and

An American March
[still from 35mm film].

cheaply. Other interests, however, already owned partial rights, and the amount finally designated for fees much exceeded the amount available from Oskar's grant-budget. Ultimately the music was not cleared for several years, during which time *An American March* could not be screened for profit.

Along with *An American March*, Oskar sent Rebay a print of the black-and-white version of the Paramount film "Radio Dynamics", which she loved. By July 1941, the Solomon R. Guggenheim Foundation offered Oskar $1,300, nominally to help him buy the rights for the Paramount film and prepare the first colour prints. Once again, however, Rebay's terms for the grant demanded not only a print of the colour version of the Paramount film, but also a print of the next film that Oskar produced – a laboratory cost nearly half of the grant.

Meanwhile, the Fischingers had faced another six-month period of

OPTICAL POETRY: *The Life and Work of Oskar Fischinger*

near starvation before the next grant money arrived [Elfriede managed to do some sewing, cleaning and babysitting for extra money, and young as he was, Karl had begun to earn a little by delivering newspapers]. Their rent at Normandy Village was so hopelessly behind that in August 1941 they were forced to move to a small bungalow house ($52-per-month) at 1010 Hammond Street, still just a block from Sunset Strip, but some 10 blocks closer to Beverly Hills, and just a block from Paul Kohner's Agency. This turned out to be a very lucky move for them, since the landlord, Nelson McGrady, became a good friend and even bought paintings from Oskar. McGrady lived on a ranch in Camarillo (about a two-hour drive from Los Angeles) where he grew avocados, and kept rabbits and chickens which he shared liberally with the Fischingers throughout the coming war years when ration stamps and food shortages would add to their chronic poverty. McGrady would often spend the night at 1010 Hammond rather than drive back home, and he was treated as a member of the family. In the yard of the Hammond Street house stood mature orange and lemon trees that bore fruit year round, and the yard was large enough for a vegetable garden, so for the first time since 1936, the Fischinger family enjoyed a degree of comfort and security. The neighbours were also friendly, especially the D'Amores (who moved in about 10 years after the Fischingers). They owned a fancy Italian restaurant, The Villa Capri, where Italian-American celebrities like Frank Sinatra would dine. They also ran an Italian food stall in the Farmer's Market. They would often bring home some delicious left-overs to share with their neighbours.

Another German emigrant, Elise Nisse, a single woman who earned excellent wages as a housekeeper and gourmet cook for Carl Laemmle

Elise Nisse (Liesschen).

Jr. and other Hollywood celebrities (George Cukor, Katherine Hepburn, Jean Renoir, etc.), loaned the Fischingers money for a down-payment to purchase the Hammond Street house, which was a stroke of good fortune. Liesschen (as the children called her with the German affectionate dimutive) remained a kind of angel for the Fischingers throughout her life. Often when an extra cake or plate of some gourmet delicacy was left over from a party or elegant dinner, she would bring it to the Fischingers, and she always tried to make sure that the children had enough things that they needed, including clothes for school. Since Karl had learned German as his primary childhood language, it was not possible for him to attend the public schools, but the Catholic school in West Hollywood was glad to accept him, and the other Fischinger children as well. Some of the fees for the Catholic school were simply overlooked or waived, and Liesschen would also donate some fees and school uniforms. Liesschen also introduced the Fischingers to some of her other families with children, who would invite them over to swim in their pools, attend parties, etc. Charles Starrett had enjoyed a long career as a star of western and action features, including a number of films such as the *Durango Kid*. One of his boys, David, would some years later take painting lessons from Oskar – the only time Oskar ever accepted a pupil. The Mendyka children Karen and Gary also remained life-long friends of the Fischingers. Betty and Leo Schoenbrunn bought a number of fine paintings from Oskar, and their daughter Mary also became a good friend of the Fischinger girls.

In September 1941 Oskar's friend/lawyer Milton Wichner finally arranged for Oskar to buy his film back from Paramount for $500 (they had wanted $1,500 originally, then $1,000 by February 1941). Ralph Rainger, the composer, kindly signed over the music rights to Oskar. By October 1941, Oskar actually received the cels and film materials from the studio vaults.

Through another stroke of good luck, Orson Welles, who admired Oskar's films very much, hired Oskar to work at Mercury Productions on an RKO feature *It's All True* that would have contained four short episodes about the history of jazz. One of them, involving Duke Ellington and Louis Armstrong, would have included some of Oskar's abstract animations to jazz music. Welles was supervising all four stories in simultaneous production, and Oskar never received an exact assignment, just as at Paramount, but was allowed to work on his own animations at the RKO studios, where he painted more cels for *Radio Dynamics*. When the United States entered World War II in December 1941, Oskar was actually designated as an "Enemy Alien" and technically forbidden to work in any job having to do with the media, however Welles continued to pay Oskar cash out of his own pocket, and allowed him to continue working on his own projects at the studio. Welles was enjoined by Nelson Rockefeller and John Hay Whitney to change the focus of his feature to South America, where they feared Nazi and anti-US influence. Welles dutifully left for Rio to film the carnival, and Oskar presently received reels of samba soundtrack to experiment with. However, monetary and administrative changes at RKO and the CIA caused Mercury Productions to be ejected from the RKO lot in July 1942, and *It's All True* was cancelled. Oskar was given the Mercury Productions bulletin board as a souvenir, and since canvas was already becoming scarce and expensive, he painted one of a series of non-objective compositions on it: hard-edged geometric forms "floating" over loosely-brushed stripes of brown and black.

The entry of the US into the war placed the Fischingers in new jeopardy. Oskar, Elfriede and their son Karl were all legally "enemy aliens" since they had been born in Germany, and were not yet US citizens. The immigration quota that Oskar had gotten in Mexico in 1937 only allowed him to be hired on contract for special productions, not to hold a regular job of any kind. Since the Fischingers now had three children born in the US, their right to stay in America was assured, but they were still categorized as "enemy aliens" and severe strictures were imposed, including a curfew at 20:00 in the evening, mail censorship, and ineligibility for employment in any job having to do with the media, which included the film industry. They were also forbidden to have a short-wave radio in their home, and since their family radio did have a short-wave band on it, they were forced to store it at Paul Kohner's office until the end of the war. After some six months, Oskar took the radio to a repair shop and had the short-wave part removed, but the repairman reported Oskar to the FBI, and agents came to the house to investigate if the Fischingers were spying. When they asked if Oskar had any weapons, Oskar pondered a moment, then went to the back porch and returned with a small hatchet, which caused the FBI men to laugh, and they left.

Fortunately for Oskar, Orson Welles chose to keep him unofficially employed after December 1941; Welles paid him privately, out of Welles' own salary, for nine months. During his time at Mercury Productions, Oskar finished his work on the Paramount film, and worked on another silent film to which he would attach the old title cards for *Radio Dynamics*.

When Mercury folded, Oskar was forced to ask Rebay for another $750 to cover the lab costs of striking another print of the Paramount film, meaning that the Solomon Guggenheim Foundation would have loaned $2,000 for the project. On 26 September 1942, Rebay wrote to Oskar: "It was not easy for me to get even $1,000 agreed to, for we get very wonderful films from Mary Ellen Bute and Norman McLaren for one half to one third of your price ... . I think it is outrageous that you speak of the starvation of your family when you spend money and time on painting, for which you are not even gifted ... something that only increases the amount of mediocrity in painting." By 8 October, however, she had "managed to arrange" the $750, but demanded in exchange for it not only the colour print of the Paramount film, but also a new print of *Komposition in Blau* and a print of the intentionally-silent

Allegretto
[still from 35mm film].

OPTICAL POETRY: *The Life and Work of Oskar Fischinger*

film with a 78-frame rhythm that Oskar had been working on – once again a value in laboratory costs almost exceeding the amount of money Rebay was offering.

Rebay disliked the Paramount title "Radio Dynamics", and insisted that Oskar make new titles reading *Allegretto*. [In Bauer's 1917 Der Sturm exhibition, out of 92 paintings, 89 had musical titles, among them five "Allegretto"s.] Since Oskar had already printed up a *Radio Dynamics* title for the Paramount film, he transfered that name to his intentionally-silent film. When Oskar delivered *Allegretto* to Rebay in February 1943, she berated him bitterly for not having the intentionally-silent film ready too, and in her 26 April letter she complains, "I found in dealing with Germans one is tricked more often than not!", apparently forgetting that she, too, was German.

During this period, the specific object of Rebay's anxiety was really not Oskar but rather Rudolf Bauer, who regarded the concept of a Museum of Non-Objective Art as his own – as it may well have been, since he insisted upon "Das Geistreich" from the earlier Berlin days. Despite the fact that Rebay continued to supply substantial support for Bauer – she had made the arrangements to have him released from a Nazi prison, shipped him and his possessions including paintings and automobile to America in 1939, bought him an estate in New Jersey, assured his continued financial security – he despised and belittled Rebay, and apparently in an attempt to discredit her, in 1942 he denounced her as a hoarder, and she spent two months in detention.

Bauer then fell in love with and secretly married a woman who lived at his house posing as a maid. When Rebay discovered this, she was heartbroken and furious. She confided in Oskar that she had gone into Bauer's house and found him lying naked on top of another woman. [The irrepressibly witty Oskar, when telling Elfriede about it, quipped, "Did she expect him to do it in a tuxedo?"]

Oskar became, unfortunately, tightly embroiled in the affair since Bauer had bragged to Karl Nierendorf in 1941 that he would depose Rebay and become director of the Solomon Guggenheim Foundation himself; Nierendorf had told Oskar to warn Rebay, and subsequently she regarded Oskar as a go-between or sympathetic ally in this matter. After Rebay and Bauer were no longer speaking to each other, she sometimes drafted letters that she ordered Oskar to re-copy in his own handwriting and send them to Bauer as if they were from Oskar himself. The pathetic, tragic truth is that, however conceited, fatuous, and sadistic Bauer was, Rebay really did depend upon him for her artistic opinions and taste. This trap of contradictions is clear in her 20 June 1943 letter to Oskar: "Somehow, Bauer is full of vanity and would like to run the Museum after his fashion, and get the credit for everything I have done, but he cannot even speak English! I do not claim in the

Right: *Hilla Rebay*.

Below: *Galka Scheyer with Barbara Fischinger*.

least to be an expert in anything; in fact, the more I learn, the less I know – but I do know one thing: that, most every day, I start to work at 3:00 a.m. for this Foundation ... You can well imagine how much I have to concentrate to get everything going and to plan it on time. It is a terrifying job considering that I cannot even discuss it with Bauer."

As friendly relations between the Baroness and Bauer became rather permanently strained, then severed, Rebay became more bitter, and she began to vent her vengeful emotions on Oskar. In June 1943, now that Bauer no longer received an extra support stipend from the Foundation, Rebay agreed to give Oskar $200 each month for a year, if he promised to finish within that time three films: one synchronized to Bach's "Brandenburg Concerto No. 3", one synchronized to John Cage percussion music, and the intentionally silent film with a 78-frame rhythmic cycle. She required Oskar to write her regular, detailed reports on his progress, and to acknowledge each of her letters by repeating back her key phrases. In order to "improve himself spiritually", she also arranged for him, starting July 1943, to attend the Institute of Mental Physics in Los

Angeles, a church run by a "guru" of Rebay's, Edwin Dingle, who had adopted the "Tibetan" name Ding Le Mei.

Rebay's letters obviously make exaggerations to humiliate Oskar in ways she would have liked to humiliate Bauer; and Oskar repeats her phrases with an exaggerated effusiveness that can only be satirical. In October 1944, for example, Rebay writes: "I had offered to loan my gorgeous canvas 'Andante Cantabile' to the Institute of Mental Physics – but the offer was ignored – Of course, when it comes to taste, one must be looking elsewhere, as their book, pamphlets, letterheads and last colour reproduction of flag and candlelight (did you see it?) are very unorganized in this respect – It is hard to believe – To my feeling, the Inner Chamber should have no purple ..." And Oskar replies: "I am quite sure Dr. Dingle will be very happy to have your great picture 'Andante Cantabile'. I think your offer is really grand. This would bring for the first time one of your really great paintings to California, so it can be seen by as many people as there are interested in it. And I think the Institute of M.P. is a good place to show it. When Dr. Dingle has given no reply to your generous offer, I think it is due to two facts: first, as a real Yogi, he shuns any involvement in other fields of expression. Second: he does not know what it is all about. The flag and candlelight colour reproduction hit me, too, in the stomach, but here maybe we have to be patient, too – The originators of Non-Objective Art are still alive, and originators are mostly not much concerned with teaching. They teach through their work – and it needs a long time before the regular teachers grasp the Idea – Many generations are necessary to teach the masses ...".

These report letters (about twice a month) had to be typed in good English, and Oskar spent days (sometimes a whole week) of anguished work on each one – amounting to a third or a half of his working time! When it came to reporting how many Bach cels he had finished, then, he felt justified in claiming about 500 each month, although he could not concentrate enough to get film work done. He did, however, continue to paint, but since Rebay's comments about his painting were so particularly cruel, he had to pretend that he did not. In addition to all this, Rebay would make other little demands, such as the letter of 27 December 1946: "We are enclosing fifty cents in stamps for which Baroness Rebay would like very much to have you buy her a copy of "Your Dog's Astrological Horoscope". We believe you can find this in any Hollywood Pet Shop. Will you please send it to her as promptly as you can? Thank you!".

To balance how the Baroness operated like an evil witch (dangling lures, but punishing more than she helped), Galka Scheyer became more and more helpful and generous. Her home, designed by immigrant architect Richard Neutra, was only a few miles away from the

Fischingers, on a hill above Sunset Strip. In the kindest, most unobtrusive way, she made sure the Fischinger family got by in hard times; she hired Oskar to maintain a "victory garden" in her yard, paid Elfriede to sew, shop and cook for her, or whatever pleasant and easy tasks she could devise. When she went on a lecture tour, Oskar would act as caretaker for her dog Tuffy and her house, where Oskar could scrutinize and touch and meditate on the splendid Klees and Kandinskys.

Unlike Rebay, Galka encouraged Oskar's own painting, and made sure he got to visit important local private collections of modern art such as Walter Arensberg's home, where hundreds of Dada, Surreal and Abstract paintings (including a near definitive selection of Marcel Duchamp) not only hung on every available inch of wall, upstairs and down, but also stood in bunches of five and six against bookshelves and closet doors. At that time Jawlensky, crippled with arthritis, painted (with the brush taped between his stiff hands) simple canvases that Galka could not sell for $10, and she herself was buying a Picasso for $800 (in $30-per-month payments). But she still arranged to sell one of Oskar's paintings (a fine geometric composition, painted on milk-glass, with triangle-points bursting out of its implied frame) to Katherine Dreier for $250. Oskar, however, stubbornly insisted on $450, and refused to sell it for less. Galka also sent all visiting celebrities to visit Oskar, so that, for example, Maya Deren and Sasha Hammid came to 1010 Hammond Street to study Oskar's art before they shot their masterpiece *Meshes of the Afternoon*. Unfortunately by 1944 Galka grew ill with cancer, and though she struggled painfully to be active until the last, she died in December 1945, a sad personal loss for the Fischingers. Galka's superb collection of paintings is now in the Norton Simon Museum in Pasadena.

Rebay's spiteful, erratic insults about Oskar's paintings were also contradicted by others. Dr. Alois Schardt had assembled important collections of modern German art as curator of the Moritzburg museum in Halle and then on Berlin's Museeninsel until the Entartete Kunst Austellung in 1938, after which he emigrated to Los Angeles, where he taught at Immaculate Heart College, while his wife, who had triumphantly played Goethe's Iphigenie in Germany, worked as a chambermaid in the Biltmore Hotel. Schardt understood and admired Oskar's paintings, and they became fast friends, which challenged Oskar with a continuing, comparative critique of his work from a trained art historian.

During the early 1940s, Oskar threw his energy ecstatically into painting, which offered him a tangible, immediate return as opposed to the long delays and cumbersome technology of film projection. He fell in love with everything uniquely belonging to painting, and demonstrated his mastery of technique and conception in dozens of splendid canvases. The 1940 "Dream" arose literally from one of Oskar's dreams: the deep blue background is applied with a spatula in heavy impasto, and vague bluish-white blotches, also scraped with spatula, add to the vagueness and the tactility of this matrix; over this context lie two broad, gestural spatula strokes of white, one from top centre pulling down to the right, the other smaller one from top right pulling down toward centre – and a few delicate smudges in lavender/wine shades upper left. The tension between the nebulous polymorphous suggestions of colour/form and the boldness of the texture and gesture maintain the vivid ambiguity of certainty and uncertainty of the dream-image, as well as its quasi-mystical serenity. The 1941 "Red Circle" uses not only spatula, but also sponges and etching tools to supply intricate textures to a rigid geometric form, while the austere 1942 "Black and White Circle" creates a dynamic momentum to the viewer's glance by imprisoning it within a white circle surrounded by black, then forcing the eye to trace dark zig-zags of thin impasto lines that cross and re-cross the feathery brushstrokes of the "white" circle which seems more textured grey the longer one looks. From 1943 one can delight in the exquisite "Finger-Painting" in which a warped checker-board of primarily blue shades with a cluster of red/yellow squares knotted in the lower right was literally smudged on to a textured celotex board with Oskar's fingertip – or revel in the flamboyant vitality of "Snowflakes" with its loose brushstroking of large white and bright-red curving lines and circles layered over an intricately multi-coloured speckled background.

These energetic and calm paintings arise partly from Oskar's film-making wisdom, modulating visual energy to create an arc to the action in his Visual Music compositions. In turn, these painting were feeding ideas into his filmmaking. The 1944 "Solo" (which Irmgard von Cube purchased) develops out of parallel curved lines, each painted in a slightly different shade from the previous, so that a spectrum leads from the bright-orange piercing wedge in the lower right through yellow and white into gently-curving tranquil blue bands in the upper left. This not only begins a series of paintings in this style, but also relates to the concentric vortex of graduated circles in *Radio Dynamics*, and provided the climactic images of Oskar's "Bach" film three years later – both of these filmic sequences highly charged with spiritual balance.

From 1942 survives a spectacular composition consisting of three transparent English-drawing-silks [such as Oskar had used for *Radio Dynamics* animations] glued together to create a wide panorama rather like the cinemascope format – and rather like Oskar's *R-1* triple projection from 1927. Each panel is an intricate mosaic of small geometric shapes, the left coloured in shades of grey/green, the centre in shades of brown/rust/yellow and the right in shades of blue. Within each "tessera" of the mosaics, the careful brushstroke follows exclusively the geometric

Major Movement, 1946, *from the collection of Angelica Fischinger.*

logic of the form it inhabits: a diagonal rhomboid brushed diagonally, a rectangle horizontal or vertical, a triangle diagonally coherent with the adjacent rectangle, etc. Over all three panels floats a sinuous cream-coloured line created with a single drip of paint gracefully turned in lissajous curves. Was this intended as a spectacular finale for the Hindemith project? or the intentionally silent film? or the John Cage film? Or was this quite simply an inventive painting? Here Fischinger the painter and Fischinger the filmmaker are already inextricable. Oskar folded this "cel" in order to get it in his suitcase when he travelled to New York in 1944, so even that late he hoped to interest someone in providing financial backing for what would have been an astonishing, splendid project.

OPTICAL POETRY: The Life and Work of Oskar Fischinger

Out of the $200-per-month stipend, Oskar rented (for $30 a month) a storefront studio on Sawtelle Boulevard in West Los Angeles, ostensibly as a work area where he could finish the three films, and he did in fact work on them. However, Oskar happened to acquire at that time 20 pieces of celotex (a composition board) which he hung in a row around the walls of the studio. Artist's canvas, by that point in the war, was largely unavailable, so Oskar could not resist the temptation to paint on the celotexes, which were mostly about three feet square. For about a year's time, during 1943/1944, he painted all 20 celotexes simultaneously, strolling about the studio making a few lines here, a dash there, sponging an area, scraping a bit, painting over something, etc. What a sight they must have been in 1944 with all nearly complete! Two, both named "Magic Mirror", with checkerboards mapped on to twisted, rippling surfaces, posit intricate geometrical illusions like M.C. Escher – as does the "Finger-Painting" already mentioned. One series involves dozens of brightly-coloured organic shapes and textures that swirl and mingle in intricate balances and fluid tensions – the closest Oskar ever got to the early "improvisations" of Kandinsky ["Birthday", now in the collection of Beverly and Pat O'Neill, is particularly fine]. Another shows merely a cluster of nine spheres floating in a neutral background. Another, in serial rapport with the earlier "Black and White Circle", shows dark zig-zag lines over a feathery textured grey/white background. And two paintings overtly reference Oskar's black-and-white *Studien*, one with a complex arrangement of comets, crescents, bars and other iconography from the films (even two "atom splittings") in harmonic balance, but with three arrows indicating the trajectory of movement – as in some of Klee's paintings.

The wonderful "Red Bowl" (also somewhat in the style of Klee, whom Oskar adored) consists of a dozen pure geometric forms on a brown background, each of the areas lightly brushed so that the texture of the celotex shows through, and several of the shapes overlapping so that blue and yellow and cinnabar almost combine to recreate the brown of the background which they cover: while the forms balance each other harmonically as an absolute composition, Oskar's playful arrangement leads one to speculate if triangles in the upper area might not be pyramids – indeed if one overlapped by a pointed oval might not be the "eye" on the pyramid familiar from Egyptian/Alchemical/Masonic mysticism, as well as the Masonic-inspired design for the United States' one dollar bill; then could the three large pointed ovals be a Nile boat, the cinnabar the hull, the blue and yellow sails, the orange triangular wedge at the back a tiller? Such whimsical speculations would undoubtedly delight Oskar (as they did Klee), but in the final analysis, the painting is a vibrant visual fugue of triangles curved and pointed, in a select range of colour. Oskar, by the way, almost never gave names to his paintings, preferring to call them all "Abstraction" with numbers to differentiate or designate a particular one. The poetic-descriptive titles suggesting some representational connection are all made up by gallery owners or curators who needed some variety of titles for exhibitions and catalogues, or by family and friends who said simply, "That one looks like a ..." and the title stuck.

In addition to the celotex paintings, Oskar did work on films quite a bit. He began the "Bach" film several times in different media, ranging from traditional cel animations (he painted about 1,000 cels and shot 500 on to 35mm film, but apparently was dissatisfied with the results), to black-and-white and colour pencil drawings on paper, to new techniques such as layering and changing coloured celophane gels in a matte that produced "Yin-Yang" images, or manipulating "tessera" in grid patterns.

5

Painting

At that time, the Baroness had become obsessed with possessing a Colour Organ, because the rival Museum of Modern Art had acquired several Lumia compositions from Thomas Wilfred, which either projected moving coloured light inside a self-contained television-like box, or occupied a large space, casting amorphous swirls and sinuous currents of coloured light surging across walls and ceiling. Rebay had accepted the Los Angeles light artist Charles Dockum as the Guggenheim's rival. Dockum's MobilColor Projector involved a large console with three moving projector units tied to a sprocketed control-tape which regulated some of the changes in imagery, while others had to be manipulated by hand. Unlike Wilfred, Dockum could produce hard-edged geometric images of an ethereal luminescence, and he choreographed the forms to move gracefully and overlap in complex layers. By using different primary image slides, he could also produce soft organic shapes, or moiré patterns of great intricacy.

Dockum received a stipend from Rebay while he was perfecting a new MobilColor Projector specially designed for performance at the Museum of Non-Objective Painting, one that would work totally automatically and continuously in the museum's galleries. Dockum experienced the same tempestuous, depressing relationship with Rebay that Oskar had, including the elaborate, time-consuming letters, from which every word would be taken wrong. When, for example, Dockum mentioned his friend, Peter Krasnow, who was a painter and sculptor, Rebay replied that "several very great artists do not like Krasnow at all", and further warned him that "sculpture is a second-rate artform anyway, so you should not really associate with an average person like Krasnow, but rather strive to impress a master like Bauer". When Dockum actually finished his new MobilColor Projector and took it to New York in 1952, he only played it one time. The Baroness hated it, especially because it

would not actually play continuously and automatically without a person tending it. Rebay had it put in storage, and later had it dismantled so that the lighting elements could be used in the museum's painting galleries. So all of the compositions that Dockum had made for this MobilColor were destroyed. Fortunately, Mary Ellen Bute shot some footage of the 1952 performance, so a few minutes of documentation survive, but the actual character of the colour-music – the intensity and luminosity of the colours, etc. – can hardly be captured on film.

In 1943, Rebay demanded that Dockum, as part of his official duties as a Guggenheim fellow, go to Oskar's studio and spy on him to find out if he were really working on the Bach film. Oskar adamantly refused to let Dockum into his studio, since he in fact was not working very much on the Bach project because he had still not arrived at the right means of expressing the baroque music. But he and Dockum became friends and exchanged anecdotes about the Baroness. Oskar did not really believe you could make art with a machine, and he wrote that to Rebay frankly, telling about his experiences with Alexander Laszlo in the 1920s. Oskar also had pictures of himself taken sitting at his animation desk with hundreds of bottles of paint, representing the many fine gradations of colours numbered so that someone else could fill them in on the cels, but nonetheless looking very much like an organ. He sent these "Color Organ" photos to Rebay 7 July 1943 with the following description: "The first thing I did was to prepare the colours used for this work in such a way that the colour used for each instrument was specially balanced and mixed. For the three bass viols a special bass scale was mixed, and for the three cellos, the three violas, and the three violins there are also special colour scales. The colours are in little bottles which are placed like a colour organ, five rows over each other, and easy to reach. The colour row scales are tuned as exactly as possible in the same mode as the instruments. The movements are free. I studied the music over and over again, reading the conductor's partitur, and I know by now every single note. I hope some day to have a cello in order to play it and get a better feeling for the bass section, which is the basis for the whole work ..."

During this period Oskar finished the film *Radio Dynamics* as well. No overt reference is made to this film in the correspondence. Since Rebay had rejected the old Paramount title which Oskar re-used, naturally he would not have referred to it by that name. The "intentionally silent film with a 78-frame rhythm" must in some way correspond to *Radio Dynamics*, since that film is preceded by a title reading "No Music please – An Experiment in Colour-Rhythm", but only about 75 per cent of that film falls into 78-frame phrases; perhaps Oskar did not offer it to Rebay because he feared she would notice the discrepancy and castigate him – or, since only a single print of the film survived in Oskar's estate, perhaps he never could afford to make a print for Rebay. A lovely, sensuous *Organic Fragment* which Oskar left unfinished from this period [the cels were finally painted and shot by his daughter Barbara in 1984] actually falls into perfect 78-frame phrases.

In any case, the principle governing the design and final composition of *Radio Dynamics* is undoubtedly mystical, and Oskar certainly finished it during the 1943/44 time when Rebay was forcing him to attend Dingle's Institute in order to (she said derisively) improve his spiritual qualities. Bauer (and Rebay) belonged to the first generation of non-objective painters, and still shuddered at the criticism that abstract art was just decoration – wall paper – and the sole defence against that charge (so brilliantly articulated by Kandinsky and Mondrian) seemed to them the spiritual values of the artist expressed in pure, "musical", Platonic, non-objective rhythms. [The Baroness refused to acquire works by Malevich since she regarded him as a communist, and hence anti-spiritual, although he also had a strong mystical bias, as it turns out.] So Rebay cautiously painted according to certain "rules" of spirituality, prime among them being: "Avoid pattern and decoration at all costs!" Fischinger was just enough younger than Bauer and Rebay that for him non-objective art seemed totally natural and obvious – and he nurtured no mystique about the primacy of "oil on canvas" as an ultimate art medium, and ornamentation (decorative pattern) fascinated him as a valid, spiritual folk-art form; so rather than suppress it, Oskar often used decoration consciously. He also broke almost every other "rule" laid down by Bauer in "Kosmische Bewegung" and Kandinsky in *Point and Line to Surface*, but everywhere in his canvases he evinces his extraordinary technical mastery and his refined sensibility. Oskar's vast experience with kinetic arrangements and durational colour mutations made him sensitive to a more adventurous range of possibilities. Oskar was not a follower, he was an original genius. But the Baroness feared Oskar's painting because it defied all her safe preconceptions. She resented his unconventionality, and hoped to tame him into painting conservative "party-line" non-objective canvases by getting him involved with an orthodox mysticism.

Since at least the 1920s in Berlin, Oskar had been fascinated by all forms of speculative scientific and mystical contemplation. Even though Oskar disliked all formal organizations and never belonged to any social groups, he avidly studied all schools of mystic thought and loved long Platonic dialogues with friends – most recently, at that time, with Galka Scheyer, who was a devotee of Krishnamurti. Quite aside from hating to attend two (time-consuming) regular religious services each week (and he had to take his daughter Barbara to Sunday School as well), Oskar found the atmosphere of Ding Le Mei's Institute of Mental Physics more akin to Protestant Puritanism (and, indeed, in 1944 its name gradually changed to International Church of the Holy Trinity, then First Church of Mystic Christianity) than to the Tibetan Buddhism (with its roots in shamanism and Hindu tantric practices) that it technically represented. Oskar, however, at this point knew better than to try to cross Rebay, although he does shyly, slyly try to suggest to her that he does have some spiritual roots, and perhaps does not need so much "training" [11 December 1943]: "I am very happy with the spiritual development through which I go now, and feel already a great improvement in my whole body, and I am very thankful for this. I wish I could write you how much this whole teaching is in line with my innermost tendency. Already in 1929 in Berlin I invented or developed and used a rotating cylinder, driven by a motor, day and night, all the time, to hold my denials and affirmations in steady motion-rotation (*An Optical Poem* reflects something of this). Years later I learned about the Buddhist prayer wheel, and discovered the existing parallel thoughts in my continuous rotating cylinders and the thousands-of-years-old prayer wheel. I was a little bit choked up to have made all on my own – as I thought – such a similar invention, and thought I was, at this time, the only one in Europe ..." [The rotating prayer-wheel cylinder, by the way, is also the source for Oskar's logo.]

Nonetheless, Rebay still required Oskar to relate to her the content of some of Dingle's sermons, and once (10 May 1944) when Oskar quoted phrases exactly out of one of Ding Le Mei's pamphlets (which had such illuminating titles as "Our Country's Future Influence in the Orient" and "Why God Permits War"), Rebay berated him: "I advise you not to mix up business letters with rather undigested ideas of Ding Le Mei".

Rebay wrote Oskar 25 February 1944: "A religious non-objective film without music seems to me ought to be done. Did you ever run a film without music? Don't you think it is just as (if not even more) beautiful – a film without music, or if not without, simply with just sounds of knocking, flat or sharp, loud or soft, varied by the rhythmic interval of speed?" Once again this documents Rebay's mental instability, since Oskar's "Without Music/78 frames per bar" was included in a contract already in October 1942, and also a film to John Cage's percussion music (which consists of plenty of irregular "knocks") appears in the June 1943 contract. Oskar, however, on 9 March 1944 patiently answers: "Your idea about the production of a religious non-objective film ought to be done, and could be done. You write in your letter that film does not need music necessarily, and can be even more beautiful without music. How true this is. The optical part, the form and motion, is visualized through the visual imagination – through the phantasy of the eye. Light is the same as sound: they are waves of different length that tell us something about the inner and outer structure of things. Non-objective expressions need no perspective. Sound is mostly an effect of the inner plastic structure of things, and also not needed for non-objective expressions."

Perhaps this interchange encouraged Oskar to edit *Radio Dynamics*. Several times he mentions that Dr. Dingle wanted him to show films at the Institute, but he never says that he actually did screen any there. And in several instances, Oskar was obviously using the Dingle screening as a pretence for getting back from Rebay his only print of *An Optical Poem*, which he had loaned to Rebay but which she now claimed was hers and would not return.

In any case, *Radio Dynamics*, painted and shot in the earlier 1940s and edited in 1943/44, may be Oskar's finest film, the one in which his craftsmanship and spiritual ideas balance into a meaningful, faultless whole. The film has the structure of yoga itself: we see first a series of exercises (for the eyes or sense of vision) in fluctuating, stretching rectangles; then icons representing meditation – a flight into an infinite vortex defined by finite movement, and an image of two "eyes" opening, expanding/contracting, while between them grows a third eye of inner cosmic consciousness. After a brief introductory statement of these three themes, each is repeated in a longer, more developed version, so that we can actually participate in the hypnotic yoga meditation, sensitizing our own eyes on the more elaborate exercises that culminate in complex stroboscopic flickers between mosaic paintings, relaxing into concentration on the hypnotic rhythms of the expanding third eye, and then challenged by the ambiguities of the meditation on the vortex whose

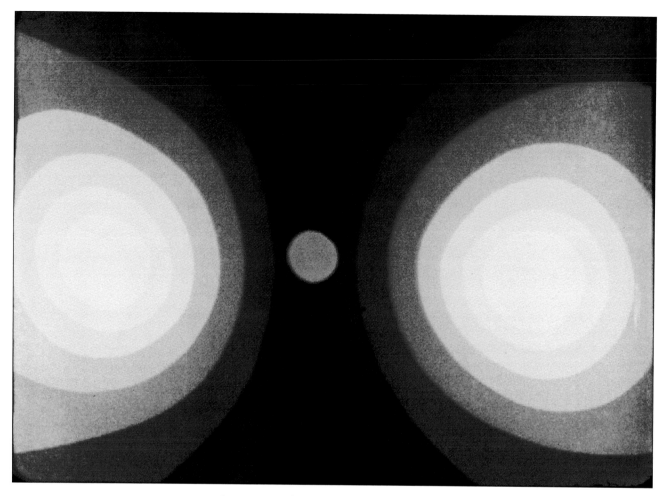

Radio Dynamics.

rings expand as we fly into it (simultaneous inward and outward flight, the eye of the observer as the eye of the universe), with changes in colour, size and sense of speed that suggest the primary cosmic dilemmas of Einstein and Heisenberg – the balance between energy, matter, velocity and observer. Oskar articulates this in wholly visual terms – clear but emotional, simple but subtle and complex – that happen to the viewer and can be understood directly with no intervening words.

Another, and perhaps more significant, spiritual factor of this period leading to the perfection of *Radio Dynamics* was a new set of friends, the Bertoias. On 25 June 1943 (in the same letter where she mentions that Frank Lloyd Wright will design the new museum), Rebay wrote to Oskar that she was having an exhibit of work she wished Oskar could see by a young Italian artist Harry Bertoia. A few months later Bertoia turned up in Hollywood, where he moved with his wife Brigitta, daughter of Dr. William Valentiner, Director of the Los Angeles County

Museum (and the same person he had visited at Detroit in 1938 seeking backing for the Dvorak film). The Bertoias lived on the beach near Topanga, where Harry (later famous for his kinetic-musical sculptures) was creating delicate woodcuts and monoprints on rice paper, and designing fine jewelry in silver. Oskar and Harry became instant comrades, and by the winter 1944/45, a great intimacy had grown between Oskar and Elfriede and Harry and Brigitta that made them constant companions. Despite gas rationing, the Fischingers would pile into their 1932 Chevy with a rumble seat and drive to the beach, and the Bertoias in turn drove to Hollywood as often as possible, especially after they moved into a house in Topanga that had no running water, so they came to wash and bathe at the Fischingers.

One Sunday when the Bertoias were visiting the Fischingers, Oskar had prepared a masonite board for a new painting, coating it with a primer of rabbit glue (thanks to hours of smelly boiling by Elfriede) and gesso. All white, the masonite lounged on an easel on the front porch, drying in the sunlight. Elfriede and Brigitta were busy preparing lunch and herding the children. Oskar had gone out to his studio-shack in the back yard to finish some film business. Harry could not resist the lure of that lorelei gesso, gleaming in a shaft of sunlight, and seizing Oskar's palette, he began a composition of bold vertical strokes.

Suddenly Oskar burst on to the porch and cried, "Hey! Wait a minute. That's *my* board! I got it ready for a certain painting I plan to do."

"I'm sorry, Oskar", Harry replied, quietly beaming. "It's my painting now".

Painting   115

Brigitta Bertoia with Elfriede's
mother, Elfriede and Gabi
Fischinger (Elfriede's niece).

"But it was my board, so it's my painting", Oskar grumbled. Materials weren't cheap or easy to find.

"But which is the more important part now?" Harry speculated. "Your board – your painting yet to be – or my painting already begun?"

Lunch interrupted their argument, but some time between the avocados and roast rabbit and the dessert of fruit, Oskar slipped out to his studio, sawed the masonite in two pieces (without cutting through any of Harry's lines) and reappeared at the dinner table to render this judgment of Solomon: "Here, Harry, this is your half; this is mine."

Harry and even more so Brigitta were deeply spiritual, mystic people – just the sort Oskar had longed to meet, but by his mid-40s, despaired of ever meeting. Brigitta revelled in the mysteries of Astronomy and Astrology, the Baghavad Gita and the Tao, and the secret rituals of tantric yoga. The couples went star-gazing and stayed up at night spinning out intricate philosophical discourse and experimenting with the possibilities of thought-transfer in meditative states. The warmth and joy and supportiveness of this new relationship may well have inspired Oskar's serenely energetic meditation film (later known as *Radio Dynamics*).

Friendships could also waste time. Brigitta played chess eagerly, and she and Oskar would sit for hours over a game – the same hours he should have been animating on his "Bach" film. Brigitta also behaved very seductively towards Oskar and though she called it "yin/yang" and "yabyum" (the Chinese and Tibetan expressions for a male/female sexual bonding), to Elfriede and Harry it seemed very much as if Oskar and Brigitta were having an affair, especially when they would disappear together for a few hours. Both Oskar and Brigitta denied that they had ever made love with each other, and insisted that they were merely meditating, contemplating the star patterns, discussing spiritual matters, etc. That seemed hard to believe since Brigitta behaved rather extravagantly, including regaling them with stories about how she, as a child, would sneak out of bed and watch from the top of the stairs while her father participated in orgies with a dozen athletic young men. Both Harry and Elfriede managed to reconcile themselves to the eccentricities of Brigitta, and came to believe that the relationship between Oskar and her was in fact completely chaste. The four of them remained best of friends throughout their lives. In 1953, when Elfriede went back to visit Gelnhausen, Brigitta happened to be visiting in Europe at the same time, and made an appearance at the Fischinger Drugstore in Gelnhausen. She flirted with Elfriede's brother Robert, just as she had done with Oskar, and one Sunday afternoon, in the presence of the entire Fischinger clan (including Elfriede's 10-year-old daughter Angie and Robert's 7-year-old daughter Gabi, as well as the grandmother) Brigitta lept on to a coffee table and demonstrated how a dervish could whirl almost endlessly – and also revealed to the astonished family that she was not wearing any undergarments. The Bertoia children, Val, Celia and Lesta, would remain friends of the Fischinger children for many years – indeed Lesta later spent several years at the Fischinger home in Laurel Canyon, which seemed idyllic and sane to her compared to the tensions and chaos of her family then in Pennsylvania.

Another avid time-wasting chess player was Carl Junghans, who had made communist films (including the famous 1930 *So ist das Leben* [That's Life!] before the Nazi era, then had his work banned by the Nazis (including a 1938 feature of Fallada's *Altes Herz geht auf die Reise* [The Old Heart Goes Wandering]). When he emigrated to Hollywood, he worked as a gardener for Kurt Weill and Robert Siodmak, but failed to establish himself in filmmaking. He did come regularly to the Fischingers to spend hours playing chess and arguing about politics, full of outrageous, provocative first-hand anecdotes about the Nazis. His wife Lotte was another kind, generous and long-suffering soul.

In November 1943 another daughter, Angelica [nicknamed "Tootsie" by the family and "Angie" by other friends], was born to the Fischingers, and the Baroness became her godmother, sending a hand-stitched, fully-lined pink silk bonnet and gown for her goddaughter to wear for the christening at Ding Le Mei's Institute. Throughout the coming years, Rebay regularly sent many kind packages of clothes and other presents (ranging from war bonds to autographed photos and reproductions of her paintings) to her godchild.

Rebay's relationship, however, with Oskar remained as equivocal, sado-masochistic as ever. On one hand, she continued to invite him to submit paintings to each group show at her museum, and often as many as six were included in one exhibition. On the other hand, she constantly scorned his painting verbally, in statements ranging from hysterical, underlined shrieks: "*You can not paint!*" [18 August 1942 and again five years later 23 August 1947], to confirmations of exacted promises: "I am glad that you will no longer waste time and money on your not so significant paintings" [6 December 1944]. The happy medium is perhaps best represented by her letter of 11 October 1943: "Many thanks for your little painting. I will try to show it in one of our shows, yet let me advise you that one chord is not a symphony or sonata yet, and I don't think painting is your most useful medium. Your ability is timed rhythm it still seems to me. Your letter to Mr. Bauer was not good. He makes constant unbelievable trouble out of 'Ehrsucht' ['greedy ambition', in German in the original] and vanity, and ignorance of earthly conditions. A dismissed employee, Menken, and housekeeper 'putsched' him up. I put a nice louse in my fur; my brother once warned me if I let him come over here."

A similar ambivalence is apparent in the events surrounding the plans for the new museum building. Rebay writes often to Oskar asking advice, for example, about the safety precautions for preserving paintings and films, and when it was feared that robot-rocket-bombers might blitz New York, she asked Oskar where the art might be stored [he recommended Denver]. In June 1943, she told Oskar confidentially that Frank Lloyd Wright would be the architect for the new museum building (Ding Le Mei was using Wright as architect for a proposed City of Mental Physics), and she solicited elaborate plans from Oskar for a film section (he designed complete production facilities and a dome theatre).

In May 1944 she paid for Oskar to come to New York to consult with Wright. Oskar was delighted to see the current Museum quarters, and amused to find that Rebay had a recording of Bach's "Brandenburg Concertos" played continuously in the galleries. The "guards" were painters whom, like Oskar, Rebay did not appreciate and consequently as punishment/training forced them to work in the museum as guards "where they would be surrounded by and learn from great art". They told him how much they hated that same recording of Bach, played over and over, and how they had worked out a system of warning signals with Rebay's chauffeur and the doorman, so that while the Baroness was away, they could shut the music off, and when she returned they would be notified in time to turn it back on. They also joked with Oskar about how Rebay had set out cards to be filled in by the museum visitors, saying which were their favourite and least-favourite paintings; each day she demanded that there be a reasonable number of these cards, and she read them all carefully, getting furious with the guards if the cards contained some negative criticisms. Therefore, they had to spend several hours each day writing these cards, faking different handwriting styles, since on some days no one at all came into the galleries, and those who did most often wrote severely critical, even mocking, commentary which had to be thrown away. Inventing new comments and handwriting styles indeed added to their Art education. The object of particular humour and scorn was a large painting by Rudolf Bauer named "Blue Balls" which Rebay habitually hung directly in front of the main doors so that visitors would see it first. On cold winter days, they inevitably burst into raucous laughter since, unbeknownst to the Baroness, "Blue Balls" was a common American slang term for "frozen testicles", either from chilly weather or an encounter with a particularly frigid sex partner. The "guards" had extra work on those winter days, as relatively many people came in just to get out of the cold.

From painter–filmmaker Marie Menken, who had worked as Rebay's secretary, Oskar also learned the tale of the handsome young painter–filmmaker Dwinell Grant, who had made two abstract films, *Themis* in 1940 and *Contrathemis* in early 1941, before approaching Rebay in 1941 for funding of a further animation project. She replied that she already had several good animators, but what she needed was a theoretical text about non-objective kinetic art, defining the aesthetics of the timed, moving abstract image in film or colour-organ projection. Grant declined at first, admitting that writing was not his strong point, but Rebay insisted that he would only get assistance from the Foundation if he did write such a tract. Finally, in desperation, he accepted a fellowship that would support him while he tried to write the treatise. Rebay warned him that he was now a representative of the Guggenheim Foundation, and insisted that he spend a substantial portion of his stipend to rent a prestige apartment and buy several business suits so that he could appear in public at all times in a decent suit. After several months, Rebay demanded to see his manuscript, and when she had read it, denounced it as unusable nonsense, and demanded that he repay his stipend money immediately. Of couse, he could not, having spent it on the expensive life-style Rebay had commanded. "Then you will have to work for me until the equivalent is paid back," she said.

"What shall I do, then?" Grant asked.

Rebay reached into her desk drawer and pulled out a handful of worn underpanties. "Wash these!" she ordered. Grant took them to the men's restroom and washed them, then brought them back to Rebay's office (she had left) and hung them on lamps and chairs and shelves to dry. He left the Guggenheim Foundation and did not come back.

Oskar confided to Menken a similar incident that had occurred to him in 1938 when he first met Rebay and she took him to her estate Green Farms in Connecticut. While they were walking in the gardens, Rebay's underpants fell to the ground, and she stepped out of them, asking Oskar to pick them up. As he handed them to her, she grasped his hand through the underwear, part clinging, part inviting. Oskar pulled loose and merely walked on, and the incident was over, but he always remembered it as an attempted seduction.

Oskar had an excellent rapport with Wright, especially as he admired Wright's fine buildings in Los Angeles. They also joked about the Baroness' temper-tantrums and her ridiculous insistence on absolute laws of colour and form in art. When Oskar left New York on 3 June 1944 he was so elated that on the three-day train ride back to Los Angeles he drafted a joyous manifesto for the Non-Objective Kinetic Group, which would be housed in the new museum, and would include all the major practitioners of abstract film including Len Lye, Mary Ellen Bute, Norman McLaren, Francis Lee and (despite the fact that Rebay had omitted his films from her collection) Dwinell Grant. Oskar dreamed of them all sharing their skills and achievements. The shared confidences about the Baroness from other artists had made him feel better, realizing that she had no special grudge against him, and apparently no serious weight lay behind her insults.

A few days after his return to Los Angeles, however, he received a chilling letter (9 June 1944) beginning: "I am glad you left when you did and wasted no further money on hotel rooms". After three paragraphs of bitter reproofs about Oskar's behaviour in New York, and his relationship with Ding Le Mei ("Please in the future stay away from Mr. Dingle ... as he, out of kindness and very likely *respect for me*, seems to give you far too much of his time ... when you have really nothing of any importance to tell or say to such an important man."), the entire second page of the letter is devoted to a repeat of her objections (written at least twice before) to *An American March*, concluding: "As long as you introduce the flag in a film, it should have been a flag film – nothing else. The flag should have appeared before the title, before the music begins. But this has never occurred to you very evidently, as in the *An American March* there was no development of the lines, the stars, or the section themes of the flag themselves. I would first have made a fugue of the main themes, then introduced the stripes, then introduced the stars. Yet you probably do not understand at all what I am writing about and you would, as you should, never say: I do not understand. Too Bad. Greetings, Sincerely yours, Hilla Rebay".

Did she not remember (as she apparently forgot the "intentionally-silent film with a 78-frame phrase") that she had written this all before? Did she simply have nothing else to say? In any case, despite her threats, she still required Oskar to attend Dingle's Institute, and she continued to solicit plans for the new museum: Oskar advised (1 October 1944) moving the dome theatre and film department to a separate structure adjacent to the circular painting-gallery-ramp on account of fire danger. And she even increased Oskar's monthly allowance to $300 once (although she also lowered it to $100 once).

In response to Rebay's harsh letter, Oskar replied with formula flattery; he had learned his lesson: "You, dear Baroness, are already far advanced and far ahead of us, in many ways, especially in the expression of artistic-creative work. I could feel this very clearly when you were sitting in your screen-house. I still see you sitting there, and I cannot forget your eyes and the beautiful light that came from you. In the train rolling away from New York, I saw you all the time, so like a wonderful white Buddha, full of fascinating light and life. When I was told to leave, I felt depressed and unhappy only because I could no longer see you ...".

Oskar could also withstand the jibes of the Baroness better because of a growing sense of artistic community in Los Angeles. At a show of Oskar's paintings and films at the Stendahl Gallery in fall 1939, he had met the Whitney brothers who had not yet made films. By 1944 they were completing their *Five Film Exercises*, and James Whitney came to visit Oskar and invite him to a private screening at his studio, one of the Frank Lloyd Wright buildings on the Barnsdall estate, Olive Hill, in Hollywood. Also at the screening were photographer Edmund Teske, Kenneth Anger, Man Ray and Bertolt Brecht. Oskar's own films were also screened with a certain regularity at the leading art schools in Los Angeles, Art Center School, Otis Art Institute and Chouinard School of Art, where he became friends with painters Lorser Feitelson and Helen Lundeberg, ceramicist Al King, and photographer Frank Judson. In 1946 Al King founded the California Color Society, and Oskar was named an honorary lifetime member for his superior achievements as a colourist; among the other members was silent movie star Harold Lloyd, who painted delightful abstract canvases that he dubbed "Landsca-pades", and he also became Oskar's admiring friend. Oskar also grew friendly with Stanton Macdonald-Wright who in 1913 in Paris made a manifesto together with another American painter Morgan Russell, for abstract colour-oriented painting: Synchromy. Now living in the Los Angeles luxury suburb Pacific Palisades, McDonald-Wright shared with Oskar his experiments to create an instrument that could project flowing colours with geometric shapes – an idea already articulated in the early Synchromy days in Paris, but only now in Los Angeles had it been realized.

From a console about three feet square, the colours were projected upwards through a translucent screen on top, while battery-powered mechanisms rotated geometric forms that inserted their shapes into the colours – remarkably like a living version of the Synchromy paintings. Impressed by Oskar films, Macdonald-Wright hoped to perfect his colour-organ so that the choreography of colours might synchronize with music, but he never managed to do that.

Filmmakers regularly made pilgrimages to Oskar as a master of the earlier Avant-Garde. Claire Parker and Alexander Alexeieff travelled to California in 1942 (when they were living in New York as refugees from the war in Paris) to visit Oskar and tell him how his *Studie Nr. 7* had first inspired them to make their visual music film *Night on Bald Mountain*. They did not know that Oskar was married, and thought that the woman dressed in black who brought in some tea and cakes but never spoke must be a servant – and guessed that the noisy children running about in the yard must be hers (and thought Oskar rather brave and kind and perhaps foolhardy to put up with it). In addition to Maya Deren and Sasha Hammid, other young makers of surrealistic-confessional psychodramas Kenneth Anger, Curtis Harrington and Gregory Markopoulos also visited Oskar.

The Filmarte Theatre in the late 1930s and early 1940s showed experimental shorts on a regular basis, including Dudley Murphy's hand-tinted print of *Ballet Mécanique* which he would bring in person and explain about the complicated genesis of the film. Aside from the sneak preview of *Composition in Blue*, a full programme of Fischinger films appeared there as early as August 1937. The American Contemporary Gallery on Hollywood Boulevard (run by Clara Grossman and Barbara Byrnes, whose husband James had been Dr. Valentiner's assistant) also held regular film screenings along with their painting shows, so that Man Ray, Fischinger, the Whitney Brothers and others could exhibit their graphics as well as their new films – at screenings often attended by D.W. Griffith and Lillian Gish, Edward G. Robinson, Vincent Price or Fritz Lang. Lang, by the way, was rather cordial with Oskar, remembering their collaboration on *Woman in the Moon* fondly. He bought one of Oskar's oil paintings, but some years later, when his eyesight began to fail, he gave it back to Oskar.

The screening of Oskar's films was unconsciously facilitated by Rebay. Because of problems with fire regulations and union projectionists, the Baroness began ordering 16mm copies of Oskar's films starting in 1942. By the end of the war, Oskar had a complete set of 16mm prints of his 12 sound films, except *An Optical Poem*, of which Rebay stubbornly retained the only (35mm) print, so Oskar could neither show it nor copy it. Due to the use of 16mm for training films and entertainment for troops at the front, 16mm sound projectors proliferated in the early 1940s, so schools, museums, galleries, clubs and private individuals could afford them.

The apogee of these screenings occurred in San Francisco in October

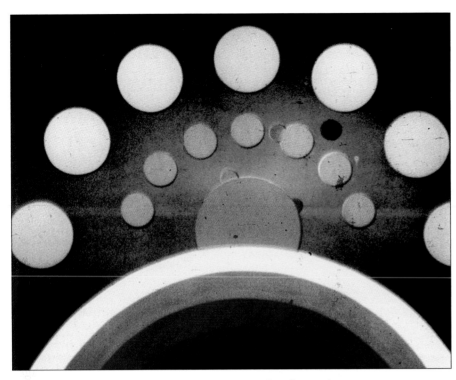

1946, when Frank Stauffacher organized a festival, Art in Cinema, at the San Francisco Museum of Art. He availed himself of the new Museum of Modern Art (New York) film collection to be able to screen Méliès and *Caligari*, *Entr'acte* and *Ballet Mécanique*, Man Ray, Marcel Duchamp and Luis Buñuel, Germaine Dulac and Jean Cocteau beside Fischinger and the Whitney brothers, Maya Deren, and the new film *Potted Psalm* by Sidney Peterson and James Broughton. Frank Stauffacher had sent Harry Smith, a young painter and anthropologist who had volunteered to help with the festival, down to Los Angeles to try to encourage Fischinger and the Whitneys to come to San Francisco. Harry was awestruck by Oskar's paintings, and dazzled by the films. He found Oskar's paintings especially exciting in relationship to his anthropological study of design and ornamentation among American Indians and other tribal peoples with a living religion: he believed Oskar's paintings demonstrated an inner spiritual truth and immediacy usually found only in peoples with shamanistic and drug-related religious ecstasies of spirit-possession. Harry began immediately to create abstract films by painting directly on the film strip, since he had no camera or other filmmaking experience, and these vivid, intricate films would première at subsequent Art in Cinema festivals, leading to a long filmmaking career (and close encounters with the Baroness Rebay).

Oskar still had not properly begun the "Bach" film by the time of this

first Art in Cinema. He made yet another attempt in a different technique: he purchased a turn-of-the-century mutoscope and tried to draw the "Bach" synchronization on the small cards that turned on the reel inside the machine, seen through a viewer, cranked by hand. He originally intended to offer the mutoscope with the complete Bach reel to Solomon Guggenheim as an 84th birthday present, February 1945, but it became apparent to Oskar that the loose synchronization, dependent on the smoothness and speed of turning the crank, would never satisfy the Baroness, who demanded very precise coordination between sound and image: she actually expected a film like *Allegretto* in which the layered cels provide a perfect analogy to the music, with background rhythms, harmonic arrangements of various shapes and colours, and bravura melodic solos. Since he had already begun with the mutoscope, Oskar proceeded to make two more reels of 670 cards, one painted in oils with brightly-coloured circles growing larger and smaller against a black background, somewhat reminiscent of *An Optical Poem*, except that in the black chamber of the mutoscope they seem to flutter a ghostly after-image that makes them magically trail off as tenuous cones. Oskar sent that reel to Solomon Guggenheim for his 85th birthday in 1946. Fortunately Oskar shot this mutoscope reel on 35mm film before he shipped it off to New York, since Rebay stored the original in her barn, where it was destroyed by rats and frost – along with several valuable paintings also stored there. Oskar's second mutoscope reel remained unfinished, although completely sketched out in coloured pencils, so it was possible to be "filled in" by his daughter Barbara for a 1970 exhibition of Oskar's paintings at the Long Beach Museum; its diverse

Composition 48, *1948*.

imagery in constant transformation includes "star-bursts" and "comets" as well as sweeping movements by large rectangles and triangles.

At this time, just after the war, a number of Europeans came to visit Los Angeles. Loni Fürst, completely exonerated of any wrong-doing by the American courts, came to Hollywood for a few days on a fact-finding tour of the film industry. As required by the Nazi government, he had married and had a couple of children. He and Oskar were thrilled to see each other again, and Oskar drove him all around the Hollywood studios, the beaches and the other worthy sights. Richard Ralfs, who

Painting

had made the musical arrangements and recordings for Oskar's colour films *Circles*, *Muratti Gets in the Act*, and *Composition in Blue*, also appeared in Hollywood. Unlike Fürst, he was very despondent and frankly alcoholic. Oskar, who rarely drank, found it difficult and depressing to be with him – as well as costly, since he insisted upon a constant refill of his gin or vodka drinks. Oskar, short of money as usual, began re-filling the liquor bottles with a little water so that the alcohol content was gradually diluted. Ralfs, already a bit drunk, got miffed at this deception, and did not return again soon.

Viege Traub, the widow of a man who had worked beside Loni Fürst in Berlin, also appeared in Hollywood at that time. She would remain for the rest of her life, and become a major figure in the Hollywood Foreign Press Association. She bought a painting from Oskar, as did her son Volker who married an English woman Jane Trevarthen. Jane's brother Colwyn would also buy a fine painting from Oskar when he visited LA some years later.

Oskar's painting had reached a ripeness and facility that made the most intricate compositions easy for him. He continued to add to his various series, pushing them into ever more complex variations, and making them in thicker and thicker layers, as if all of the previous members of a certain series needed to be recreated in order to arrive at this newest manifestation of the imagery. The interrupted lines (drawn by discrete bars) that covered the 1936 "Experiment" in even parallel rows from top to bottom, in front of and behind circular forms, have by 1946 become "Woven Square" and "Counteraction" [dense layers of triangular configurations, all browns, blacks, greys and whites], and "Strata" with curved and irregular diagonal layers overlapping like the twisted tensions of geological formations in the earthquake-ridden hills of Los Angeles. The "Tapestry No. 1" of 1938 has multiplied into the "Layers Outlined" of 1946 with transparent rectangles pulled in tension between the overlapping colours of several occlusions and the taut opposition of various diagonals. The grids are also crossbred with the parallel spectra of "Solo" to create another series of canvases emphasizing depth, such as the 1946 "Abstraction No. 669", in which nearly-concentric grids seem to form perspective alignments, and then "Tunnel" in which the perspective lines themselves struggle to maintain their integrity against improbable juxtapositions. And "Solo" will also develop the 1947 "Swirls" with its concentric graduated spectra applied to organic shapes reminiscent of cross-sections of bone and tissue, perhaps the spinal column – as well as the cross-sections of Oskar's *Wax Experiments*.

6

Oskar and Bach

$\mathcal{J}$t is possible that Oskar saw at the Art in Cinema a screening of a film *Glens Falls Sequence* by the New York filmmaker Douglass Crockwell, who also animated with mutoscope reels and slicing wax. The fragments of experiments collected in *Glens Falls Sequence* were painted on several layers of glass and filmed frame-by-frame as each alteration in the painting occurred. If he did see it, Oskar would probably not have liked the film, since it consists of loose figurative images with a sense of Surrealist landscape about them, but little consciousness about harmonies of colour or shapes, and no development or planned choreography leading to a resolution or climax. But it may have reminded Oskar about Walther Ruttmann's *Opus* films painted on glass. In any case, a month after Art in Cinema, Oskar decided to make the "Bach" film by recording one of his paintings with a single-frame exposure each time he made a brushstroke.

Oskar knew the Bach "Brandenburg Concerto No. 3" very well. He had selected it for the Swiss walking-trip in 1934, and bought the rights to a version conducted by his friend Wilhelm Furtwängler; then, when the Swiss film was not actually released, Oskar had reconsidered the "Brandenburg 3" for a possible *Lichtkonzert Nr. 3*. He had analysed the score in minute detail, charting and graphing the exact duration of each note by each instrument, so that he could have done an *Allegretto*-type cel animation with exact correspondences between each aspect of the sound and image. But he did not want to. His own silent *Radio Dynamics* pleased him most, and the lovely 8mm films James Whitney had shown him confirmed the validity if not superiority of silent non-objective animation. He had also experienced the Whitney brothers' *Film Exercises* with their experimental soundtracks of pendulum-generated "electronic" music, which he found terrifying, often ugly, but powerful – and an absolute break with 20th-century imagery enslaved to music from centuries past. He would, since the Baroness insisted, use the Bach

music, but he would only time the film to correspond to the change between the two movements of the concerto and the end of the music; the relationship between the visual and auditory would be loose and conceptual – a parallel type of architectonics, not an illustration.

Oskar worked for nine months on *Motion Painting No. 1*, finishing his painting August 1947. He painted on one board for several months, before he noticed that the thickness of paint was beginning to catch reflections from the lights, so six times he placed a sheet of plexiglas over the painting and continued on the fresh surface. Yet *Motion Painting No. 1* consists of a single "take", one single seamless flow of action lasting more than 10 minutes, and had it been just a regular painting unfilmed, Oskar would have done it on a single canvas, so we would now see only the final mandala. In fact, many of Oskar's canvases are indeed painted in just this fashion, with faint traces of invisible shapes hiding behind the beautiful final image on display – Oskar said these hidden images were the soul of the painting ... so in *Motion Painting*, the soul is laid bare.

On one hand, *Motion Painting* is a document of a painter painting, pre-dating by several years the famous documentaries of Jackson Pol-

lock and Picasso at work, but more important, *Motion Painting* shows
the growth of the painting without the painter, as a mystical spiritual
act, which for Fischinger it was. Twice at least Oskar told friends, Harry
Bertoia and James Whitney, "I feel sorry for Jackson Pollock, and the
other Abstract Expressionists, who are so maladjusted, so tortured in
ways they can't resolve, that they have to express themselves with
violent gestures, with aggressive chaos of sudden glaring gestures hap-
hazardly colliding with other spills and spasms of anxiety. I make
Abstract Expressionism, too, but for me, I feel such inner peace that I
can reach out calmly and draw a perfect circle or a straight line in a
gesture of serenity."

As an exercise in the painter's art, *Motion Painting* demonstrates a
mastery of a variety of styles, from the soft, muted polymorphous
blossoming of the beginning, to the hard-edged colour rhythms of the
spirals (at one point in six distinct shades of blue), to the intricate
geometric architectonics of the central section, to the inevitable sweeping gestures of the parallel wedges at the end.

The film, as the title suggests, is also a painting of or about "motion"
itself, and the element of motion is exploited in many forms and
variations. During the opening sequence, we see the literal motion of
the comet-like bodies ascending; in the spiral sequence, we see the
impressionistic motion of changing colours, which seems to speed up

Motion Painting No. 1
[still from 35mm film].

as it draws toward the tight centre of the spiral – the variable dynamic tension of music and painting; in the central geometric sequence, the appearance and placement of static objects becomes an instrument for manipulating the motion of our eyes – the motion of sculpture, happening and pageant; and the final dramatic sweeps of the great wedges, motion by accretion, forming the climactic mandala, are rendered more exciting by the relative static scenes that precede them – theatrical motion of dynamic duration in time.

An iconic analysis of *Motion Painting* reinforces the spiritual agenda of the piece. The field of the opening sequence contains a shape like the human brain, while the soft forms and sensuous action are amorphous like the thoughts of a child or untrained thinker. Out of this develop connections first in the form of slow, logical enlargements of basic kernels, then by the direct connection of the kernels themselves. Paths

OPTICAL POETRY: The Life and Work of Oskar Fischinger

almost like a road-map explode out of this and large blocks of neutral material create a "tabula rasa" field for new action: architectonic designs that grow and connect and overlap, with the slow deliberation of logical

Oskar's collage of Kandinsky and Mickey, ca. 1940 [from the collection of The Elfriede Fischinger Trust].

construction – cogitation and contemplation – which gradually become more cohesive and significant, finally engendering grand structures of depth and power and beauty which collide to form the peaceful balance of the mandala – creativity and transcendent meditation. This archetypal pattern – childhood through initiation to maturity – has a validity on many levels, for example, the raising of spiritual energy through the chakras in kundalini yoga. However, the absolute experience of the film says much without requiring any verbal explanation.

Oskar had difficulty getting *Motion Painting No. 1* printed, since it was shot on a Technicolor (three-colour separation) negative, and the laboratory, used to dealing with major studios, would only make prints in multiples of 50. Oskar, with the tattered remains of his stipend, could hardly afford one print. After three months of attempts, he managed to convince Ub Iwerks (who remembered him fondly from *Fantasia* days) to allow him to make six 16mm prints at the laboratories of the Disney Studios.

Oskar sent the Baroness a copy of *Motion Painting No. 1* on 2 December 1947. She hated it. She angrily scorned it as "Fischinger's awful little spaghettis", and screamed that he really owed her a 45-minute film for all the money she had given him. She expected a cel-animated synchronization, with cels she could display [perhaps because she had already "lost" the *Allegretto* cels, or neglected them until they decomposed]. She had repeatedly forbidden Oskar to paint, which he not only continued to do, but flaunted it to her by filming it. She refused to pay for the prints, and did not offer Oskar any further support from the Foundation. Oskar at last wrote her a letter expressing his true feelings: "I always began to pray for you because I thought you went crazy. I hope you will get well again, and become your real self again ... If I

Above: *Original poster for première of* Motion Painting *at Art Center School.*

Left: *Oskar with Frederick Kahn, Robert van Young, Lorser Feitelson, and Boris Deutsch at première of* Motion Painting, *1948.*

would be in your shoes, I would concentrate on being *real humble* – but humble throughout your heart, not only saying so ...".

Oskar also made a series of seven collages, which perfectly catch his sense of humour, even about the most tragic events. He snipped from old Guggenheim Foundation catalogues reproductions of paintings by Kandinsky and Bauer, then cut out figures of Mickey and Minnie Mouse from *Walt Disney Comics and Stories* and pasted them over the non-objective images in "realistic" positions that make them seem to comment on the abstract art: a furious Minnie pointing behind her as if to say "Clean that up!", or a sweating Mickey on the telephone as if he were calling to report that something had gone wrong with the Bauer behind him. Thus Oskar parodied at the same time Disney and the Baroness, both of whom gave him trouble because his abstraction did not conform to their taste.

Rebay's taste was roundly contradicted by the wild success of *Motion Painting No. 1*. When the film screened at Art Center School in 1948, the students, struck breathless with admiration, elated, beat on the stools and cheered. More students struggled and pounded the locked doors of the full lecture hall, and the film had to be screened twice, after which Oskar was mobbed with praises and questions. Lorser Feitelson and other members of the California Color Society (including Boris Deutsch, who in addition to his painting, had made an experimental expressionist film *Lullaby* in 1929 using actors from Yiddish theatre troupes) held a

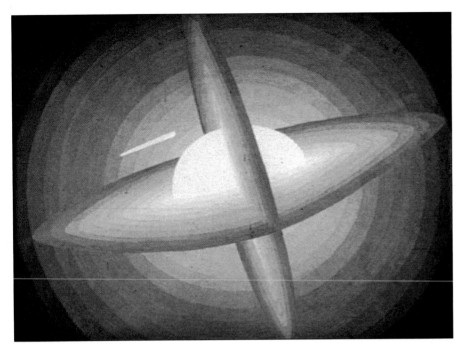

Muntz TV commercial
[still from 35mm film].

discussion of the genius of Oskar's new film immediately after the screening. *Motion Painting* enjoyed similar triumphs at Art in Cinema (inspiring Jordan Belson, Hy Hirsh and others), and in 1949 would win the Grand Prize at the International Experimental Film Competition in Brussels (where the Whitney brothers' *Film Exercises* also won a prize for best sound).

Unfortunately, without the Guggenheim support, Oskar would never again be able to afford to make another film. He continually submitted proposals for projects, but no one believed, quite rightly, that they could regain their investment in an abstract film. In 1952, hoping to capitalize on the fad for 3-D films, he proposed a Stereo Motion Painting, and shot a 30-second test to show that he could actually conceptualize and paint in three dimensions. In 1957 he tried a *Motion Painting No. 2* in 16mm, and in 1961 a *Motion Painting No. 3* in 35mm, plus a few other brief undated 35mm "Motion Painting" fragments. He used the "Motion Painting" technique for the 1953 *Muntz TV* ad, and carefully shot the action so that he could have made a pure abstract version (as he had with *Kreise* twenty years before), but he never had enough money to do so.

With the obstacle of the Guggenheim Foundation removed, Oskar did give his films to the Museum of Modern Art to be distributed. Edward Steichen telegraphed him 16 January 1952: "Abstract evening unqualified success. Your *Motion Painting* received tremendous ovation by packed auditorium. Would like to propose permanent acquisition of a set of your films if feasible." But the rental income from his films proved heart-breakingly little; though steady and nonetheless welcome, it was never enough to finance a new film. The income Oskar earned from film rental and sales of his paintings just barely paid for the expenses of his art supplies and film materials (fresh prints, and raw-stock for shooting movie tests and samples, as well as colour and black-and-white film for making publicity stills, and documentation of paintings).

A parallel frustration occurred with film rental in Germany. Hubert Schongar (for whose film *Das Hohelied der Kraft* Oskar had made special effects in 1930) now operated a film rental agency, and Oskar consented to allow him the rights to distribute his films in Europe. Schonger arranged a mini-retrospective of Fischinger films at the 1953 Göttingen Deutsche Filmtage, where *Motion Painting No. 1* was acclaimed as the highpoint of the festival in the press. Yet again the practical financial results were negligible. After several years of pathetically small income, someone notified Oskar that his films had actually been playing quite widely, including on television, and he was simply not being paid for most of the screenings. Oskar felt crushed and embittered, and never after 1962 offered his films for rental. Barbara Fischinger was studying in Heidelberg, and with the aid of Aunt Maria Rauch sued Schongar and managed to recover some money.

In addition to *Muntz TV*, Oskar worked on four other television commercials, and did special effects [the old *Frau im Mond* rocket trick] for a television series *Space Patrol*. He also drew some *Synthetic Sound* in 1948 for Alexander Laszlo as part of a dispute with the Musicians Union over the issue of recorded versus live music, and how many musicians should constitute a minimum [Oskar's film proved that music, Khachaturian's "Sabre Dance", could be performed without any musicians at all!]. Oskar also sold some "synthetic drawn sound" to be used as sound effects on the soundtrack of a *Northern Tissue* TV commercial which showed naughty (cartoon) children tossing rolls of toilet paper into the air. But none of these commercial projects brought in enough money to finance a new film either.

Neither did Oskar's work provide enough money to support the family. Elfriede worked constantly, designing clothes and shoes for Mascot Studios, Susie's Sweaters, and Andrea of Beverly Hills – as well as baby-sitting and other odd jobs that she could squeeze in. One day in the early 1950s, a Mrs. Merrill stepped out of a limousine in front of the Hammond Street house, followed by a black maid carrying some baskets of wool. She said (between compulsive inhaling of her cigarette) that Elfriede had been recommended to her as someone who knew how to card and prepare wool as well as design and knit sweaters. Elfriede replied "yes". The wool came from Mr. Merrill's sheep in Maine, and

Mrs. Merrill wanted to use it to make sweaters for herself and her husband and two children – as surprise Christmas presents. The fee she offered was quite substantial, and Elfriede agreed immediately. She measured Mrs. Merrill right then, and Mrs. Merrill brought along a sample garment of Mr. Merrill's and the two children, so Elfriede could take measurements from them. With only a few weeks until Christmas, Elfriede set to work and managed to finish all four sweaters on time. When Mrs. Merrill came to pick them up (still in the limousine with the black maid, still inhaling her cigarette compulsively), she tried hers on and de-lightedly threw her arms around Elfriede and proclaimed, "Darling, they're just perfect!" As El-friede packed the sweater up, she said, "You know, there's something about you, Mrs. Merrill, that reminds me of Bette Davis." Holding her cigarette to one side, Mrs. Merrill threw one arm around Elfriede in a warm embrace, saying, "But, my dear, I *am* Bette Davis!"

All of the children also worked: as box-boys and babysitters, as vacation-time workers at Farmer's Market stalls, newspaper delivery, pulling weeds and mowing lawns, and whatever else they could find to do.

In 1950 Oskar invented and patented the Lumi-graph, an instrument for playing light images. It consists of a frame enclosing a three-foot-square screen area; the lighting elements are inside the frame, which only allows the light to escape through thin slits, so that just a thin area a quarter of an inch in front of the screen contains coloured light. If the performer and the area behind the screen are blackened, then only something protruding into the light area will be visible, whether it be a screen pushed forward, or the hands of the performer (wearing white gloves) without a screen. Oskar gave sensitive performances on the Lumigraph, playing to music such as Sibelius' "Valse Triste", at the Coronet Theater and Frank Perls Gallery in Los Angeles, in connection with painting exhibitions, in 1951. He hoped to get financial backing to produce and sell the instrument, but none ever appeared. The Lumigraph was transported to the San Francisco Museum of Art for a one-man show of Oskar's paintings in February 1953, where it was enthusiastically received [Jordan Belson gave a particularly fine descrip-tion of Oskar's performance (see Testimonials, page 168)]. But during

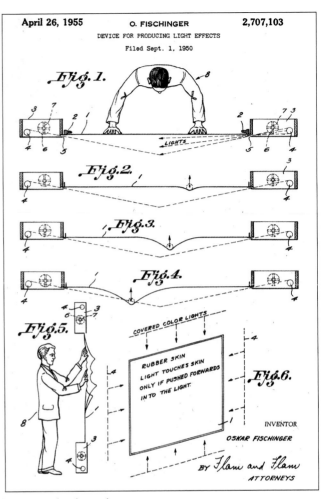

Patent sketch for Lumigraph.

a rehearsal, a speaker fell from above the stage and struck Oskar on the head, forehead and nose, causing considerable bleeding, although he was well enough to perform that evening. Oskar, however, was superstitious, and took the falling speaker to be a bad omen. He never played the Lumigraph publicly again.

Painting became the only enduring, and immediate, wholly-satisfying artform that Oskar could practice. In the wake of his triumph with *Motion Painting No. 1*, and his release from the troubling bondage to the Baroness, Oskar created some of his greatest paintings, especially a set of large canvases each about 4 feet high by 3 feet wide: the 1948 "Outward Movement", the 1949 "Furnace", the 1950 "Square Spiral", the 1952 "Mosaic", the 1954 "Yellow Moon", the 1957 "Space Spiral", and the 1964 "Space Abstraction". Although the imagery in these paintings is quite different in some respects, they all share a certain formal pattern – an emanation from just above the centre – which begs to have them considered as a serial composition.

Outward Movement, begun immediately after *Motion Painting No. 1*, presents the image of infinite layering, but denies the resolving mandala of

Oskar with Outward Movement, *1948 [from the collection of Barbara and Angie Fischinger].*

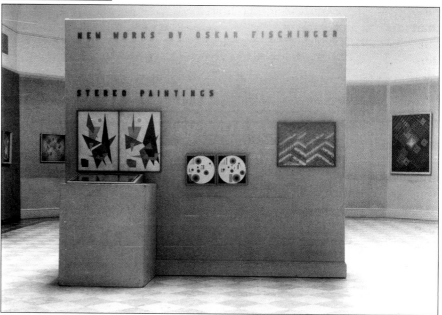

Oskar's one man show at San Francisco Museum of Modern Art, 1953.

OPTICAL POETRY: *The Life and Work of Oskar Fischinger*

the film. Square grids composed of fine lines, in shades of grey, blue and pink, progress in alignments toward the viewer. Each grid is literally painted on top of another completed grid, with only a slight displacement allowing the edges of each grid beneath to show. The strong sense of *outward movement* of these grid-alignments forces the viewer to "enter" the painting (like the Einstein/Heisenberg layered vortex of *Radio Dynamics*) and focus on the seeming centre of this explosion or rampant construction: one grid just above centre which has not been covered by an alignment, and through which we can see tantalizing evidence of a completely different composition hidden behind the existing painting. Other traces of brushstrokes also suggest an alternate reality buried beneath this surface: the lovely painting as veil of Maya, a splendid illusion masking another, perhaps more significant, reality.

The equally spectacular "Furnace" consists of multiple layers of rectangles, woven together and overlapping, in warm shades of green and brown; even the seemingly solid thick bands on some of the rectangles are composed of fine-line grids. Just above centre hangs a dark thick-framed square with creamy light texture inside. Three dull-red rectangles radiate from the central square. The title "Furnace" refers to the core of a reactor in which atomic reactions are bred, so the somber idea of the red radiation spreading out over the intricate brown and green Earth adds a melancholy premonition to the painting's mood.

"Square Spiral" places layers of predominately-brown squared spirals on a diagonal axis, so that the sensation of the composition as a whole is (especially because the "eccentric" central spiral winds unevenly with more space between the upper lines and less between the lower) of diamond formation. Again, not only the interstices between spiral lines but also the transparency of many of those lines allow us to glimpse dense fine-lined grids in the background, in addition to the labyrinthine arrangement of overlapping spirals in the foreground, the topmost (youngest?) in brighter rust/ orange/yellow. And just above centre subtly appears the sole non-rectangular figure: two joined rounded forms, one long thin orange with dots at each end, the other, overlapping the middle of the first, is the same shape (but bluish) bent double so that both the dots are close together on the right. For all the imposing architectonic grandeur of the square spirals, new sensuous bodies have appeared above them.

"Mosaic No. 2", like others of the mosaic series, consists of an even grid of uniform tessera, 2 cm square, each painted individually in a slightly different shade of blue, with certain configurations painted in hues of red and yellow. The central configuration resembles architecture, with a sharp red horizontal base and triangular blue "roofs" over yellow and burgundy-red diamond clusters. The push-pull action of the sharply-defined colours creates considerable 3-D illusion in this main

Yellow Moon Painting, *1954.*

area, but above this, in bold contrast pushing forward of the multi-shaded blue field surrounding it, stands one square composed of a yellow centre, burgundy cross, and red corners – and hovering over it is a large "Y" of yellow and burgundy stretching from upper right, joining just across from the bright square, and continuing as a single line down to lower left. This great curve pushes most strongly, arching forward, ahead, as if flying, and somehow contradicting the rigidity of the mosaic format itself.

OPTICAL POETRY: The Life and Work of Oskar Fischinger

"Yellow Moon" is again a "folk name", but it is easy to see how the luminous creamy circle just above right-centre, floating in a field of aquamarine, with a hundred curving lines sectioning spiral circles, must have seemed to the children like a moon over a nocturnal garden with blossoms and spiderwebs. Once again, however, the intricate optical composition requires no scenario to create delight: behind the primary image lies a mostly-hidden world of purple grids, which helps make the circular forms seem to push forward, while the gracefully curving white lines suggest a gentle rotation that is aided by the irregular sectioning of the circular spirals. Surrounded by this delicate swirling, the serene cream disc floats ethereally, firm in a fluctuating ambience, true in a net of illusions.

In "Space Spiral" the certainty of shapes is denied by the irregularity of spatula smudges and stippling. The same creamy circle floats in the right-centre, but here it is a loose, virtual circle, while the spirals of smaller circles that surround it suggest the nebulousness of galaxies. Beside the luminous circle waits a black smudge almost as big, like a black hole, or a dark partner star, or, were not the celestial analogy so prominent, like the Jungian "shadow". Again aquamarine shades predominate, but subtle touches of yellow and burgundy help define the spiral curves.

"Space Abstraction" follows the series of graduated concentric band imagery which was developed in *Radio Dynamics* and *Motion Painting No. 1* as an icon of spiritual expansion and concentration. Oskar worked more frequently in this style during the 1960s, possibly because he believed in beginning a new painting on the night of every full moon, and as he was often sickly and feeble in the 1960s, the simplicity of these concentric bands could be outlined in a dot pattern on full-moon-night, and filled in with colour later. "Space Abstraction" corresponds to the format of "Outward Movement", "Mosaic", "Yellow Moon", etc. in its horizontal bluish graduations interrupted by a circular configuration floating just above the centre, with again the warmer colour effects on the circle pushing it forward, while the gentle shades of blue seem to fade off in the distance.

While each of these large paintings share the same contemplative format (as well as brilliant technical finesse and sheer physical beauty) with each other, each also bears connections with other of Oskar's paintings. Other mosaics – such as the 1951 "Near and Far" with its tiny tessera, mostly in brown shades, crowded into irregular, map-like formations; or the sublime 1952 "Contemplation" with its small tessera in a perfect graduation from the brown of the frame to the pure white tessera in the exact centre; or the two stereo mosaics from 1951, the large "Stereo Mosaic" and the small but thrilling "Distant Rectangular Forms" which offer us exact right and left eye information so that tessera

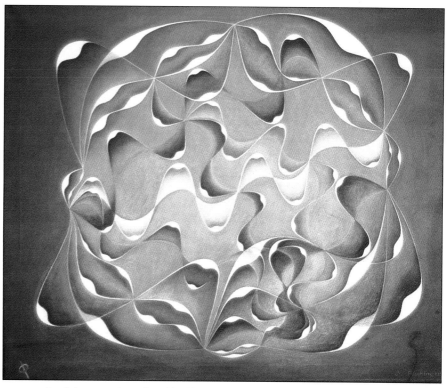

are pushed forward and pulled back not only by colour balance, but also by crafted displacement – make us appreciate how unique and ingenious is the flying arch of "Mosaic No. 2". And the logical conclusion of our contemplative series is actually a canvas of the same dimensions, but turned horizontally: the 1966 "Nirvana" which was Oskar's last large canvas. It consists entirely of small dots, each a hand gesture, stippled in the divisionist style of Seurat, but in an unbelievable profusion, layers and layers thick. Creamy golden shades predominate from a distance, but a complete spectrum of colours actually appear among the thousands of dots, giving a rich texture to polymorphous cloudy apparitions as well as to an oval, a triangle and a paisley curved manifestation just above centre which seems to promise that even in the great sea of uniform units, moments of cooperative configuration can occur.

The approximately 800 paintings that Oskar Fischinger created contain so many surprises and delights – a large canvas bent to fit in a corner, a canvas painted with millet mixed into the paint when Oskar dreamed he was a bird, a mandala made of soundwaves in vibrant harmony, a diamond-shaped white canvas with a single black line delineating a labyrinth on it – that an entire book could hardly do them justice. While the paintings are perfectly valid as still images, it can be hard not to sigh and wish that some farsighted studio had provided

Oskar with the means to animate some of the paintings, so that the "windmills" of "Yellow Moon" could really whirl past us, that we could really fly into the vortex of "Outward Movement", or that the nebulae of "Nirvana" could begin to swirl gently and breathe forth an apotheosis.

During his lifetime, Oskar enjoyed considerable success with his paintings, selling many at gallery shows (Frank Perls 1951, Ernst Raboff 1963/4, etc.), and he participated regularly in the annual Jewish Community Center Art Sale. He was chosen for group shows (Museum of Non-Objective Painting, 1944–1947, Los Angeles County Museum of Art 1948–1953, Art Institute of Chicago 1947, etc.) and one-man shows (Pasadena Museum 1956, San Francisco Museum 1953, etc.). Oskar was shy about promoting himself, and never played "gallery politics" or tried to curry favour with critics; had he done so, he might have become even more of a prominent painter – but he would also have had less time to paint! Once a painting show had very negative results: the 1950 "Operation Peace" show at the Fraymart Gallery in Los Angeles was attacked as a "communist propaganda plot" [this was the heyday of the House Un-American Activities trials] and Oskar fell under suspicion.

Oskar, especially after his experiences with the Baroness' peculiar kind of criticism, actually avoided critics and discussions of theory. But he often let his sly viewpoint out in jokes. In 1938 he drew a hilarious Cubist parody, and around 1950 painted a portrait of Salvador Dalí on a lampshade "because he needs inner light". Once at a gallery opening, the actor Vincent Price (who was a rather prominent figure in the Los Angeles art world) gushed to Oskar, "Oh, Fischinger, you're 50 years ahead of your time!", and Oskar calmly answered, "No, Mr. Price, I'm right here: you're evidently 50 years behind." Oskar's wit was most often profound: when a student at Art Center College asked him if he had ever composed music to go with one of his films, he answered, "It's taken me all my life to refine my art and technique for visual imagery; it would take me another lifetime to really become an auditory music composer. You notice, when Schoenberg paints his self-portraits, he never paints on his ears. And Van Gogh – he cut his ear off because he didn't need it!"

A number of other events in the last decades of his life took time away from Oskar's creative efforts. In 1953, Elfriede and 10-year-old daughter Angie sailed to Europe due to a family illness in Gelnhausen, so Oskar was left with handling some practical household affairs, from which Oskar was ordinarily shielded by Elfriede's hard work. Liesschen gave a "Bon Voyage" party for Angie and her friends, and Oskar made a short documentary film of the occasion. Elfriede also used her weeks in Germany as an opportunity to go through all the film and papers stored there to make sure they were surviving in decent shape. During the war a stray bomb had fallen on the Fischinger Drugstore (apparently accidentally, since the village of Gelnhausen was never a combat zone), but fortunately a sewing machine in the attic had detonated the bomb right on the roof, so the damage to Oskar's things was minimal. However time and the elements had wreaked a bit of damage on some of the films and paper. Elfriede had to dispose of a few film prints that had nitrate decay, and a few of the animation drawings were either torn or pilfered (since paper was in very short supply during and immediately after the war). But the bulk of the materials were preserved quite well. Barbara Fischinger would spend a school-year in Gelnhausen in 1956, and once again checked all of Oskar's things and found them mostly in good shape.

By 1957 the property values around the fashionable Sunset Strip had risen so high that the Fischingers sold their home on Hammond Street and bought a new house on Wonderland Park Avenue in the quiet Laurel Canyon. It had large glass windows on all sides of the house, so that nature (and orange and lemon trees and flowers that were planted) was visible from every room. There were high ceilings which gave a nice illusion of space, but were hard to keep warm in the winter, and most of the rooms opened into this communal space, so there was virtually no sound privacy in the house – but there were three bedrooms and two

The Fischinger Children at Wonderland Park.

bathrooms, an improvement over Hammond street. The process of moving the vast amount of equipment and paintings to the new house, as well as the numerous alterations and additions necesary to make it practical (including a workroom studio for Oskar added [with much

Full Moon painting [from the collection of Cindy Keefer].

help from Conrad] to the side of the garage) consumed considerable time and energy. But it was worth it. The house was situated near the top of a mountain range, in a valley, so it was very quiet and pastoral. Deer and coyotes, skunks and possums, roadrunners and quail roamed the hills, especially at night. And by night much of the artificial light from the city was subdued by the mountains, so one could see the stars clearly. Oskar often did spend all night contemplating the skies, and began to make a series of special paintings for which he would prepare a black background ahead of time, then he would stipple in patterns of white dots by moonlight with the fine tip of a brush. Some of these "full moon" paintings would be finished later by creating coloured areas following the white-dot templates, but many of them remained as Oskar first painted them, like arcane astronomic observations.

The neighbours on Wonderland Park were also quite nice. Bob and Sandy Crain (and their three children) across the street, Zona and Ed Mann (who played the bagpipe one house above the Fischingers), and Lee and Mickey Walker one house below all acquired paintings from Oskar.

In 1961, Karl Fischinger, who had been stationed in Germany with the US occupation troops and had married a German girl, Hedi, was allowed to bring back to the US a substantaial amount of "household goods" that would be shipped to LA in government boats. Hedi said she would rather have new American furniture and things, so they offered to bring instead all of Oskar's films, papers and animation drawings which had been stored in Gelnhausen. Barbara Fischinger was studying at Heidelberg University (and staying with Elfriede's sister Ria) at the time, so she was able to help them pack everything. It was all shipped safely to Hollywood. Oskar naturally spent a great deal of time going over the cans of film to see what was in good condition, and he built a special storage vault to preserve the nitrate films at a continuous uniform cold temperature – a simple building out in the yard with double cinder-block walls and a metal roof placed a foot above this bunker, so that the air could circulate and keep cool even during the heat of summers. For more than 30 years it did in fact preserve the nitrates in perfect condition at an optimal temperature. Then Oskar began to build an optical printer so that he could copy the best prints on to safety film – but he was never able to finish this task, and never saw his silent films projected again.

In 1964, Oskar's friend Ib Melchior [son of the famous Heldentenor (heroic tenor) Lauritz Melchior] wrote and directed a science fiction feature *The Time Travelers* in which he wanted to use Oskar's Lumigraph as the ultimate home entertainment of the future – something so enjoyable and sensual that it could substitute for other erotic pleasures during an era in which strict population control was necessary. Since

Oskar's original Lumigraph used a cold light source which was not bright enough to film, his son Conrad built a new, larger, more glamorous instrument to use during the filming. It would get hot quickly and could only be filmed for 20 or 30 seconds in operation. When the film was finally released, the lurid posters showed a sexy woman playing the Lumigraph with bold letters announcing "See the Love Machine". Elfriede and the children made sure Oskar didn't see any of the posters or newspaper ads, because they knew he would be upset to see his instrument used this way, and he was rather ill at the time. The income from this film came in handy. Later the Lumigraph also appeared on Andy Williams' television show, this time using a larger model built by Conrad which did produce a bright enough image for television cameras.

Last photo of Oskar, already quite ill.

The last, and by no means the least important, factor in Oskar's difficulties was his poor health. Already in the 1950s, he began to have mild strokes, which became gradually more severe, until they sometimes left him temporarily paralysed. Diabetes complicated the condition. He finally died of a heart attack 31 January 1967, aged 66. One of his last canvases, a small 13 cm high by 18 cm wide, seems at first to be just a solid background of Oskar's favourite celestial blue, a painting just begun, and left unfinished. But closer inspection shows that the brushstrokes, all horizontal, wave gently and contain many subtle hints of whitish and bluish shades – a crafted composition of a pure colour field. It is carefully signed and dated, with the prayer-wheel logo.

Within a few months, Guy Coté from the Cinémathèque Québécoise called Elfriede, inviting her to come to Montréal for the Expo, and asked if any of Oskar's films needed restoring. Angie drove Elfriede across America to Montréal that summer, and newly-restored prints of Oskar's *Studie Nr. 7* and *Studie Nr. 11* were screened for an enthusiastic, adoring audience. More retrospectives and homages followed at the Berlin Film Festival and around the world in museums, colleges, film clubs, and festivals.

Posthumous glory is nice, but Oskar also got to enjoy some during his lifetime. On 24 March 1957 Oskar appeared on the television show of prominent Los Angeles painter Lorser Feitelson, who had known Oskar personally and professionally for some twenty years. Feitelson introduced Oskar with these words: "Like all great artists, Fischinger is a solitary figure. He has not created any cult around himself; he does not play the rôle of yogi with little ones worshiping him: he is too busy being a true artist – a completely sincere man, a man with a deep knowledge of music and physics, and at heart, a poet and mystic. All in all, he sums up for me the personification of the word *Genius*." Oskar also appeared on two other media events, one an interview for *The Voice of Democracy*, a series supported by the US government and designed for broadcast in foreign countries to acquaint people with American customs, and the pleasant adventures of emigrants who settled in the US. Unfortunately no copy of Oskar's interview seems to survive. Elfriede and Oskar also auditioned for Groucho Marx's mock quiz show, but that tape is also missing.

New generations of younger artists – Sara Petty and Robert Darroll in traditional drawn animation, Larry Cuba and Vibeke Sorensen in computer graphics, Michael Scroggins in videographics, to name a few – continue to fall under the spell of Oskar Fischinger's enchanting films. Oskar suspected this would happen: when he was praised or asked about the importance of his abstract films, Oskar would often answer modestly, "Perhaps they will be primitive. I think I am mostly a catalyst." He had the hopeful aspiration of a pioneer settler on a new continent: he knew that the non-objective world had always existed, even though European art was just re-discovering it – and he felt comfortable in its absolute landscape of geometric colour fields, organic auroras and mathematical trajectories, for he had heard about this wondrous land from Plato and the Tibetan painter of yantras, Einstein and Heisenberg and the Hopi Shaman, even as others would learn it from him.

Epilogue

I first saw a film of Oskar Fischinger's in 1958, when I was a student at the University of Southern California, and took a course in Film History from Arthur Knight. As Arthur Rosenheimer, he had been early involved with the Museum of Modern Art Film Department. As Arthur Knight he became film critic for *Saturday Review* magazine, and wrote a splendid history of cinema *The Liveliest Art* which, like his classes, covered not only Griffith and Eisenstein, but also Fischinger and Maya Deren. That time was also a glorious era for world cinema, and often Mr. Knight would get review prints of a new Antonioni, or Bergman, or Resnais which would be screened in class. Knight told me that most filmmakers (especially independent experimental creative filmmakers) really lived somewhat lonely lives, and they usually enjoyed meeting and talking with people who knew and admired their work. I tried calling Fischinger several times, but on each occasion he was ill. However, on Knight's advice I did visit Maya Deren when I went to New York as part of the GE College Bowl team for USC.

In 1965 I began teaching at Occidental College in Los Angeles, and I showed Fischinger films to my classes, which I rented from The Creative Film Society, a 16mm film rental company that had begun as a California-based filmmakers cooperative. It had become a business for one of the filmmakers, Bob Pike, who had received his Masters of Art degree from the University of California at Los Angeles Film School with a fine thesis paper on Experimental Film in California. In April 1968 Bob Pike prepared a retrospective of experimental films, The Yankee Underground Film Festival, for Occidental College, and Elfriede Fischinger attended the screenings with one of her daughters. She talked frequently in her best whisper voice, which, although not really loud, had an absolutely piercing quality that made it audible throughout the auditorium. One of the films screened, Will Hindle's *Chinese Firedrill* (a new film with many intricate optical effects, layers of overlapping imagery) returned several times to a shot of the filmmaker urinating. About the fourth or fifth time this reappeared, Elfriede's comment "If he has kidney problems, he should go to the doctor instead of just filming it!", which generated a sizable chuckle in the audience, much to the detriment of this somber psychodrama confession. I had intended to speak with Elfriede after the screening, but this made me decide not to.

In 1969, I went to work for Creative Film Society. It was the height of a craze for film in general, and "underground film" in particular, since not only was it being praised in books like Sheldon Renan's *Guide to Underground Film* and the art-world publications, but also much animation and experimental film seemed to foreshadow the psychedelic perception which came into prominence on the wings of rock music, light shows and easy supplies of recreational drugs. And in that pre-video time, seeing films meant seeing them in a theatre (including many midnight movie series), or renting them on 16mm film. After Oskar Fischinger's death, Bob Pike had made a contract with Elfriede to distribute the Fischinger films, and he had advanced money to make new 16mm prints, which in some cases meant making new negatives from surviving nitrate prints. Bob was an all-business person: he worked very hard to build up the Creative Film Society collection, which included hundreds of titles from all over the world, including many of the classic "art" films, from the silent era to recent experimental work. And he had a family to support with the income from this business. One day in the fall of 1969, Elfriede called Bob on the phone. He was tired and out of sorts, and recognizing her voice immediately, he put his hand over the receiver and said to me "It's the widow Fischinger; I can't deal with her right now – you talk to her". She had called to ask for help in dealing with all the nitrate film prints in Oskar's storage shed. "I don't even know what most of them are", she said to me. She dropped the receiver, and slipped into German language for a moment: "verdammt noch mal!" and I answered her in German. I had learned some German as a child from opera librettos, and when I was seven, my grandmother had come from Germany and I learned more conversational phrases. In college I had studied German as a literary language, and a subtitled-film language. I had also travelled in Germany six times, visiting relatives, screening my films, and just sightseeing. Elfriede was enchanted that I knew something about film as well as speaking some German, and invited me to her house in Laurel Canyon for New Years Eve, to meet her family and friends. It was a charming evening, with Elfriede's legal advisor Eva Mason and her witty husband Leo, and the Fischinger daughter "Tootsie" (aka Angelica) and a wonderful chow named Amika.

Elfriede called the next day to indicate that I had "passed muster" with flying colours, and would I please come to inspect the nitrates as soon as possible. So began a life-long entanglement.

I would go to the Fischinger house almost every day, before work or after work and all day on the weekends and holidays. As I rolled through the contents of the first 15 cans of film, it became clear that these films could only be properly identified and restored with a great deal of research, since most of the labels were brief, enigmatic and even wrong (that is, the label obviously refered to some other film that had once been in this can, but the current contents were something else quite unrelated, sometimes quite enigmatic).

Elfriede had as many boxes of papers as she did cans of films, and I began trying to read and sort all of the papers – but that turned out to be almost impossible. I bought boxes of file-folders and labels, and tried to place each document [personal letters, invoices and business corre-spondence, clippings, whole issues of certain magazines or newspapers that contained some review or reference to Oskar, photographs] in a sensibly categorized and labelled folder, reflecting some sort of chrono-logical as well as alphabetical order. But I quickly found that, like the 1001 nights, what I finished each day managed to get undone in the following week. Labelled files would suddenly be empty. I would ask Elfriede what had happened to the contents. She would at first deny ever having touched them, would claim to know nothing about them, etc. Then it might come out that she had taken the item to make a xerox copy, or to show someone – but where was it now? Sometimes she had made a new file for it with a different identification tab, but sometimes the missing document might not surface for months – perhaps used as a bookmark in a magazine or novel that she was reading. Elfriede also tended to make multiple files with different names for the same item: *Canada*, *Cinémathèque* Québécoise, *Québec*, *Montréal*, *Beaudet* (the curator at the Cinémathèque) or *Louise* (Beaudet, the curator at the Cinémathèque). Elfriede also had the bad habit of "dropping every-thing" when the phone rang or the doorbell buzzed, so a given document might lie in a stack of newspapers or on an unrelated shelf for months before being re-discovered. Fortunately, hardly anything ever got thrown away.

It seems important to note here that Elfriede was a completely remarkable woman – her problem with "order" was a particular pecca-dillo, and she had some others, but she was extraordinarily healthy and energetic, endlessly curious and willing to try almost anything, inquisi-tive and adventurous to see every kind of art and movie, and sample all sorts of ethnic foods and cultural events, and eager to travel everywhere in the world. Her love of talking and interrupting still led her occasion-ally into the socially awkward situations that had bothered Oskar so much 40 years before, but on the other hand she was so girlish and obviously well-intentioned that it was hard to hold something against her for long.

For a while she fell quite madly in love with me, convinced herself that I was some sort of re-incarnation of Oskar (or rather a "transplant" since I was in my late 20s when Oskar died). Elfriede had a tracing of Oskar's hands, and convinced herself that my hands were exactly like them – although it was clear to me that my hands were quite awkwardly different, with a sort of crookedness to some of my fingers. She still fancied that somehow Oskar's spirit had flown out of the hospital when he died and entered my body as I drove past on the freeway. I must say in her favour that several other people whom I met later in Europe, who had known Oskar, also said that I bore some eerie hint of resemblance to him. In any case, it took me several years to convince Elfriede that I was homosexual, and would not be marrying her. And to her credit, she was usually quite accepting and warm with my gay friends, although she remained unrelentingly suspicious and antagonistic to most of my female friends: "Oh, that Linda is no good!", she would grumble, "Oh, that Priscilla, I can't stand her!"

As I identified each of the nitrates, I began to make safety copies of them and attempted to restore them to their original form. At that time my nephew Bob Curtis was working in an optical house as a film technician. Two special effects companies, Illuminator and Spunbuggy, worked out of the studio [an old house behind the Cinerama Dome] doing 35mm and 16mm optical printing. Pat O'Neill, one of Los Angeles' greatest experimental filmmakers and artists, had hired Bob as an assistant. The optical printer was in use 24 hours a day, for in addition to commissioned film magic-tricks and titles, Pat was working on his own personal brilliant art films, such as *Runs Good*, which contained a multiplicity of images matted together in surreal layers, combinations, and juxtapositions – and other experimental filmmakers like Chick Strand would also appear occasionally to create some optical effect for a new film. Bob Curtis and Pat O'Neill transferred some of the most fragile Fischinger nitrates on to safety masters, slowly and delicately, frame by frame. At that time the film laboratory Fotokem also still worked directly with nitrate film, so the longer films, in generally good condition, could be taken there to have a new 16mm and 35mm safety negatives struck, from which it would be possible to make many prints for sales or rental.

I did finish cataloguing the papers and the films, and made enough cross-references to be able to identify most of the films, and begin to appreciate the great breadth of Oskar's work, including many films that had never been seen in America, and a number of films that did not seem to have survived. As each one of the "new" films was screened, I was dazzled and impressed, and became more curious about the context. Over the next 10 years, I developed a steady pattern: I would work for one of the Los Angeles area colleges [Art Center, Chouinard, Pitzer, UCLA, etc.] during the school year while also working on the Fischinger restorations (and occasionally my own experimental films). Then in the summer vacation, I would travel to Europe, where I would screen films, and do research in film archives. I had been at the Cinémathèque Française several times researching (with Henri Langlois, Marie Epstein, Lotte Eisner and Mary Meerson) Germaine Dulac, *Ballet Mécanique*, and *Entr'acte*, which I used to screen for my students at Occidental College, and I had wished to properly restore them to the original lengths, synchronized with the original musical scores. I also had a little screening of my own films at the Cinémathèque in 1969. Now I began a systematic search for Fischinger materials, and fortunately I was able to speak with the golden-age generation of curators including Lotte Eisner (who told me much about Fischinger and the Kamera cinema in Berlin), Jacques Ledoux at the Cinémathèque Belgique, Ib Monty of Det Danske Filmmuseum, Jan DeVal at the Filmmuseum in Amsterdam, Mme. Prolo in Turin, Freddy Buache in Cinémathèque Suisse Lausanne, and Dorothea Gebauer at the Deutsches Institut fur Filmkunde. The summer of 1970 I had finished restoring a print of *Spiritual Constructions*, and I took it to London to show Lotte Reiniger, who had not seen it before, but liked it very much. She generously regaled me with anecdotes about Oskar (whom she knew only casually) as well as Bert Bartosch, Walther Ruttmann, Bert Brecht, and Jean Renoir. And she cut some silhouette figures for me as well.

More importantly, I interviewed several members of the Fischinger family, including Oskar's older brother and sister Joseph and Maria who shared with me photos and drawings of Oskar's as well as many colourful details of Gelnhausen and the Fischinger drugstore. I also saw Oskar's younger brother Karl, who had worked at Louis Seel with Oskar – and who had a jolly wagishness about many of his anecdotes, which paralleled, I believe, the witty side of Oskar. His son Dieter bore an uncanny resemblance to Oskar's son Richard. And I visited the Fischinger Drugstore, where I was generously hosted by Elfriede's brother Robert and his Belgian wife Jeanette, who is an excellent gourmet cook, and very warm and witty as well – as were her wonderful son and daughter Joachim and Gabi – all of whom would welcome me (and supply valuable help with transportation, translation, etc. many times over the next decade). I also spoke with an "amateur" film collector/connoisseur Paul Sauerlander (who had a charming baroque movie theatre built into his home) whose film print collection contained many fascinating animation and experimental films (as well as rare and restored features) among them some documentary footage of Hans Fischinger which also contained a few test shots for unfinished film projects. He graciously gave me the Hans Fischinger footage to include with the other Fischinger family films. I also enjoyed visiting with Lou Linde-mann, one of Elfriede's friends from girlhood (and her witty son Karl and his lovely wife Ellen). And Elfriede's "Trudl", now Gertrude Mende, who was not only kind and gracious, but also a remarkable goldmine of information: she remembered dates and details of all kinds, and patiently spent hour after hour sketching little images of vanished places, playing old 78rpm records, and re-telling events with a slow patience so that I could understand all the circumstances and qualities of events and situations.

Back in Los Angeles, I sought out and interviewed as many people as I could find who had worked with Oskar or spent a substantial time with him, ranging from Alexander Laszlo (who gave me invaluable information about the multiple-projection films), Richard Ralfs, and John Cage, to friends like the saintly Liesschen, the Bertoias, Hedwig Traub, Milton Wishner (Oskar's lawyer in the early years), various members of the California Color Society, Jan and Ursula DeSwart, Oskar's gallerists (including Ernst Reboff, Herbert Palmer, and Jim and Barbara Byrnes), and any other friends, neighbours or artists I could find. Elfriede often accompanied me, and she carefully took me around to visit all of the locations where the Fischingers had lived, worked, gone to school, etc.

Elfriede also began to accompany me on my summer adventures. She showed me all of the places in Gelnhausen, Frankfurt and Berlin where Oskar had lived and worked, and introduced me to dozens of Fischinger relatives, way back to elderly women who still tilled the soil of Kurzell in the Black Forest from whence the Fischingers had originated. We went to Munich in search of some remnant of the Wax Machine, but found no traces of Emmy Scharff. But we did drive from Munich to Berlin, looking for the villages and landscapes Oskar had filmed in 1927. Over the next three years I interviewed Alexandre Alexeieff and Claire Parker, Rolf Badenhausen, Maria Bartosch, Albert and Elfriede Benitz, Thorold Dickinson (of London Film Society, which Oskar had visited), Leonhard Fürst, Hans Gensmer and Oscar Sala (who had composed scores to Oskar's *Studie Nr. 6*), Lore Leudesdorf (co-worker with Ruttmann), Erna Niemeyer now Re Soupault (co-worker with Viking Eggeling), Gerd Opfermann (who as a young man had attended all of the Color-Music Conferences in Hamburg), Gertrude Pabst (who reminisced about the severe difficulties with the Nazi film control), Peter Sachs (one time worker in Oskar's Berlin studio, now a college professor in England) and Martha Seeber, the widow of Oskar's friend and technical idol, film pioneer Guido Seeber.

When Elfriede and I visited Leonhard Fürst, his wife and children were present and we all shared coffee and cakes. Elfriede very much dominated the conversation, asking such things as "What was the name of that other guy you were living with before you met Oskar?" and "Remember how you came to our wedding almost an hour late, and you were all unshaven and obviously had been drunk?...". He denied everything, or brushed it off by saying he didn't remember anything about that. As we were leaving (on our way to Munich, where we had an appointment with Enno Patalas at the film archive in the Munich Stadtsmuseum) Leonhard cautiously pressed a folded note into my hand. It said "Please, please, call me at this number, at 7 o'clock this evening." I did. He apologized, and explained that he was embarrassed to discuss such things in front of his wife and children.

As soon as I had finished with the cataloguing of the Fischinger papers, I began to set out the template for a biography of Oskar. Elfriede was again extremely helpful, establishing correct chronologies, supplying anecdotes and snapshots and correct spelling. She recounted all the grim details of her difficulties during the Nazi era, and even supplied me with photographs of Roland and Ernst Schimanek, saying "I know you will want this for the biography." But at the same time, she asked me not to print any of those things while she was still alive. "When I go to a screening of Oskar's films, I don't want someone asking how much an abortion cost in 1930 – it should all be about Oskar's art." Indeed, when people at a screening did ask questions about how things were during the Nazi era in Germany, Elfriede would calmly lie. "We never had any problems", she would say. "We were artists, and it had nothing to do with us."

In 1973, the United States Information Agency (which provided libraries and auditoriums for cultural events in foreign countries) sent me on a tour with a package of experimental films, including three of Fischinger's, as well as Maya Deren's *Meshes of the Afternoon*, Kenneth Anger's *Eaux d'artifice*, James Whitney's *Lapis*, Jordan Belson's *Allures*, Pat O'Neill's *Runs Good*, and some films of my own. The screening and lecture appeared in Tokyo, Taipei, Kuala Lumpur, Bangkok, Calcutta, Dehli, Bombay, Teheran, Beirut and Athens. Then they sent me back to Calcutta for a month to teach an experimental filmmaking workshop for college students. During all my free time, the plane flights and waiting rooms and jet-lagged nights stark raving awake, I continued to work on the Fischinger biography, and essentially finished it. When Elfriede read through the biography, other problems unexpectedly emerged. Elfriede had always insisted that she had inspired Oskar's drawn-sound experiments by dropping a key. The information that I had verified concerning Rudolph Pfenninger's experiments with drawn sound seemed to have preceded Oskar's, as well as less documented Russian experiments around that same time. Moholy-Nagy also fiddled

William Moritz with Elfriede Fischinger, Montreal 1977. [Photo courtesy of Yves Bellemare, Musée des Beaux-Arts de Montréal.]

with drawn sound, as did the Fleischer studio, and the young Norman McLaren. It seemed to me that the idea was just natural, in the wind. But Elfriede became furious and hysterical about the matter. "I know Oskar did it first! I was there! Those other people must have just copied from Oskar! They must be lying about their dates!" When *Film Culture* offered to print my Fischinger biography in their 1974 issue, Elfriede's tension escalated. She insisted that I list one of Oskar's nitrate prints as having been lost by Fotokem, because she could not find the print (although a receipt indicated that she had received it back). And when I submitted to her a dated newspaper review of a screening of Rudolph Pfenninger's drawn sound in 1931, she insisted that I change the date of Oskar's première screening to 1931 in my text, even though her own newspaper clippings from Oskar's first screening were clearly dated 1932. Elfriede threatened to sue both *Film Culture* and me personally unless the change was made, and had Eva Mason draw up formal legal documents which were served to me and Jonas Mekas. Jonas called me to say that since they had already set all the type for the Fischinger biography, if Elfriede did sue, *Film Culture* would quite simply go broke, and have to close down. "Please, can we just accept her demands?" he asked. "Anyone who is reading the text will just think it is a typographical error, since the actual chronology is so clear." So we let the little "errors" stand. Years later, Elfriede did find the nitrate print tucked away in one of her drawers.

As more and more of Oskar's films were restored, we had more and more screenings in Europe and America, often with two or three programmes to accommodate all the films. Sheldon Renan, for the opening of the Pacific Film Archive in Berkeley, gave us funds to restore two films so that they could have a première in their new theatre. Similarly Louise Beaudet, curator at the Cinémathèque Québécoise, always arranged to restore something so that a few "brand new" films would also be seen beside the known classics.

As a sample of our typical tours: for an exhibition in the Museum of Fine Arts in Montréal in 1977, Elfriede and I drove Conrad Fischinger's van from Los Angeles to Canada with a selection of Oskar's oil paintings packed in the back, along with a number of film prints. We stopped at the Bertoias' country home in Pennsylvania, and had to dry out the paintings which had got wet from rainstorms (and leaks in the camper) during our travels. Brigitta got out of the attic a dozen paintings (mostly fine German expressionist canvases) which had been damaged by water leaks and mildew – just so we would not feel too depressed about our relatively mild "accident". She also showed us her exquisite little Michelangelo marble, and Harry treated us to a thrilling concert of his sounding bronze sculptures in the barn. We stopped in New York city to screen some Fischinger films at the Museum of Modern Art, and I screened some of my own films at Anthology Film Archive. Elfriede and

I slept in the car (parked outside Anthology) to guard the paintings, but someone tried to break in anyway, and only ran away when Elfriede emitted a piercing scream (which she said she had learned from the Wandervogel in her girlhood) and threatened them with instant death. We also appeared on the New York television broadcast Camera Three, talking about Oskar and his artworks, with John Canemaker as the host. John published a charming article about the weekend in New York in the magazine *Funny World*. We arrived safely in Montréal, and the exhibition was fine. Elfriede and I created an exact-size model of the animation table which Oskar had used for *Composition in Blue* and the colour Muratti commercial, with an image from each film on the two sides. The paintings were cleaned and displayed beautifully. And Louise Beaudet arranged for a special screening of Oskar's films, with his *Studie Nr. 3* accompanied by the original musical score performed live from sheet music by Maurice Blackburn and other musicians from the National Film Board of Canada.

When we were in New York, I took Elfriede to visit Harry Smith, whom she had not seen since 1946. He lived then at the Chelsea Hotel, in a room crowded from floor to ceiling with boxes and stacks of books, artworks, and other things, so that one could hardly get around much. I had visited him twice before, so I knew what to expect, but Elfriede was flabbergasted, and then thrilled at the dozens of curious and priceless things that kept emerging from the seeming chaos which, however, Harry knew down to the last scrap and could retrieve any particular item with relative ease. He spoke glowingly of how inspirational Oskar had been for him, and said that it must be nice to have his legacy so well preserved. Elfriede told him frankly how many things – films, paintings and papers – had not been properly preserved yet. "Well, something should be done about that!" Harry proclaimed, and disappeared for a moment into his "archive". He emerged with a few magical instruments and a live chicken, and proceeded to perform a ritual, chanting, dancing around and sacrificing the chicken to use its blood to mark symbols on various objects including Elfriede's hand. "Now", he said in conclusion, "you should not be having so much financial worry, and most of your precious things will be taken care of in the next few years". Indeed, within the next years, the Frankfurt Filmmuseum paid a substantial amount of money to acquire a representative cross-section of Oskar's work (films, paintings, documents, photos, and animation materials including the *Motion Painting* originals and Oskar's original Lumigraph) for their museum. That money made it possible to finish much of the necessary preservation work on Oskar's things, and also made things much easier for Elfriede in general. Barbara Fischinger sorted and copied all the materials that were shipped, so that the Fischinger Archive in Los Angeles maintained a duplicate of all the

essential information. In 1993 the Frankfurt Filmmuseum presented a major exhibition of Fischinger's works, with a catalogue, regular screenings of the whole Fischinger film canon, and Elfriede, Barbara and I played the Lumigraph at the opening.

Elfriede and I made dozens of tours like the LA to Montreal adventures described above. We went "behind the Iron Curtain" to visit Zagreb, Hungary, Czechoslovakia and East Germany. We went to Rome and Stockholm, and everywhere in between. Although many of our screenings took place in film archives, we also appeared at festivals and colleges (in Würzburg we performed a reconstruction of the *R-1* with five 16mm projectors). When the new ZKM [The Center for Art and New Media] opened in Karlsruhe (where artists like Larry Cuba and Robert Darroll would be artist-in-residence to use the computer facilities for new films), Elfriede and I presented some of Oskar's films and graphics, and spent a wonderful week with Elfriede's brother Werner and his family. Even in her 80s, Elfriede went to Caracas and Mexico City.

In 1989 Martina Dillmann chose to make a catalogue *raisonne* of Oskar Fischinger's paintings and graphic works for her doctoral dissertation at the Goethe University of Frankfurt. She came to California several times, and Elfriede and I travelled around with her to Denver and San Francisco and many other places where art collectors owned Fischinger paintings. She also sent dozens of letters to collectors in distant or inaccessible places asking for photos and exact details of the paintings they owned, and travelled around on her own tracking down the paintings belonging to collectors like Marian Messenger. The results of her research yielded a two-volume dissertation (one with a [German-language] essay on Oskar's paintings, and a listing of all exhibitions containing Fischinger paintings; the second volume with a complete listing of Oskar's paintings, most of them accompanied by a small identifying picture). Her Doctorate was conferred in 1995, but unfortunately only a few copies of the catalogue were made, one of which is on file at the University in Frankfurt, and another copy is available for research at The Fischinger Archive or The Center for Visual Music in Los Angeles.

In 1995 I was diagnosed with cancer in my neck region. Over the next five years I had repeated episodes of radiation, chemotherapy and surgery. At one point I weighed only 90 pounds and had no hair at all – and could not speak because my throat was so dry and swollen. Just about then, I had to move, because the house on Wonderland Park Avenue where I was living at that time had been sold. Fortunately Larry Cuba had created a non-profit foundation, The Iota Fund, dedicated to the preservation and dissemination of abstract film and Visual Music. Most of my files, film copies, paintings and ceramics I had collected from Fischinger, James Whitney, Jules Engel and other visual-music artists were moved directly to iota, where they lived for several years until 2003, and then to The Center for Visual Music and The Fischinger Archive. The Center for Visual Music is open to scholars for research, and continues to preserve and provide access to visual music through its screening series and videotape/dvd distribution on line, as well as other online services. The foundation operates a web-site www. centerforvisualmusic.org.

Elfriede continued to travel until the last year of her life. At the Anthology Film Archives in New York, in the fall of 1998, she introduced some of Oskar's films at the First Light programme, and Cindy Keefer (the director of iota) recorded her on video. Elfriede Fischinger died in May of 1999, and was buried beside Oskar at Holy Cross Cemetery in Los Angeles.

For Oskar's 100th birthday in the year 2000, iota created a traveling show, KINETICA 2, which included two evenings of Fischinger's own films, most of them newly restored by the Academy Film Archive. [Full details of the preservation of each film is included in the Filmography section at the end of this book.] A third programme included the work of other abstract filmmakers inspired by Fischinger. Cindy Keefer made a short documentary to accompany the programmes, which included some of the footage of Elfriede at Anthology – capturing quite well her charm and energy – and also her careful evasiveness, saying "Oh, we didn't know anything about the nazis, we were just artists ...".

KINETICA 2 screened in many venues including The Centre

Pompidou in Paris, Harvard University and the Museum of Modern Art in New York, the National Gallery of Art in Washington DC, Pacific Film Archive in Berkeley, the Los Angeles County Museum of Art (which also included one of Oskar's oil paintings in their millenium exhibition in their galleries), The Nederlands Filmmuseum in Amsterdam, The Royal Film Archive in Brussels and The Swedish Film Institute in Stockholm.

I still sleep every night under blankets knitted by Liesschen, and every day I keep my head and neck warm with scarves and caps knitted by Elfriede.

Testimonials for
Oskar Fischinger

All the persons below are filmmakers/artists unless otherwise noted

LOTTE REINIGER (1970)

I never saw Fischinger's silhouette animations, but I saw several types of his abstractions, and I was very impressed. Walther Ruttmann had some of the films, and he admired Fischinger so much, he told me Fischinger was a real genius of animation. Of course, I thought, well, why not get him to work with me like Bartosch and Ruttmann? But each time I tried to arrange a meeting with Fischinger, Ruttmann managed to cause some snag, so it never came about. Finally Ruttmann admitted that he had done it on purpose, because he was afraid that if I once worked with Fischinger, I would never want to work with Ruttmann again!

MARY ELLEN BUTE (1969)

I wanted to make some kind of Visual Music, so I was studying with Mr. Joseph Schillinger, actually struggling along, because he had very complex mathematical ideas about the correspondences of musical and visual structures. One day, worn out by this hard concentration, I decided to just go to the movies and relax. I've forgotten what the feature was, but in those days, the early 1930s, it was probably full of songs and dances – but I don't remember because first came a short subject, a little animation by Fischinger set to a jazz song "I've Never Seen a Smile Like Yours". It was the simplest thing, drawn lines fluttering about in graceful swirls in perfect time to the music. Suddenly it all made sense for me. That was how to do it, not by mathematical theories, but rather an intuitive choreography.

I was happy to meet Mr. Oskar Fischinger half-a-dozen years later when he visited New York. He was a very sweet man, modest, with a good sense of humour. I suggested we might work together on something, but it never worked out ... .

ALEXANDER ALEXEIEFF and CLAIRE PARKER (1970)

We actually met at a screening of a Fischinger film. It was the "Brahms Hungarian Dance No. 5", and it was playing as a short in an ordinary cinema, so it was quite a surprise. We were both so stunned that we just sat there after everyone else had left. After a few minutes, we noticed, and silently went out and sat down at a corner café. We didn't say much to each other, just things like, "Quite wonderful, wasn't it?". We didn't even exchange names, so when Alexeieff received a letter from a Claire Parker asking to be his student in engraving, he didn't even know it was her, and made a formal appointment to meet her. What a delightful surprise!

We knew we could never rival Fischinger in his own field of pure abstractions, but his films did make you want to create a kind of Visual Music. Then Bartosch inspired us to use a graphic technique closer to engraving, but still, whatever we did, it was bound to be compared with Fischinger – and how often we got commissions for advertising films "in the Fischinger manner"! Sometimes we were very proud to have succeeded in equalling him.

LORSER FEITELSON (*Art Critic*) (1951)

Oskar Fischinger's constant achievements in animated abstract films have distinguished him as the leading figure in this newest Art. His importance in this kinetic medium is comparable to that of Cézanne in modern painting. From his earliest to his latest films, we witness the unfolding of the many-faceted talent of an ingenious craftsman, impeccable designer and creative artist. He is at once artist–poet and scientist.

GERALD NORDLAND (*Museum Curator*) (1970)

I am very pleased to write a few words about the distinguished filmmaker and painter, Oskar Fischinger. From my first meeting with him, at the apartment of another filmmaker and painter Jules Engel, I sensed an idealism and breadth of intelligence in Oskar's conversation that marked him as a man of sensitivity and brilliance. He was a person uniquely prepared and qualified to play an important rôle in the evolution of the Art Film. He was an artist who needed to control all of the elements of his production, and he had instinctive feelings for his media. His concern for rhythmic lines, special textures and overlapping planes is equally graphic in film or in painting. Oskar Fischinger is an important pioneer of Modernism, and he is still alive as an influence.

HERMAN WEINBERG (*Critic/Author*) (1980)

At the Museum of Modern Art Film Department in New York, there is a big fat file on Oskar Fischinger, full of fascinating clippings of statements by him and about him, reviews, commentaries, etc., attesting to how he stirred things up with his little abstract films. They may have been little in the sense that they were short films, but in the way they were done – the ingenuity, bravado and, one must say it, charm – they made a big mark in the field of abstract film animation. Nothing to match them had been done before, nor since. But Oskar Fischinger was above all (above all the scintillating films he made) a most charming and jolly companion. In the brief years I knew him in New York, we became good friends, and I have an endearingly inscribed photo of himself that he gave me as a tender souvenir of those happy days. I think it is characteristic of the warmth of his spirit, in even so cerebral a medium as the abstract animated film, to know that he could do such delicate things as his rococo divertimento *Studie Nr. 11* or the exquisite little *Liebesspiel*, and to show the richness of that spirit that he could do such opposite things as the jubilant *An American March* which almost "raises the roof".

JOHN CAGE (*Composer*) (1974/1980)

forgive me

        when yOu
           Said
         eaCh
          inAnimate object
      has a spiRit

that can take the Form of sound
        by beIng
            Set into vibration
         i beCame a musician
      it was as tHough
you had set me on fIre
         i raN
    without thinkinG
      and thrEw myself
   into the wateR

This mesostic refers to an incident that occurred in 1937. Galka Scheyer had suggested that I compose a musical score for one of Fischinger's films, and Fischinger himself suggested that I learn about animation by assisting on his current work-in-progress, *An Optical Poem*. Dozens of paper circles were suspended on fine strings from a scaffolding over a deep stage. For each single exposure (of which thousands seemed to be necessary), every one of these circles had to be moved a very slight increment, and then they all had to be steadied so that there would be no blurry movement when the frame was shot. Fischinger had a long pole with a chicken feather fixed to the end, which was to be used to steady the circles after they had been moved. He sat, round and jolly as a Chinese Buddha, beside the camera, puffing cigar smoke, and giving me directions concerning exactly how far each circle should be moved. Moving was not such a problem, but steadying the paper discs to motionlessness, in the hands of a novice like me, took such a long time that gradually Fischinger dozed off. The cigar fell from his lips and rolled over to a little bunch of papers and rags. The paper had ignited before I noticed it, and in a sudden panic, I seized a bucket of water to splash over the fire. Much to Oskar's chagrin, the water doused him, as well as the camera, although I don't believe either were really damaged. My career in animation ended that day, but Fischinger's whimsical notions about sight and sound opened a new door for me, something that stays with me always.

NORMAN McLAREN (1975/1980)

Fischinger was one of the great formative influences in my life. Around 1935, when I was about 20, in my student days at the Glasgow School of Art in Scotland, I saw for the first time an "abstract" movie. It was Oskar Fischinger's film done to Brahms' "Hungarian Dance No. 5". It is difficult to describe adequately the impact it had on me: I was thrilled and euphoric by the film's fluent kinesthesia, which so potently portrayed the movement and spirit of the music. The experience made an indelible impression on me, excited a yearning in me, and was to have a profound, long-lasting influence on many of my films.

Several years later, at the Guggenheim Museum of Art in New York, I was further enriched by the experience of seeing many more of Fischinger's works. Each impressed me by his mastery of motion, and all intensified my desire to make this kind of abstract film.

In the early 1950s, I had the opportunity and great pleasure of visiting Fischinger and his wife at their home in California. That was a most memorable day for me, when I became aware of the many-faceted nature of his genius and artistry. I discovered that Oskar was interested not just in filmmaking, but was into all kinds of other experiments, the most intriguing of which for me was his stereoscopic paintings, for I myself had been dabbling in binocular drawings. On leaving their house, I felt I had met someone with a truly inventive and exploratory spirit, and an artist who had pioneered a new path in the history of cinema.

LEN LYE (1977)

My first film, *Tusalava*, was based on aboriginal Dreamtime imagery, and it took two years to make. It was black and white, and very slow, since I wanted that slow-motion quality of dreams, but maybe too slow. Jack Ellit composed a nice score for it, but we could not afford to record it and put a soundtrack on the film. Anyway, it was shown once at the London Film Society in 1929, and that was it. I was a bit discouraged that so much work would have such tiny yield – of course, the ten-minute film still exists and we can still see it now, but at that time the situation seemed pretty depressing, and I didn't consider making any more films for several years. Then I saw Fischinger's *Studie Nr. 7* as a short at a regular cinema, and the dynamic dance of abstract light wouldn't go out of my mind. I knew I had to try again, and since I didn't have any money for cameras and cels, I started drawing directly on film, in experiments that led to *Colour Box*. Whenever I had a chance, I would go out of my way to see Fischinger films. He was a true, natural genius. He ought to be sainted, but I guess they don't have Art Saints.

JULES ENGEL (1976)

I first met Fischinger in 1939 at the Walt Disney Studios, while we were both working on *Fantasia* ... Fischinger was designing the Bach "Toccata and Fugue" as a totally non-objective piece, but all of his work was being changed because the Director wanted something softer and more representational. No one had the least sympathy for his ideals or his concepts of how to make a Visual Music, and least of all his desire to use animation as a medium for absolute art. I arranged to meet him at lunch, since I was already making small abstract paintings, and I wanted to show them to him to find out what he thought about them. He was practically the only person in this milieu with a passion for abstract art. He strongly encouraged me, urged me to pursue my career as a painter or abstract animator, and so he became, as they say, my mentor.

Fischinger was a very nice and sensitive man. He believed in the highest ideals, but at that time he still had some difficulty with the English language, and he could not argue well enough to combat the other animators at the studio. And his integrity made it hard for him to remain in this environment. He believed that creativity was an act of intense belief, almost an act of religious faith in the true sense.

JAMES WHITNEY (1970)

I was still a painter and my brother John was photographing real objects in the *Ballet Mécanique* tradition when we first saw Fischinger's films at the Stendhal Gallery in 1939 or early 1940. Only four or five films were shown – a few black-and-white *Studies*, *Circles* and *Composition in Blue*. John, who was mad for Schönberg then, hated the traditional classical music tracks, but I hardly heard the music at all. I only saw the pure moving light, and after that, still painting would never be enough for me: I had to make real non-objective imagery in motion. And I was strengthened in my resolve by a certain tragic grandeur about Fischinger himself: how brave he seemed, to defy the artistic conventions of the 1920s, the political restrictions of the Nazi era, and now the mediocrity of Hollywood, to insist on the quality of his absolute films, of the ideals he believed in.

Subsequently I visited him several times at his studio, and we had some wonderful and profound conversations – about the primal geometry of organic forms like seashells, for example – but I regret not speaking to him more about spiritual matters. In those days, a devotion to mysticism or some spiritual discipline was frowned upon by society at large, so you got in the habit of hiding it – and I never dreamed that poor Fischinger, surrounded by a swarm of children, would have time or peace to practice meditation or philosophical contemplations.

HARRY SMITH (1977)

You can tell how much I admire Fischinger: the only film of mine that I ever gave a real title to was "Homage to Oskar Fischinger" (*Film No. 5*, in the current scheme of things). I learned concentration from him – visiting his home and seeing how he could sit serenely in that small house, crawling with what seemed like a dozen children, and still paint those stunning pictures. That great film *Motion Painting* makes the process seem deceptively simple – and it was simple for him: the images really did just flow from his brush, never a ruler or compass, all free-hand – but you can't see all the obstacles he had to overcome in order to even work at all. Something so wonderful happened in that film, and in those paintings, something so much better than all the Pollocks and other stuff that the museums fight to get hold of. Did anyone ever fight to save Fischinger's things?

JORDAN BELSON (1971)

I was just graduating from college in painting when I saw Fischinger's films at the 1946 *Art in Cinema* festival at the San Francisco Museum of Art, and that inspired me to start making films instead of just painting canvases. He was very supportive of my work, and recommended me for a Guggenheim Fellowship on the basis of my first film.

My most impresive memory of him is the lingering imagery of the Lumigraph show he performed, also at the San Francisco Museum of Art, in 1953. His films had been shown in the auditorium, which was treat enough, and then the curtains were closed for a brief intermission. Then the lights faded out slowly, and the hall was completely black for several mintutes, so your eyes began to adjust. Some music – I think Sibelius' "Valse Triste" – arose out of the darkness, and in mysterious synchronization with the sounds appeared soft, glowing images where the movie screen had been. I could tell that this was not a film: the luminous presence of these lithe colours was quite different even from the illusions of the high-contrast black-and-white films we had just seen. These irregular, always-changing shapes could flicker and pulsate, and when they swirled around, they could leave a vague trail like a comet's tail. The bright, saturated colours had a ghostly three-dimensional presence. The shapes changed so easily – occasionally resembling some hard, complex object, but most often amorphous clusters or discrete points of light – however they seemed so dimensional, so solid. Sometimes the lights would disappear and appear suddenly, but other times they would fade in and out extremely slowly – just as one colour might glow exquisitely in saturated duration or suddenly jump to another hue, with brilliant, tasteful timing.

When the music was over, we were plunged into total darkness again. The audience erupted with wild applause. Fischinger wouldn't let anyone backstage to inspect the Lumigraph because it would have destroyed the magic (just as he didn't like to tell about his filmic techniques – and I have followed his wisdom in that). Actually, the mechanism of the Lumigraph was rather primitive, hand-made, but the way he performed proved his innate artistry, his natural sensitivity, that could turn even the simplest things into a luxurious, magical illusion of cosmic elegance. That was very inspirational to me: much of my work after that had more of the quality of Lumia, and relied more on simple, hand-made devices.

MICHAEL SCROGGINS (1984)

When I worked with *Single Wing Turquoise Bird* light show for rock concerts in the late 1960s, we used to rent Fischinger films to use in our performances, so I would see them over and over again. Miraculously, their integrity was such that they survived in almost every context in which they were shown. Those films had a lot to do with inspiring me to continue my career as an artist in moving non-objective art and performance, rather than painting. I suppose even the series of *Studie* I am now working on in video synthesis reflects the serial structure of Fischinger's black-and-white film *Studie*. Fischinger is truly the first master of Visual Music.

VIBEKE SORENSEN (1992)

Oskar Fischinger's work continues to inspire me. His brilliance and inventiveness, the magic and poetry of his works, the range and reach of his vision, and the timelessness and passion of his works attest to the realization of his dream: the creation of a purely visual music. His abstract animation resonates so deeply in my heart. Upon repeated viewings, I see each piece differently each time, with an increasingly deeper understanding and affection for his work. A part of my attraction to it lies in its mystery, where his soul dances in colour and light, a soul that is entwined amid, embodied in, and transcendent of the craft he both mastered and invented. Each gesture, each shape, each transformation simultaneously maintains and reveals the mystery of his spirit, becoming both elusive (as it is temporal) and tangible (in that it is visual). Oskar's work is intellectual, emotional, philosophical and spiritual. The sheer range and variety of the ways he translates musical ideas into visual form (and vice versa: he early created synthesized sound by filming abstract shapes on to the optical soundtrack of film) has spawned countless admirers and followers, generation after generation, thus transcending his own time – a sure sign of greatness. His spirit continues to live in his works and in the hearts and minds of those he continues to touch. I am one of his many children, nurtured by his passion.

PAUL GLABICKI (2000)

Seeing Fischinger's work for the first time was a revelation. *An Optical Poem*, *Radio Dynamics*, *Motion Painting No. 1*, and *Composition in Blue* had a life and energy that I hadn't seen before in animated film. They seemed to embody the music that accompanied them, producing the impression that the moving abstract shapes and forms were creating the music as you watched. They also created their own visual language which synthesized the contemporary experiments in abstract painting that surrounded Fischinger with his own idiosyncratic style and vivid imagination. His films seemed at once new, modern, pure, eccentric, innocent, and visionary. The unusual and inventive techniques employed by Fischinger to create his lyrical works displayed an intimate knowledge of the mechanics of cinema, motion, rhythm, and how camera and viewpoint could transform our perception of scale and space.

I was once treated to the privilege of visiting the home of the late Oskar Fischinger and his dedicated wife Elfriede. I was completely overwhelmed by the sheer volume of work that inhabited that house. Remnants of experimental light machines, artifacts of his classic films, and what seemed to be hundreds of paintings, filled every available space. Beautiful paintings that I had never seen or even thought had existed were stacked in the hallways, closets, and even under the dinner table. The legacy of Fischinger's career literally inhabited the space. This legacy continues to resonate with the sense of joyous discovery and creative exploration that characterized early 20th-century cinematic form and, in many ways, parallels the excitement and experimentation now emerging in digital media.

BAERBEL NEUBAUER (2000)

I love the rhythmical elements of Oskar and Hans Fischinger's films. The rhythms they used also fit perfectly to modern music, including Jazz, Pop and Techno. I know, because I tried it out in my own films! *Spiritual Constructions*, with its images of drunk men struggling, is just as rhythmic as the abstract animations. It is especially exciting for me to see figurative/storytelling elements perform in perfect rhythm.

Mathematically exact rhythm is, of course, very musical. But I was also very impressed and inspired by the *Wax Experiments* with their flowing, organic textures. But the beautiful choreography and colours of the great abstract works are hard to beat.

ROBERT DARROLL (2000)

I have always considered Oskar Fischinger to be one of my principal artistic sources. Oskar was not merely a formalist, playfully juggling with forms and colours. There is also a profounder aspect to his work, in which his inner vision of the real nature of the world is expressed through his personal visual language. It was his striving towards a visual expression of his existential perspective which enabled me to identify so strongly with his work.

Here, I am referring to Oskar's formulation in visual terms of archetypal relationships and processes. He was amongst the first animators to set real aesthetic standards in the field of abstract cinema. He achieved this firstly through his extraordinary abilities in both musical as well as visual fields, and secondly through a sovereign command over the technical possibilities of his time. Now I look at his work, many decades after it was produced, and I am still deeply impressed by its convincing liveliness and expressiveness.

Statements by
Oskar Fischinger

My statements are in my work (1947)

To write about my work in absolute film is rather difficult. The only thing to do is to write why I made these films. When I was 19 years old I had to talk about a certain work by William Shakespeare in our literary club. In preparing for this speech, I began to analyse the work in a graphic way. On large sheets of drawing paper, along a horizontal line, I put down all the feelings and happenings, scene after scene, in graphic lines and curves. The lines and curves showed the dramatic development of the whole work, and the emotional moods, very clearly.

It was quite an interesting beginning, but not very many could understand this graphic, absolute expression. To make it more convincing, more easily understood, the drawings needed movement, the same speed and tempo that the feeling originally possessed. The *cinematic* element had to be added. To do this, motion picture film was the logical medium, so it happened that I made my first absolute film.

When sound was added to film, faster progress was possible on the wings of music. The flood of feeling created through music intensified the sensation and the effectiveness of this graphic cinematic expression, and helped to make the absolute film understandable. Under the guidance of music, which was already highly developed, there came the speedy discovery of new laws – the application of accoustical laws to optical expression was possible. As in the dance, new emotions and rhythms sprang out of the music – and the rhythms became more and more important.

I named these absolute films "Studie" – and I numbered them *Studie Nr. 1*, *Studie Nr. 2*, and so forth. These early black-and-white studies drew enthusiastic response at that time from the most famous art critics of England and Europe.

Then came colour film. Of course, the temptation was great to work in colour, and I made thereafter a number of absolute colour films. But I soon found out that the simplicity of my own black-and-white films could never be surpassed.

The colour film proved itself to be an entirely new artform with its own artistic problems, as far removed from black-and-white film as music itself – as an art medium – is removed from painting. Searching for the last thirteen years, to find the ideal solution to this problem, I truly believe I have found it now, and my new, forthcoming work will show it.

Now a few words about the usual motion-picture film which is shown to the masses everywhere, in countless moving picture theatres all over the world. It is photographed realism: photographed surface realism-in-motion ... There is nothing of an absolute artistic creative sense in it. It copies only nature with realistic conceptions, destroying the deep and absolute creative force with substitutes and surface realisms. Even the cartoon film is today on a very low artistic level. It is a mass product of factory proportions, and this, of course, cuts down the creative purity of a work of art. No sensible creative artist could create a sensible work of art if a staff of co-workers of all kinds each had his or her say in the final creation – producer, story director, story writer, music director, conductor, composers, sound men, gag men, effect men, layout men, background directors, animators, inbetweeners, inkers, cameramen, technicians, publicity directors, managers, box office managers, and many others. They change the ideas, kill the ideas before they are born, prevent the ideas from being born, and substitute for the absolute creative motives only the cheapest ideas to accommodate the lowest among them.

The creative artist of the highest level always works at his best alone, moving far ahead of his time. And this shall be our basis: that the Creative Spirit shall be unobstructed through realities or anything that spoils his absolute pure creation.

And so we cut out the tremendous mountains of valueless motion picture productions of the past and the future – the mountain ranges of soap bubbles – and we must concentrate on the tiny golden thread underneath which is hardly visible beneath the glamorous, sensational excitement, securely buried for a long time, especially in our own time when the big producing and distributing monopolies control every motion picture screen with an airtight grip.

Consequently, there is only one way for the creative artist: to produce only for the highest ideals – not thinking in terms of money or sensations or to please the masses.

The real artist should not care if he is understood, or misunderstood, by the masses. He should listen only to his Creative Spirit and satisfy his highest ideals, and trust that this will be the best service that he can render humanity.

It is the only hope for the creative artist that the art lovers, the art collectors, the art institutes, and the art museums develop increasingly greater interest in this direction, and make it possible for the artist to produce works of art through the medium of film.

In this connection, I wish to express my deep gratitude to one great American institution which has in the past helped so many artists in an idealistic, unselfish way, and which has made it possible for me to do a great amount of research work in the direction of the absolute, non-objective film. I am speaking of the Solomon R. Guggenheim Foundation in New York, under the direction of Curator Hilla Rebay.

[Printed in the programme of *Art in Cinema*, San Francisco Museum of Art, 1947.]

1. A NOTE ABOUT *R-1* (1927)

"... An intoxication by light from a thousand sources ... A happening of the soul, of the eyes, of the eye's waves, waves, wave streams, Sun flowing, a level vanishing, a sudden eruption, an awakening, ceremonial, sunrising, effervescent, Star rhythms, star lustre, a singing, surf breaking over chasms, a world of illusions of movements of lights, sound and song tamed – leaping breath [*Atem*], Atman, a wandering through clouds ...".

– from a letter dated 13 September 1927.

2. A DOCUMENT RELATED TO *R-2*

In the absence of the full document recording Fischinger's own description of *R-1*, I have chosen this work-plan for *R-2*, written during the same period. I find this interesting primarily in that it demonstrates Fischinger's romantic, quasi-anthropomorphic attitude toward "abstract" action. The staffs are seen as acting out a situation, and the flow of the time–space lapse (ultimately the "meaning" of the film) is determined by the working out of that situation. I am reminded of the writings of Rabindranath Tagore, who also clothes his complex philosophical ideas in natural events so simple that they become abstract; I have no idea if Fischinger was familiar with Tagore's work, but it would be reasonable to assume he might be, since Tagore had won a Nobel prize, and his philosophy is rather parallel to Fischinger's. A film *R-2*, by the way, is not known *per se*. Perhaps the film in question was never completed, but in any case, the description clearly relates to the various films discussed in the Filmography as No. 2, *Staffs* [William Moritz].
[*The translation (by Linda Hoag) is followed by the original German text.*]

R-2

First a quiet beginning. Points of Staffs start to dance slowly, rhythmically, and arise gradually up to the middle of the picture. The tempo is at first practically non-existent, and then begins only slowly to become perceptible. Now single bunches grow out above the general line and take the lead in a particular way. Then they destroy the uniform line and attempt to lead an individual, independent life. They succeed only to a certain degree, whereupon they then fall back again and revert to their original tempo, i.e. the inferior rhythm of the masses trumps and kills their independent attempt. Nevertheless, this attempt was an elevation not without influence on the rest of the masses of staffs, which now beat out a quicker tempo and become livelier. Now begins a livelier dance, a lighter hopping and soaring. The rhythm slackens, becoming visibly bolder and more spirited, until a certain group again seizes the lead and the tempo, slackened now, tries to restrain itself and the earlier, graver calm is enforced. However, even at this point things don't remain at a standstill. Immediately an opposing group breaks through to a new tempo and gradually the increasing tempo begins to become bolder and bolder. The tempo becomes more vigorous, bolder, wilder. They follow one another in quick succession now and wild, steep dives occur. Till when, with a crash, complete peace reigns. Of course, I could already have ended here, but it occurs to me now for the first time that the really final, really most important climax should happen next. After the calm has arrived, a gentler tremor of excitement begins to run through the points. This recurs over and over until single staffs break loose wildly. The tempo rises furiously in a steep ascent and attains such wild strength that it takes your breath away. Now the violent storm rages in all its power and beauty before the eyes of the viewer. It rages and rages and finally reaches its climax. Now, however, it does not subside back into its earlier calm, but merely levels off gradually in its force. The strongest blow must be the rush, the place where the last, most surging motion rises in speedy tempo, loosening itself like a breaking storm. After the passing of the climax, these outbreaks now become only more infrequent, not weaker, and die off into the distance. Just as when a thunderstorm subsides, that storm itself continually rages with the same vehemence, but it is merely no longer perceivable by the spectator, even so, this is no common conclusion, when you reconcile yourself with everyone and vain peace and love prevail, rather it finishes, but it lasts forever on and on.

The music for this will be composed of "noises" which will be produced by all kinds of percussion instruments.
Munich, 29 March 1927

Zunächst ruhiger Beginn. Spitzen von Stäben beginnen langsam rhythmisch zu tanzen und erheben sich nach und nach bis zur Mitte des Bildes. Das Tempo ist zunächst so gut wie gar nicht vorhanden und beginnt nun erst langsam fuhlbar zu werden.

Nun wachsen einzelne Partien über die allgemeine Linie hinaus und nehmen in gewissem Masse die Führung. Sie zerstören zunächst die einheitliche Linie und versuchen ein eigenes eigenwilliges Leben zu führen. Dies gelingt Ihnen nur bis zu einem gewissen Grade, alsdann fallen sie wieder zurück und nehmen ihr altes Tempo wieder auf, das heisst der geringere Rythmus der Masse übertrupft und erschlägt ihren eigenwilligen Versuch. Jedoch war dieser Versuch einer Hebung nicht ohne Einfluss auf die übrige Masse der Stäbe, die nun ehr aus sich heraus ein schnelleres Tempo einschlagen und lebhafter werden. Nun beginnt ein lebhafter Tanz, ein leichteres Hupfen und schweben. Der Rythmus lockert sich zusehens wird kühner und mutiger, bis alsdann widerum eine besonder Gruppe die Fuhrung an sich reisst und das nun gelocherte Tempo zu bändigen sucht und die frühere schwerere Ruhe erzwingt. Jedoch bleibt auch hier kein Stillstand. Sofort schlägt eine gegengruppe zu neuem Tempo durch und beginnt allmählich eine imer kühner werdend Steigerung. Die Tempos werden heftiger kühner wilder. Sie überschlagen sich schon und wilde stelle Stürtze vollziehen sich. Bis dann mit einem Schlage föllige Ruhe herscht.

Ich könnte zwar hier schon schliessen, dedoch erscheint mir nun erst die richtige endgültige wirklich grosste Steigerung am Platz . Nach den die Ruhe also einge ehrt ist, beginnt ein leichter Errregungsschauer durch die Spitzen zu fliessen. Dieser Wiederholt sich mehrfach bis dann einzelne Stäbe wild ausbrechen. Rassend steigert sich nun das Tempo in stilem Anstig und erreicht eine solche wilde Macht dass es den Atem berrückt. Nun tobt sich das Unwetter in aller Pracht und schonheit vor den Augen der Beschauer aus. Tobt und tobt und erreicht endlich seinen Höhepunkt. = = == =: Nun sinkt es jedoch nicht mehr in seine frühere Ruhe zurück, sondern ebt nur in seiner stärke allmählich ab. Der stärkste Anschlag muss der Andrang sein die Stelle, wo der letzte gesteigerste Bewegung anhebt in raschem Tempo loslegt wie ein anbrechender Sturm. Die Ausbrüche werden nunmehr nach überschreiten des Höhepunktes nur noch seltener, nicht schwächer. und klingen in die Ferne ab. So als ob sich ein Gewitter verziehe, das an sich jedoch in gleicher heftigkeit imer noch weiter tobt, nur dass es nicht mehr für den Beschauer wahrnehmbar ist. Also kein üblicher Schluss wo sich alles versöhnt und eitel Friede und Liebe ist, sondern es ist vorüber aber es dauert immervort weiter.

Die Musik herzu setzt sich wiederum aus Geräuschen zu sammen die durch Schlagzeug-instrumente aller Art erzeugt werden.
München, den 29. März 1927.

MUNICH TO BERLIN (1927)

Walking from Munich to Berlin is such a sizeable challenge that anyone who undertakes it must have a very good reason. I was motivated mostly by a longing for freedom. I wanted to break ties that bound me, and I wanted to become healthy from this long hike at the same time that I broke all the ties binding me to Munich. I succeeded in walking over 1,000 km [620 miles] to Berlin, taking the back roads, all on foot, with no trains or conveyances used. Daily I put long stretches of road behind me. I saw many beautiful landscapes, met friendly people, farmers and workers, and here and there Gypsies. I got along well with all of them, and we had good conversations. There is a lot less difference between people than is commonly supposed. I must say that people are the same everywhere. There are some differences, of course, but these stem primarily from character and temperament, and those same variations occur everywhere.

For an airplane, this is a laughable stretch, only about two and a half hours from Munich to Berlin. But it took me three and a half weeks, wandering as I did through hop-fields, over mountains, across the Danube, through forests and little villages, and again over mountains, from the heights of which everything looks so terribly tiny.

THE BLACK-AND-WHITE STUDIES (1932)

People are curious. They're unsatisfied, and ask me how I, Fischinger, came to make such films – how the crazy idea occurred to me to make with lines – simple, cheap lines on a dark screen (yes, that's how my films look!) – something without the least resemblance to a person, a house, a fountain, a chimneysweep, a cat or a mouse?

Well, it's hard to say, but sooner or later one has to state such basic principles. So here it is: I thought – or rather, it seemed to me – that, after all, a line is actually something in and of itself, and when it moves, it can say quite a bit – that is, by changing its outer shape or expression, it can alter its inner impression: a round, beautiful, harmonious line, a vibrant circle or a lovely crescent doesn't just seem like that, it is actually in fact that, and correspondingly gives a full, effective strong impression. Now, when I think how this line, which is so nicely round and delicate and fine, can suddenly change into something pointed, angry, jagged and nervous, thorny, steep and violent – in short, when it totally abandons its beautiful character and displays a different side of its nature, then it also expresses that other temperament in a thoroughly understandable fashion. So I extrapolated from that. I conceived and produced these lines – and made an absolute cinema.

SOUNDING ORNAMENTS (1932)

Between ornament and music persist direct connections, which means that ornaments are music. If you look at a strip of film from my experiments with synthetic sound, you will see along one edge a thin stripe of jagged ornamental patterns. These ornaments are drawn music – they are sound: when run through a projector, these graphic sounds broadcast tones of a hitherto unheard of purity, and thus, quite obviously, fantastic possibilities open up for the composition of music in the future. Undoubtedly, the composer of tomorrow will no longer write mere notes, which the composer himself can never realize definitively, but which rather must languish, abandoned to various capricious reproducers. Now control of every fine gradation and nuance is granted to the music-painting artist, who bases everything exclusively on the primary fundamental of music, namely the wave-vibration or oscillation in and of itself. In the process, surface new perceptions that until now were overlooked and remain neglected. Possibilities that are definitely significant for a scrupulous and profound creator of music, for example, precise overtones or timbres characteristic of a certain voice or instrument can be reproduced with accurate fidelity through these drawn patterns. Or, when desirable, the profile of sound waves could be synchronized exactly, wave-trough with wave-trough, so that their dead-centres would coincide, sounding in perfect accord. Or, furthermore, new musical sounds are now possible, pure tones with a precision of definition in their musical vibrations that could not be obtained formerly from the manipulation of traditional instruments.

A number of experiments that I have just made confirm the unprecidented range and significance of this method. The soundtrack on present-day films is only three millimetres wide, but the artist of the future will naturally require the full width of the film-strip just for his musical composition. It would be essential for a complex and distinct composition, with the abstract, diverse effect of an orchestra, to utilize several 3mm soundtracks running parallel to each other. Each track would produce a different, well-defined sound, and planning them together, the composer could design and organize overlapping and intersecting wave patterns, on the minutest level.

In reference to the general physical properties of drawn sounds, we can note that flat and shallow figures produce soft or distant-sounding tones, while moderate triangulation give an ordinary volume, and sharply-pointed shapes with deep troughs create the loudest volume. Shades of grey can also play a significant role in drawn music-ornaments. High-contrast definition of the wave form decisively creates the prevalent sound effect, but as long as one places such a "positive" (well-defined) wave somewhere in the foreground, one can simply overlay other wave patterns simultaneously by using grey shades for the secondary sound effects. Study of sample soundtracks containing these complex tonal patterns reveals that not only do the layered ornaments produce refined, intricate musical sounds but also they appear unexpectedly as attractive abstract visual images.

A combination of any chosen sound-images is readily imaginable. The potential in this area is unlimited. But there are also other possible uses for graphic sound ornaments. Personal and national characteristics should be able to be identified by their corresponding ornament manifestations. The German style of singing, for example, with its emphasis on loud and ringing chest tones, creates a much sharper visual profile on the soundtrack than the softer, more melodic French style of singing with its emphasis on limpid head tones that produce rounder optical wave undulations.

The new methods introduced here offer new, fruitful stimulation that should be provocative to the whole musical world. Perhaps through the development explained here, the creative artist, the composer, will not only find a completely new way of working, but also he himself can simultaneously produce his creative expression in an indelible direct graphic which will be definitive in that he shall not be dependent on any reproduction by foreign hands, since his creation, his work, can speak for itself directly through the film projector.

The basis of designing a graphic art that can be actuated by a beam of brightest light will be the definitive, direct building blocks of music. Now it is the task of Industry to produce practical equipment that will enable every competent person to work in this manner. Besides a camera with the appropriate apertures for such soundtracks, the new equipment must include, certainly, the ability to play back the recorded sound on some speaker at any time, as often as the composer may want. These music artists must also be concerned with combining their musical compositions created in this new manner together with appropriate optical imagery. This should result in the potential for combination of sounding ornaments with visible filmic, spatial forms and movements. With that union, the unity of all the arts is definitively, finally achieved, is become unquestionable fact.

[Oskar Fischinger: First published in the *Deutsche Allgemeine Zeitung* 8 July 1932, then widely syndicated in other newspapers.]

COMPOSITION IN BLUE (1935)

Composition in Blue is more than merely an optical "illustration" of music. It pictures a new, higher Oneness. It aspires to a Colour-Light-Concert. It is a breakthrough, a further developmental step towards a new art of the future, the nature and effect of which we people of today can only vaguely dream at first, even as our grandparents 50 or 60 years ago could hardly have fit into their frame of reference something as powerful and persuasive as the Film Art of today.

FOUR DOCUMENTS RELATED TO RADIO DYNAMICS –
Document No. 1

This passage is written on one of the animation sheets itself; the scene is that of the three growing circular shapes, and the inscription is squeezed into the upper area between the registration holes, indicating that it was probably written at the same time that the drawing was done, when it would be still necessary to keep the picture area clear [William Moritz].

"Grenzbildungen im Biologischen Keimvorgang sind Mittel zeitlicher Konzentrationen in die Zukunft die lediglich zu Formveränderungen führen und für das einzelne Grenzgebilde notwendigerweise zum Tode führen.

"Wissenschaft und Technik verfolgen entgegengesetzte Richtungen, nämlich, Grenzen erweitern, Grenzen niederlegen, das Weltbild fortgesetzt erweitern.

"Die Biologische Entwicklungsweise kann ihre Richtung nicht ändern (nach innen konzentrieren immer neue Grenzen bilden).

"Die geistige Entwicklung versucht es fort in entgegengesetzter Richtung und kann ihre Richtung ebenfalls nicht ändern, oder?"

It is not really possible to translate this passage, since it is quite ambiguous and complex, containing a kind of play-on-words which does not exist in English. Two crucial ambivalent terms are *grenz* and *bild*. *Grenz* means "frontier", "border", or "edge", and Fischinger exploits the word for both positive and negative values, e.g. frontier as a threshold of progressive achievement, and frontier as a limitation of activity. *Bild* means "image" (or "form", "idea", etc.), but also in its verbal manifestations means things like "educate", "mold", "develop", and "imagine", i.e. "to formulate the image". Furthermore, Fischinger compounds these two words together to mean something like "ultimate achievement". A generalized rendition might read thus:

"Frontier-images in biological evolution are the means of temporal concentrations into the future, which lead solely to form-changing, and, for each individual frontier-image, necessarily lead to death.

"Science and Technology follow opposite directions, namely to extend frontiers, to establish frontiers, to extend incessantly the World-image.

"The biological way of developing cannot change its direction (concentrating inwardly, always imagining new frontiers).

"Spiritual development strongly pursues the opposite direction, and can nevertheless not change its direction, or ...?"

In the first paragraph, physical, biological development is seen as an overlapping sequence of individuals each of which is an ultimate achievement until it produces a successor which then becomes the new ultimate achievement while the older one dies.

In the second paragraph, science and technology are subtly played off against each other as well as against organic, natural development. Ideas and machines are seen as equivalents of the living individuals, i.e. temporary ultimate achievements which foster new discoveries that in turn supersede the original achievements. The word *entgegengesetzte*, "opposite" or "contrary", reinforces the tension between frontiers as limitations and thresholds, reminding us that formulas and tools are simultaneously help and hindrance. The word *Weltbild* [World-image], by the way, is a fairly common expression meaning "world-view" or "philosophy of life".

In the third paragraph, the strands of the argument are drawn together: physical forms (including technology by implication) are bound to reproduce themselves mechanically, but spiritual forms (including speculative science) can, through creative imagination, actually foster something quite irregular and genuinely new. Is, thus, Thought superior to Action? Essence to Existence?

Behind the word-play in this passage lies a philosophical language-game in Wittgenstein's sense. This form of contemplation was dear to Fischinger. The connection with the visual logic of *Radio Dynamics*, where the changing forms are spiritual gestures, is obvious. I am also reminded somewhat of the poems of Kandinsky which are printed at the end of the American edition of his *Concerning the Spiritual in Art*.

RADIO DYNAMICS – Document No. 2

This invocation is written on scrap animation paper from the early 1940s, containing (along with various scribbled telephone numbers, etc.) a doodle of concentric circles reminiscent of the eye-mandala-vortex of *Radio Dynamics*. This tone of mantric incantation was also dear to Fischinger.

"The world within, tremendous in size, complicated ring in space, in going on infinite in every direction. Look in the night at the stars, the blue depth of space, the milky way as you see it from a high desert plateau, when the stars almost become a mass of glowing material, radiating matter from one end of the horizon to the other, a luminous mass radiating alive glowing and there may be Jupiter the planet or Mars or Venus wandering around in that glowing radiating mass and the Moon may be somewhere between and some shooting stars shoot across that fast illuminous radiating infinity of the outer world of endless space. And the sun may rise in the morning on the horizon bathing in light, blotting out the stars and the daylight is all around you and the pupil of your eye narrows down to a small point and still the light of the sun seems to be a million times stronger than the fast distant glow of the stars and total luminosity of the heavens at night – but look into your eye, go down into your own eye – and going – "

RADIO DYNAMICS – Document No. 3

This fragment from the *Radio Dynamics* period shows that some dozen years later Fischinger still interprets non-objective forms, colours, and movements in romantic, quasi-anthropomorphic terms. Comparison with Klee's *Pedagogical Sketchbook* is interesting.

Creative necessity
unescapable need of expression
dictated by higher forces —
remains ————— of creative efforts
unfinished as such ———
Color ——— harmonys ——————

	Red room
	red hammer
or the shining victory	blue/red murder of the Blue body
of the blue body in	swarming over with red
a red room	little bodies
he refused to reflect	infiltration by red/
red became more	corpuscles
and more blue	and
radiating blue	decay — of the
till red	blue body first
changed	purple / then
to blue	red — fading
	away in red

RADIO DYNAMICS – Document No. 4 (1944)

A film can be even more beautiful without music. The optical part – the form and motion – is visualized through the visual imagination, through the fantasy of the Eye. If there is sound necessary, then the music has to go with the movement of the image, the motion of the forms. Light is the same as Sound, and Sound is the same as Light. Sound and Light are merely waves of different length. Sound and Light waves tell us something about the inner and the outer structure of things. Non-objective expressions need no perspective. Sound is mostly an expression of the inner plastic structure of things, and should also not be needed for non-objective expressions. The more unessential material we can take away, the more the essential, the non-objective absolute truth, can come forth.

[Another letter (1940) to the Baroness Rebay about *Radio Dynamics* appears in the main text (William Moritz).]

A DOCUMENT RELATED TO *MOTION PAINTING I*

On eight narrow strips of paper, Fischinger recorded his meditations about *Motion Painting No. 1*. The first three deal with the Bach music and its structural analogies to the perception of natural forms and events. The next two deal with Hindu philosophy, being passages copied from Book 14 ff. of the *Bhagavad Gita*. The last three pages (not reproduced here) deal with the advantages of kinetic painting over still canvas painting. The juxtaposition of the scriptural passages with the practical discussion of film and technique seems neither accidental nor gratuitous. As mentioned in the Filmography, Fischinger continues some of his quasi-Hindu iconography in *Motion Painting No. 1*, and perhaps even the three sections of the film represent the experience of tamasika, rajasika, and sattvika as described in the passage. Furthermore, the last paragraph contains an exhortation to carry on with one's karma despite all obstacles, ending with a repeated phrase that represents very closely Fischinger's attitude towards himself, Abstraction, and his artistic activity: "Only he whose senses are shielded from the object of senses by the protection of the knowledge of the spirit, only he is possessed of Wisdom" [William Moritz].

1.

This music, concerto by Bach, is like a smooth river flowing on the side of open fields –
"And what you see – is not translated music, because music doesn't need to be translated on the screen – to the Eyes music is in itself enough – but the optical part is like we walk on the side of the river – sometimes we go a little bit farther off (away) but we come back and go along on this river, the concerto by Bach."
   The optical part is no perfect synchronization of every wave of the river – it is a very free walk, nothing is forced, nothing is synchronized except in great steps.

2.

The film is in some parts perfectly synchronized with the music, but in other parts it runs free – without caring much about the music – it is like a pleasant walk on the side of a river – If the river springs, we on the side do not necessarily spring to it – but go our own free way – sometimes we even go a little bit away from the river and later come back to it and love it so much more – because we were away from it. Sometimes we go up a little while while on the side of the river and the river goes low through a tunnel or under a bridge but we are all the time with the river near the river we hear the sound of the river, and we love it and the river is the music of Bach. And what we see are the fields

3.

The optical thought the optical dance to the sound of the river of your soul The flowers of a mind The dance of handwriting and the song of flowers and the white of the clouds and the blue of the sky – Sometimes it is dark and you see in the darkness nothing but your own feeling your own movements your own pulse and the rapture of your heart your blood this is what you see – what goes with the music – The Stars the Heaven the Darkness and the Light of your own love your own heart. The Light of your mind, The Dancing Light of your blood – and your feeling

4.

The three great GUNAS, or Principles of Nature, oft times called the Three Qualities, and which are inherent in, and which spring from Nature are known by these names:
Sattvas, or *Truth*
Rajas, or Passion; Tamas, or Indifference.
Sattvas or Truth being pure and stainless bindeth the Soul by attachment to Wisdom and Harmony, and bringeth it back to rebirth because of the bonds of Knowledge and Understanding. *And Rajas or Passion* is of the Nature of burning Desire, and both bind the Soul by attachment to Action and Things and Objects, and doth bring it back to rebirth because of the bonds of worldly Hunger and Thirst for Having and Doing.
And *Tamas*, or *Indifference* is of an ignorant, dark stupid and heavy nature and bindeth the soul by attachment to sloth and idleness, and Folly and Indolence bringing it back to rebirth because of the bonds of Ignorance, Stupidity, Heedlessness, and Low-Content.

When one overcometh the Tamas and the Rajas then the Sattvas reigneth – When the Rajas and the Sattvas are overcome then reigneth the Tamas. When Tamas and Sattvas have been overcome then reigneth the Rajas.

5.

"Then rise in thy might, seize thy bright and gleaming sword, thy bright and gleaming sword of spiritual Wisdom and cut thou, with one strong sweep of thy blade the bonds of doubt and un-belief which confine thy mind and heart. Arise O Prince and perform thy appointed action:

He who hath divorced himself from *the effects of desires* and abandoned the *Lust of the Flesh*, in *thought as in action* walketh straight to peace.

He who hath left behind him *Pride, Vain-glory*, and *Selfishness, goeth straight to happiness*. Yea, so goeth he!
Verily, only he whose senses are shielded from the object of Senses, by the protection of the knowledge of the Spirit – only he is possessed of Wisdom.
Only *he whose Senses are shielded* from the *object of Senses*, by the *protection of the knowledge* of the Spirit only he is *possessed of Wisdom*.

A STATEMENT ABOUT PAINTING
(1951, for an exhibition at the Frank Perls Gallery)

The stereo paintings in this exhibition are a more recent development than my other paintings, perhaps still too new to be fully understood and appreciated. But they will be very exciting for everyone who has the patience to look at them and study them, and really see them in their stereo quality and space reality as they are meant to be seen.

To see the space paintings, the following suggestions may help you: Stand (or sit) at a comfortable distance, squarely in front of the painting. Eyes horizontal, parallel with the paintings. Look and focus and put all your attention at a nearby point (reading distance) in line with the paintings. To make it easier at the beginning, hold your finger or a pencil at reading distance. This will help you to focus at that point in space.

Adjust the distance of that point slightly by moving backwards or forwards until you have the impression that the two panels of the stereo painting on the wall have moved apart from each other. Then between them a new, a third painting of equal size appears, slightly more brilliant than the images at its right and left. However, please do not take your attention away from the nearby point upon which you have focused all your attention. This means – in spite of the temptation to look at the real surfaces of the paintings on the wall (we are naturally conditioned to look at things where they are) – keep all your attention at the focal point.

Now observe with your mind the illusive painting in the middle. This is the space illusion. It seems to be on the wall between the real paintings, but actually it appears nearby and around the focal point upon which your eyes have been fixed. Don't look away. Observe, and if your eyes are normal (i.e. not of unequal vision – the two independent images must fall – and click – together) then you should actually see and be able to wander around in that space painting and feel the exact location and position of each form and the distance behind them in all sharpness, precision, exactness and perfection.

If you should not succeed at first, don't feel discouraged. Perhaps at another time you will succeed. You are only postponing the moment of your discovery and joy. You still have it ahead of you.

New conclusions, ideas, consequences spring out of space paintings. Compositions must not only be two-dimensional or three-dimensional (as in perspective compositions) but must also be dimensionally composed into actual space. Thus space painting opens up a tremendous new field for future artists.

The space stereo paintings are an outgrowth of *Motion Painting No. 1*, my film which was awarded the Grand Prix at the International Film Festival in Brussels, 1949. This film is a continuous oil painting, not of course a usual painting, but one done with the ideas of cinematic form, colour, rhythm and movement. The progress of the ideas and inventions in the painting was faithfully recorded by a stop-motion camera throughout more than a year, though the film rolls off before your eyes in ten minutes. The effectiveness of its execution is the result of continuous work in this field since 1919.

As to the conclusion I might draw from this film, it is only that *Motion Painting No. 1*, as it unfolds itself, offers the viewer the same deep emotional feeling that he can receive from good music. Thus we find that music is not limited to the world of sound; there also exists a music of the visual world.

A DOCUMENT CONCERNING *PAINTING* (1956, for an exhibition of Fischinger's paintings at the Pasadena Art Museum [now the Norton Simon Museum]

Paintings and painters today face a world stranger and more confusing than ever before in history. Until the beginning of this century, painters had a definite, well-established place. A painter's problems could be solved in slow-moving fashion, and until he solved them, he was expressing, portraying, creating in accordance with the spirit of his time. Since about 1900, everything has changed with increasing speed. New techniques and sciences have produced a series of convulsions, upheavals and revolutions – continuous changes whose rate and speed were unequaled in all the history of our planet.

The painter, as he appeared to be before the 20th century, has been left alone, high and dry. He has become an almost pathetic figure, floating in a turbulence with his feet off the ground.

But, as in nightmares, there is always a way out – in mastering conditions by making use of them and their forces. Fast-moving times are exciting times. In times rich in producing inventions there is also a challenge and quickening in all fields of human endeavour.

So the painter, the creative artist as such, found himself equipped with new tools and thoughts as never before. Cinema was developed, silent at first, then suddenly adding sound. Images could speak music, and the very motion of visual creations opened a new world – a great world of possibilities for the creative force within the contemporary artist.

But painting in motion, combined with music, or painting *without* motion: that is the problem. The difference is tremendous. "Motion paintings" give to the painter a new potentiality. He must develop and become something like a "visual-motionist" creating not only in space but also in time. Within sixty seconds or sixty minutes he must present not only one static, framable two or three dimensional creation of a visual nature, but he must also create sentence after sentence of moving, developing visual images changing and changing, in continuously different ways. At times these may be composed of successive ideas, bringing new life into images. Forms are basic, but changes develop from the orchestration of forms and lines and colours. This is a tremendous new world – a tremendous new tool – a challenge to creativeness comparable only to music.

There are two conceivable types of the new creative artist. Those who create only visually in motion, and those who also create their own acoustical or musical soundtrack. The trouble here is that to develop either faculty to a great height asks for complete dedication and excludes everything else. A great painter, a great master in his field, has never been a great musical genius and vice versa. It may turn out to be too difficult to develop both faculties in one man so that he can create a complete work of his own. But it might be done.

So why do I still paint in two or three dimensions after making abstract films since 1919? It is a way out. Just as Columbus, after discovering America, lived out the rest of his life in misery, so have pioneers in most cases throughout history, after their first achievements, had periods of quietness and solitude, pushed aside by the eager rush of an excited mankind.

Besides, the devil always gets his foot in at the same time! Cinema was created first as *graphic art in motion*, but quickly became a *life-photo, story-telling affair*, in which the creativeness of the painter was not at all necessary. It became the fascination of the great masses to have themselves portrayed in motion by photographic means, and the creative artist, the painter, again became the fifth wheel – or a removed, unnecessary, seemingly-high-flying highbrow.

Another Mohammed must come to set into motion a new *Bildersturm* [Iconoclast] and to destroy all the films of "reality" and, I hope, at the same time all the *reproductions of paintings* – the substitutes which poison the creative channels of art.

Fischinger – November 1956

True creation

A t the beginning of the great unknown of all beginnings there is the Idea, a knowledge profound and unconscious, a feeling, a vision of the Ideal, of a path to follow, of everything, of the conclusion and of the end – of which there never is one.

The arena of the experimental is the arena of consciousness that awakes and stretches, the time of searching, the discovery of a method of doing things, of developing methods and techniques – which must correspond to the meaning and harmonize with it. Unconscious vision of the beginning.

Then comes a period of studying the possibilities of a satisfactory or ideal technique, or of a method that will grow into the completeness, the recognition, the control of the means of expression until that can become a work of art. Finally comes the moment to reject all that which becomes the tool of the creator – the humble hand through which the artist expresses and reveals himself.

If the cinema one day becomes an artform, we will owe it to poor, unknown men who have born great suffering within them: men comparable to Grünewald, Van Gogh, Rembrandt, Mozart and Beethoven. These interpreters of the creator, the artists, will be recognized through their creations, some generations later, often after their bodies have rotted and disintegrated in the earth.

We will only find true artists and masterpieces among the so-called experimental films and filmmakers. They actually use creative processes. The film isn't "cut", it is a continuity, the absolute truth, the creative truth. Any observer can verify that, and I consider myself an observer.

I worked nine months on a film, *Motion Painting No. 1*, without ever seeing a piece of it. All I did was check the exposure level of each roll that came back from the lab, so I only saw the film when the first colour composite release print was ready. Fortunately, I was relieved to see that all my anxieties about those hundreds of "little technical devils" that could have spoiled so many months' of work were quite unjustified. I was very happy, and felt a deep emotion that I cannot describe – but it is probably something that others feel on similar occasions.

I want this work to fulfill the spiritual and emotional needs of our era. For there is something we all seek – something we try for during a lifetime working at filmmaking, always unsatisfied, always cheated, always taken for an idiot by the film industry, but hoping despite all that, here and there, one day, perchance, something will be revealed, arising from the unknown, something that will reveal the True Creation: the Creative Truth!

The usual motion picture which is shown to the masses everywhere in countless motion picture theatres all over the world is photographed realism – photographed surface realism-in-motion ... There is nothing of an absolute artistic creative sense in it. It copies only nature with realistic conceptions, destroying the deep and absolute creative force with substitutes and surface realisms. Even the animated film today is on a very low artistic level. It is a mass product of factory proportions, and this, of course, cuts down the creative purity of the work of art. No sensible creative artist could create a sensible work of art if a staff of co-workers of all kinds each has his or her say in the final creation – producer, story director, story writer, music director, conductor, composer, sound men, gag men, effect men, layout men, background directors, animators, inbetweeners, inkers, cameramen, technicians, publicity directors, managers, box office managers, and many others. They change the ideas, kill the ideas before they are born, prevent ideas from being born, and substitute for the absolute creative motives only cheap ideas to fit the lowest common denominator.

The creative artist of the highest level always works at his best alone, moving far ahead of his time. And this shall be our basic tenet: that the Creative Spirit shall be unobstructed by realities or anything else that spoils this absolute *pure* creation.

And so we must cut out the tremendous mountains of valueless motion picture productions of the past and future – the mountain ranges of soap bubbles – and we must concentrate on the tiny golden thread underneath which is hardly visible beneath the glamorous, sensational excitement, securely buried for a long time, especially in our own era when the big producing and distributing monopolies control every motion picture screen in an airtight grip.

So only one way remains for the creative artist: to produce only for the *highest* ideals – not thinking in terms of money or sensational success or to please the masses. The real artist should not care if he is understood, or misunderstood, by the masses. He should listen only to his *Creative Spirit* and satisfy his highest ideals, and trust that this will be the best service that he can render humanity.

Oskar Fishinger
[Written for the Knokke-le-Zoute film festival, 1949, when *Motion Painting No. 1* received the Grand Prize.]

Selected list of public and private collections of Fischinger artworks

Margarete Ackermark, New York, New York
Ingrid Badenhausen-Knoll, Munich, Germany
Mr. and Mrs. Harry Bertoia, Barto, Pennsylvania
George and Lotte Brasloff, Nice, France
Mr. and Mrs. Sol Brill, Beverly Hills, California
Buck Collection, Laguna Niguel, California
Coca Cola Barbee Collection, Los Angeles, California
Sidney Coleman, Cambridge, England
Mr. and Mrs. Albert Fineberg, Los Angeles, California
Giuliana Haight, Gerrards Cross, England
Gisela Geyer and Ronny Loewy, Frankfurt, Germany
Mr. Solomon R. Guggenheim, New York
Mr. and Mrs. Mark Jordan, Hollywood, California
Toshi Kawahara, Tokyo, Japan
Dr. and Mrs. Robert Kuhn, Beverly Hills, California
Peter Kunstadter, Honolulu, Hawaii
Bert and Monique Ihlenfeldt, San Francisco, California
Mr. and Mrs. Augusto Lodi, Altadena, California
Eva and Leo Mason, Los Angeles, California
Karl and Helen Lindemann, Frankfurt, Germany
Mr. and Mrs. Robert Mcintosh, Bel-Air, California
Mr. and Mrs. Bernhard Messinger, Sherman Oaks, California
Mr. Frank Nierendorf, New York
Mr. and Mrs. Pierce Ommanney, Fullerton, California
Mr. and Mrs. John Paxton, Hollywood, California
Takako and Dolfi Pfau, Zurich, Switzerland
Korinna and Lothar Prox, Bonn, Germany
Gordon Rosenblum, Denver, Colorado

Mr. and Mrs. Terry Sanders, West Los Angeles, California
Thomas Schamoni, Munich, Germany
Walter Schobert, Hanau, Germany
Mr. and Mrs. Leo Schoenbrun, West Los Angeles, California
Dr. and Mrs. Roger Sperry, Altadena, California
Mr. and Mrs. A. Stendhal, Los Angeles, California
Mr. and Mrs. Folker Traub, Altadena, California
Heinz Trauboth, Weingarten, Germany
Corry and Ernst Tross, Denver, Colorado
Mr. and Mrs. Colwyn Trewarthen, Altadena, California
Mr. and Mrs. Perce Ullmann, Brentwood, California
Mr. and Mrs. Lee Walker, Hollywood, California
All Fischinger relatives in Europe and America
Solomon Guggenheim Museum, New York
Pasadena Museum, now Norton Simon Museum, Pasadena, California
National Gallery of Art, Washington DC
National Museum of American Art, Smithsonion Institution, Washington DC
Los Angeles County Museum of Art, Los Angeles, California
La Jolla Museum of Art, La Jolla, California
Deutsches Filmmuseum, Frankfurt, Germany
Moritzburg Museum, Halle, Germany
Milwaukee Museum of Art, Milwaukee, Wisconsin

One man exhibitions of Oskar Fischinger paintings

1938   Karl Nierendorf Gallery, New York
1938   Phillip C. Boyer Gallery, New York
1947   American Contemporary Gallery, Hollywood, California
1949   Arts Center School, Los Angeles, California
1951   Frank Perls Gallery, Los Angeles, California
1953   San Francisco Museum of Art, San Francisco, California
1956   Pasadena Art Museum, Pasadena, California
1963   Ernest Raboff Gallery, Los Angeles, California
1965   American City Bank, Los Angeles, California
1966   Drew Gallery, Pasadena, California
1970   Long Beach Museum of Art, California
1971   Goethe Center, San Francisco, California
1973   Occidental College Gallery, Los Angeles, California
1977   Goethe Center, Montreal, Canada

1981 Fischinger: A Retrospective- Gallery 609, Denver, Colorado
1990 Galerie Kroner, Wiesbaden, Germany
1994 Luckman Fine Arts Gallery, California State College at
      Los Angeles, California
1998 Jack Rutberg Fine Arts, Los Angeles, California

Selected group exhibitions

1945 The Solomon R. Guggenheim Museum, New York
1947 Art Institute of Chicago (Abstract and Surrealist American Art)
1947 San Francisco Museum of Art, California
1949 Los Angeles County Museum of Art
1959 Pasadena Art Museum, California
1961 Downey Museum of Art, Downey, California
1963 Long Beach Museum of Art, California
1963 Dickson Art Center, University of California at Los Angeles
1963 Fischer Art Gallery, University of Southern California,
      Los Angeles
1964 Long Beach Museum of Art, Long Beach, California
1976 Painting and Sculpture in California: The Modern Era,
      San Francisco and Washington DC
1990 & 1992   Turning the Tide: Early Los Angeles Modernists
      (travelling, seven museums)
1992/3 Theme and Improvization: Kandinsky and the
      American Avantgarde (five museums)
2000 Los Angeles County Museum of Art: Made in California
      1900–2000
2001 Jack Rutberg Fine Arts, Los Angeles, California
2002 Pasadena Museum of California Art, Pasadena, California

Oskar Fischinger Filmography

1. *WAX EXPERIMENTS*, 1921–1926, 35mm, b/w-tinted, silent,
   lengths unknown; Moritz reconstruction, 1971, 16mm, b/w,
   silent, 11:15 min

Properly speaking, "wax experiments" should refer to two different types of technical experiments – those with wax modeling and those with wax slicing – and in both cases "wax" actually refers to a mixture of fine porcelain "kaolin"clay and wax, since plain wax by itself melted too easily and showed fingerprints and other blemishes too easily.

Of the first type, very little remains except a dozen still photos. One of these shows rows of geometric forms in staggered sizes, which most likely represent animation steps for making the forms – pyramids, for example – seem to grow larger and smaller. Half a dozen more photos show complex landscape or seascape surfaces with many ridges and furrows, probably made by pouring hot wax into cold water. Still half a dozen more show semi-abstract, amorphous forms which sometimes seem to represent grotesque figures hiding in caves, or microscopic lung tissue sections. The only example of the modelled wax footage to survive on film (two short, decayed pieces from a negative) is a brief one-minute fragment, *The Boxer*, which shows two fighters (wax puppets) beating each other out of shape while two water-boys, remarkably pre-figuring Donald Duck and Mickey Mouse, look on. The original of this film seemed very old (ca. 1922), and due to its brevity and representational mode, it is now attached to *Seelische Konstruktionen*.

Of the sliced-wax imagery, dozens of reels, mostly positive prints containing one or two minutes of footage each, were discovered among the Fischinger films. Most of these looked very old because of signs of decay and shrinkage. None of them seems to be coherent or whole, though most have been heavily edited. Probably film decay had caused many of them to be cut in pieces since, when a section of film within a reel melts together, as is often the case with old nitrate film too tightly wound, one can unreel the film up to that point and then cut away the damaged section, thus creating two smaller reels – the before and the after. However, we also know that Fischinger was still using wax footage in the 1926–27 light shows, and as backgrounds for *Seelische Konstruktionen*, and that selections of wax were included in the *Querschnitt aus Experimenten* [Selections from Experiments] reel which Fischinger ordinarily showed along with his other films during the early 1930s. So Oskar may have cut out some exceptionally nice parts for use then, and these parts would most likely be lost to us now, since the last print of a *Querschnitt* reel, a 1000-foot, tightly-wound copy, decomposed and had to be disposed of by Elfriede Fischinger in 1953.

From these surviving wax fragments, three batches have been transferred to 16mm safety masters. In 1968, through the help of the Creative Film Society, the longest wax reel was transferred and shown at a Fischinger retrospective in London; this reel, in fact, is quite atypical since it contains only a single basic image – a beautiful cluster of concentric irregular circles – with almost no movement throughout two minutes; perhaps this was an experiment with shooting two or three images for each slice of wax instead of the usual one-to-one ratio – and perhaps it remained intact because Oskar knew it was not dynamic and didn't want to use it later.

In 1970 I transferred a second reel composed of three fragments, together about two minutes long, containing a wide variety of imagery and movements, considerably edited. Most of these were pure wax-sliced images with forms ranging from irregular circles (like the first reel but faster moving) to rolling parallel bars. All of these are characterized by exquisite multi-hued texture and an interesting pattern of fluctuating motion. In 1971 I transferred three more pieces, a six-minute selection, which is now combined with the 1970 footage to form an 8-minute film, which is being screened and rented with the title *Wax Experiments*. This selection shows the variety of ways Fischinger used the sliced wax, and may approximate a film that Oskar would have edited and shown as his first film. It begins with a sequence of pure wax imagery from the second reel transferred in 1970, an image like a rose slowly opening its petals – perhaps the alchemical rose. Then follows a longer sequence composed of two fragments showing wax imagery combined with overlays of animated circle patterns, and a few moments of pure circle animation (presumably drawn on paper) which Oskar himself had edited into the wax footage; this sequence makes use of positive and negative images, as well as forward and backward printing of the same image, and some tinting, including a brief bit of "Stromlinien", Oskar's experiments with mixing coloured liquids. Finally a brief sequence shows some thin line animation similar to that in *Studie Nr. 1* and *Studie Nr. 2* superimposed over a wax background [including a moment in which three lines momentarily transform into "snakes" and bite each other's tails, like a ouroboros triad, then another sequence of the "alchemical rose" closing its petals again. In 2000, the Academy Film Archive made a 35mm preservation negative from the nitrate of a 400-foot *Wax Experiments* compilation.

The wax-sliced imagery has a rare beauty and complexity, and a lush softness matched only by the later films of Jordan Belson – who, by the way, had never seen any of Fischinger's wax films. It is a shame that Fischinger never returned to this technique during his mature period, although a number of late paintings (Space Spiral, Vortex, Space Abstraction, etc.) show that he kept the feeling and textures of these extraordinary films in mind. We must remember also that it is possible Fischinger had edited from wax imagery a memorable structured film which is now lost to us, perhaps with quite different visual textures and effects.

2. *ORGELSTABE/STAFFS*, 1923–27, 35mm, b/w, silent, 3 min

Thousands of feet, mostly positive, few negative, survive of the *Staffs* [Oskar's own translation of "Orgelstabe", which literally means "organ pipes". Like *Wax Experiments*, "Staffs" covers a variety of different experiments made with roughly the same technique during the Munich period. All of them are characterized by the basic imagery of hard-edged parallel bars moving up and down in rhythmic patterns; all were, I believe, prepared with cut-outs from paper, cardboard or wood. Sometimes the staffs are broad, sometimes thin; sometimes pointed, sometimes flat or rounded on top; sometimes black, sometimes white; sometimes simple, sometimes doubled in layers or doubled from both top and bottom of the film frame; sometimes moving against plain blank fields, sometimes combined with figured backgrounds ranging from live-action footage to amorphous, wax-like images.

I have transferred only two different selections of *Staffs* to 16mm masters. One of these is a three-minute reel showing the very simplest, basic staffs: white pointed bars (like a picket fence) moving up and down in an even row of waves against a plain black background [or, of course, if this were a negative, white staffs moving against a black background, which is how I prefer it ...]. In the closing moments of the reel, the size of some staffs escalates to a larger format, and they cross at diagonals. This may have been meant merely as an element in a more complex film image, but even so it exudes a classical simplicity (like Eggeling's *Diagonal Symphony*) which is very satisfying, and deserves to be seen on its own.

Additional "Staffs" imagery is encorporated into *R-1, a Formplay* (Filmography No. 6).

3. MISCELLANEOUS EXPERIMENTS, 1921–27

Also dating from the Munich period are fragments of other experiments besides the wax and staffs. A pitifully small amount of *Stromlinien* (*Currents*) survives: only a few feet of tinted images among the Wax footage. Since some of the chemicals used to dye film various colours may hasten decomposition, a considerable amount of this footage may have been lost. These few fragments and a few still photos and a five differently-tinted film frames mounted like slides in a cardboard display [perhaps to demonstrate available tints to customers] show swirling coloured liquids such as Fischinger had already experimented with in Frankfurt. Other stills from the Munich period show liquid flows superimposed either with modelled wax figures or with the title *Fieber* (Fever), about which we have newspaper comments but no known fragments: along with *Vacuum* and *Energy*, it was apparently planned as a multiple projector show [see Filmography No. 6] which may have included wax and staffs imagery as well as Stromlinien, although these three titles might also represent names for these three types of footage ...

There are also a number of very short fragments, only two or three feet long, including one in which a live cat jumps (probably by accident) on to the image of a surrealistic landscape which is lying flat on the animation stand; and one scene of a time-drawing of a series of overlapping arches, each progressively larger, which we can see on Fischinger's animation table in one still photo from Munich, and which appears in exactly the same form in the Bach segment of Walt Disney's *Fantasia* fifteen years later. Most of these fragments are probably trims, outs, or trials.

4. *SPIRALS*, ca. 1926, 35mm, b/w, silent, 6 min

One of these experimental pieces is so exquisite that it must have been planned as a film in its own right. *Spirals* seems to have been shot from pairs of glass discs which were painted in intricate configurations that create moiré patterns when they move against each other. As in Fischinger's best films, the imagery has a dynamic, cumulative effect, sometimes seemingly drawing you into a vortex, then suddenly reversing or shocking with a dramatic change of perspective, as when a bent vortex seems to focus us downward towards the bottom centre of the screen, causing curious sparkles of afterimages amongst the intersecting arcs above. Bursts of a few frames of footage here and there provide other surprises. At the end, a black circle grows in size to neutralize the hypnotic sensation of plunging forward. This seems to pre-figure the hypnotic meditational strategy of Oskar's silent *Radio Dynamics* from the early 1940s, and this spiritual orientation is not impossible, since we know that Oskar was exposed to Tibetan Buddhism at least as early as 1923 when Ruttmann worked on special effects [possibly including "wax slice" imagery] for the Wegener feature *Living Buddhas*.

I did not find any documentation that specifically seemed to refer to this film, but the footage seemed to have more integrity than random special effects or fragments of other films might produce. The film definitely dates from the middle 1920s, since some glass-plate photos from the Munich period show this "spiral" imagery. A still from Oskar's 1930 special effects for a documentary *Hohelied der Kraft* also shows imagery similar to some of the later sequences in the film – however, we know Oskar frequently re-used footage later to create backgrounds for colour films, etc. Elfriede Fischinger suggested the title *"Spirals"*.

I made a 16mm safety negative of *Spirals* in 1970. In 2000, the Academy Film Archive made a 35mm negative from the nitrate.

5. *MÜNCHENER BILDERBOGEN*, 1924–26, 35mm
PIERRETTE 1, 1924, 35mm, b/w, silent, length unknown

As discussed above (and in Filmography No. 9) Fischinger's exact role in the production of these films has not been proven, but it seems likely that he was largely responsible for basic design and artistic control, since Louis Seel himself seems mostly to have been out of town on business.

Fischinger and Seel signed a contract to produce films in March, 1924. The distribution company Messter-Ostermayr began to issue their Münchener Bilderbogen series in October 1924 with *Pierrette No. 1*. *Pierrette No. 2* followed in March 1925; *Amor und Almanach No. 1* [Love Almanach No. 1] appeared in January 1926; *Amor-und-Almanach No. 2* in March 1926; and *Pierrette No.3* in June 1926. A *Pierrette No. 4* was apparently in production in late 1926 when the company was dissolved. These films were distributed in Germany, Switzerland and Italy by Messter-Ostermayr and apparently Seel and his wife also took sales prints to America and Austria. In addition to the titles mentioned above, both Oskar and his brother Karl mention Oskar's having worked on a version of Gulliver's Travels; perhaps one of the "Amor" shorts might be a brief comic variation on the lilliputian theme.

In May 1927, just before leaving for Berlin, Fischinger corresponded with Kopia lab in Munich about getting a print of his film *Pierrette No. 1*, along with a German translation of the titles. I assume this is the one positive print which survives among his films, since that print is cut apart at many points where titles would have been. In the can (marked simply "Louis Seel Co.") I found twenty pieces of film, one about three minutes long and the rest much shorter segments. The longer piece contained about thirty splices which I assumed must preserve the proper order of scenes since Fischinger himself had made these splices; so I set about trying to attach the other fragments [always separated by five black frames to distinguish my splices from Oskar's] to either end of the longer piece to form some reasonable, sequential whole. Although one piece clearly represents the beginning (hands drawing Pierrette and her room) and many other pieces clearly fit together with each other, I have not been able to work out an intelligible plot or order. I am now sure Fischinger's spliced reel is not in sequential order (probably he merely spliced them together at random some time in order to have a duplicate negative or work-print made), and I am reasonably sure that the nearly complete footage (except the titles) is represented since the length is seven-and-a-half minutes as is.

There are five characters : Pierrette, Harlequin, Polichinelle, a romantic hero who is probably Mezzetin or Scaramouche, and the ugly, fat old villain-captain. The basic scenes seem to be as follows:

(1) Hands draw Pierrette and her room.

(2) Pierrette is lying on her bed; Polichinelle enters and they talk; noise of someone approaching; Polichinelle tries to hide under the bed, but it turns out to be only Harlequin; the three of them, after a conversation, dance off happily, arm-in-arm.

(3) [probably sequential to #2] Pierrette, Harlequin and Polichinelle dance into a stylized setting probably representing a forest or garden. Polichinelle draws on a "wall" a "screen" in which appears Harlequin playing his lute in a garret room, Polichinelle enters, the two change clothes, and dance off happily. They dance into Scaramouche's room where he languishes sadly. Then Scaramouche puts on the black cloak, hat and mask of a villain and stalks off. As this inset image and its "screen" fade out, the three viewers dance around with joy.

(4) Full-frame scenes show presumably the real actions which were just described or planned in the previous scene: Polichinelle and Harlequin exchange clothes, and go to visit Scaramouche who sits sadly playing the lute; they cajole Scaramouche into disguising himself as a villain.

(5) Harlequin, Pierrette and Polichinelle dance joyously into Pierrette's bedroom; a dark-cloaked villain enters; they greet him happily, and Harlequin and Polichinelle seem to "steal" (quite with her consent) Pierrette's ring and necklace, and give them to the villain.

(6) [perhaps a continuation] With Pierrette, Harlequin and Polichinelle sitting on the bed and a villain standing by, a second villain enters, and the first villain runs behind the bed. Pierrette, Harlequin and Polichinelle seize the second villain and begin to beat him; his mask comes off to reveal him to be Scaramouche.

(7) [probably sequential to # 6] Close-up of Scaramouche in his villain disguise, with titles reading "It was him again" and "the real fool". Cut to the old fat villain laughing in the back of Pierrette's bedroom.

(8) [parallel scene which probably happened earlier] Scaramouche in villain's disguise rises up from the bottom of the frame. The mask dissolves away to reveal his face. Cut to a shot of the old villain aghast [probably relates to scene # 12 and 15 below].

(9) In an extended scene, Harlequin, Polichinelle and Pierrette beat a villain. Finally, in anger, Pierrette throws out Harlequin and Polichinelle, and the villain, who must be Scaramouche. They wander off together weeping, and Pierrette throws herself down on her bed, also weeping.

(10) Pierrette is lying on her bed. Scaramouche enters, throws himself on his knees beside her bed and pleads with her. A live-action still photo of Polichinelle inside a heart appears, apparently indicating that Scaramouche is pleading for Polichinelle. Pierrette is adamant and Scaramouche leaves sadly. The same process is repeated twice more: Polichinelle pleads for Harlequin, and Harlequin pleads for Scaramouche, each represented by a photograph. Pierrette remains weeping after all three have gone.

(11) A ladder lies on the ground near a wall. A villain enters, raises the ladder stealthily and climbs up.

(12) The ladder is already up. A villain enters, looks around stealthily and climbs up.

(13) A villain climbs down the ladder, with a title, "As fast as he could".

(14) A villain enters a room in Pierrette's house, steals a necklace from a box on a small expressionist table, and leaves.

(15) In another room in Pierrette's house [we can tell from the "wallpaper"] two villains run into each other. They face one another menacingly and try to scare each other with threatening shudders. They fight. One loses and runs away [perhaps to scene #13].

In addition to these well-defined scenes, there are a few shots which could be inserted in several places: a close-up of Pierrette looking into an empty box, a close-up of Harlequin looking aghast, a scene of Scaramouche stalking down a Caligari-esque alley, and a close-up of the old villain frowning, then unmasked, then laughing.

The general arc of the story is clear – for some reason, Pierrette allows her jewels to be stolen [perhaps they were to be pawned and the proceeds would fund an escapade?], but a real thief actually steals them, and Pierrette is angry with all her suitors ... But the exact reasons and conclusions are not clear with most of the title cards missing, and possibly a few scenes of the picture as well. Any suggestions regarding logical plot lines from this material would be gratefully appreciated.

Fischinger's own scenario for *Pierrette No. 1* (see the Document section) shows that his original idea was considerably different from the finished material described above, with little concern for plot, full of imaginative and fantastic transformations. This also suggests a rapport between the Münchener Bilder -bogen and the series of fantastic drawings (see photos) from this period.

6. *R-1*, a Form-Play, 1926/27, 35mm, b/w and tinted, Possibly multiple projection piece, length unknown. Moritz interpretation: ca. 1980, 35mm, Cinemascope, colour, accompanied by sound on cassette tape, 7 min

The title *R-1, ein Formspiel von Oskar Fischinger* survived on two different films, one composed entirely of "Staffs" (q.v., no. 2 above) and one composed of small fragments of many different experiments – wax, model planets, atoms, etc. – including a great deal of staffs footage. Also seven other cans contained shorter fragments of edited footage of both types. From a title on one of the film cans (reading "regenbogen" [rainbow] in Oskar's handwriting) and the tinted fragments that survive, I suspected that the "R" in *R-1* was short for "Regenbogen", though it might also have represented "rolle" [reel], or "Raidon" [a private pseudonym of Oskar's, which occurred to him in a dream, and which he used on a number of works during the late 1920s.

In one can I found a consistent [unspliced] negative of about four minutes length which was cut unevenly in the middle of a frame, both at the beginning and the ending; in the same can were titles reading "R-1, Ein Formspiel von Oskar Fischinger" and a fragment of a few feet in length containing one shot tracking towards a stylized sun. Since there was extra room in this can which could have been used for more film (something almost unique among the 200 cans that Fischinger usually crammed full with little tightly-rolled fragments), I assumed Fischinger had meant these three pieces of film to go together. Consequently I spliced the title at the beginning and the tracking sun at the end, and transferred this to a 16mm master. In another can marked "regenbogen" were a dozen tinted fragments including one spliced positive print of about one minute length which corresponds to one section of the consistent negative print, but with certain shots tinted various colours. There also survived on GasparColor film a one-minute fragment corresponding to the central "staffs" section of *R-1* in which the footage has been tinted and printed on colour stock in several layers of superimposition so that one sees bright, multi-coloured staffs moving in front of a wine-coloured background. This fragment of coloured film was spliced together with some colour tests shot for Bela Gaspar in the fall of 1933 while the new GasparColor film and equipment were being perfected and tested. Half of these coloured staffs were silent, and half with a brief repeated phrase of delicate and soft orchestral music (a bridge passage from a popular Tosti concert aria "Ideale"). I assumed from this that the coloured staffs were also part of the GasparColor tests and that Oskar must have cut apart his old copies of *R-1* and had the laboratory print the tinted strips together to test this out as a possible colouring device, with silent and sound-tracked images. Another early colour experiment of Oskar's, the *Studie Nr. 11A*, also uses some coloured "Staffs" as background material, so he must have "dismembered" some of these older *R-1* prints to plunder that footage as well.

To judge from this evidence, then, *R-1* probably was a tinted film, and to further extrapolate from the large number of tinted fragments that survive, it may well have been one of the multiple-projector films *Fever*, *Power* or *Vacuum* which were mentioned several times in 1926 and 1927 in letters and newspaper articles, with mention of diverse musical accompaniment ranging from Erich Korngold's lush symphonic music to a "percussion ensemble". I carefully copied all of the nitrates related to *R-1* on to 16mm masters in 1970. Fortunately I was able to interview Alexander Laszlo, who had prepared performances of "Colour-Light-Music" in 1925 using only slides and conventional theatre spotlights with changing colour filters. Critics to his first attempts had observed that the colour projections were too static juxtaposed to the flowing Chopinesque music Laszlo composed. Laszlo then hired Oskar to create some moving images for him, but these proved overpoweringly modern and dynamic, so the Laszlo/Fischinger collaboration was cancelled after a few performances. Fischinger then went on to perform several multiple-projector visual-music concerts of his own, including an *R-1, a Form-Play* which Laszlo saw in Munich – went to see for the purpose of making sure Oskar was not using any of Laszlo's own material ... Laszlo confirmed that Oskar used five 35 mm projectors, three forming a triptych and two additional overlapping during the last minutes to provide additional colour effects – as well as some slide projectors with painted glass slides that provided framing and other coloured effects. That helps explain the large number of separate reels for this material. Since I had done some work with Light-Shows for Rock concerts in the 1960s, I also prepared a simulation of the multiple-projection performance (using five 16mm projectors and slides) which I performed about six times (including three perform-ances in Europe). For the closing section I used the GasparColor footage, which is undoubtedly more vivid and colourful than two layers of tinted film could have been in 1927. In 1980, Walter Schobert of the Deutsches Filmmuseum in Frankfurt, who had seen one of my reconstruction performances, offered me the funding to attempt a restoration of *R-1* on to a single 35 mm Cinemascope film. With the help of one of the Hollywood optical houses, I was able to prepare that 35 mm Cinemascope reconstruction, which has been shown regularly with Fischinger retrospectives world-wide. The negative is in the Frankfurt Filmmuseum. Laszlo said that the "percussion music" mentioned in documents from the 1920s as accompanying *R-1* was hardly music at all, rather a group of people trying to make more noise than the seven projectors [remember Laszlo was a confirmed symphonic romantic]. The oldest piece of percussion music I could find recorded was a piece called *Double Music* written and performed by Lou Harrison and John Cage in

1941. Since Fischinger knew these young composers at that time, it did not seem inappropriate to use the *Double Music* as a soundtrack for *R-1*. Both of the composers were quite gracious about allowing us the rights to use their music with the film.

In a letter dated 1927, Fischinger describes *R-1* in extravagant spiritual terms which seem quite suitable to describe this film as we have it (see documents section).

7. *SEELISCHE KONSTRUKTIONEN* (*Spiritual Constructions*), ca. 1927, 35mm, b/w, silent, length unknown; Moritz reconstruction, 1970, 16mm, b/w, sound, 7 min

Fischinger had several cans containing fragments of representational animation, mostly in a silhouette mode. I preserved a number of these on 16mm masters as examples of experiments, and three particular examples have been attached to the beginning of the 16mm master for the longer film *Seelische Konstruktionen* [Spiritual Constructions] to represent three different technical alternatives to the style finally adopted by Fischinger for one of his masterpieces. One of these examples is The Boxer (already mentioned under *Wax Experiments* above), two fragments from a film in which three-dimensional puppet figures were modelled out of kaolin and wax and bent into different positions; the film stock itself looked quite old, ca. 1922, yet the blend of form and content wherein two fighting men beat each other into various grotesque shapes prefigures *Spiritual Constructions* strongly, and might even have been a preliminary test to see if the whole film might have been animated in this technique.

The second example is a brief fragment of a scene that appears in *Spiritual Constructions* but rendered here in another technique: drawn on paper with charcoal, a man staggers into a room where the floor, table and clock all droop, warp and undulate so that the man falls. These charcoal drawings are much less satisfactory than the process finally adopted for the main film, namely figures are modelled and manipulated in a layer of kaolin/wax on a glass sheet with lighting from beneath, which renders opaque shapes in silhouette with smooth movements.

The third example is a brief scene in which much if not all of the animation is done with cut-outs from paper. In one scenario, Fischinger calls this sequence *Irene Tanzt* [Irene dances] and describes it as "Circus: Foxtrot" and "Circus: A Rhythmic Filmplay". The spectators and their boxes as well as the staffs are obviously cut-outs. Whether Irene herself (who also appears in this same dance movement in *Spiritual Constructions* where "he" changes into an ostrich instead of into staffs) is animated by cut-outs or wax is a moot point.

The long (nine minutes, silent speed) film *Spiritual Constructions* is the only substantial silhouette film to survive among Fischinger's films, and it survived only in poor condition. Three large reels contained fragments from two positive and one negative prints. The positives showed signs of tinting, and in each case the tinted film was badly decayed and had been cut away except for a few frames. The negative print had been cut apart at many places as well, sometimes to remove damaged footage and sometimes because I assumed it had once been edited in some A and B roll format and then later the blank footage (which seemed to be colour coded with orange and blue-green tint) had been removed. In addition to these three larger rolls, dozens of smaller rolls contained elements of individual scenes – figures without backgrounds, backgrounds without figures, figures with different backgrounds from those found in the final film, etc. By chance, these shorter fragments fell into my hands before I became aware of the longer rolls, so that when I came to the remains of the finished film itself, I at first assumed they were just further rolls of short pieces reeled together. However, as I began to unroll them, noting their subject matter and sequence, I realized that the scenes on the larger reels were consistently more finished and more often edited in a meaningful fashion, and that furthermore the three rolls each overlapped the others by about one half in subject matter and sequence, so that almost every scene was confirmed by a duplication. Through careful collation of the three prints, I was able to assemble a complete positive print (sometimes using a substitute scene from one of the short fragments when it was more complete or in better condition) except for one sequence which had to be supplied from a negative.

Let me stress that the editing of *Spiritual Constructions* is entirely Fischinger's – and entirely consistent with the experimental editing in Fischinger's other films of the period such as *R-1* and *Spirals*. One brilliant editing touch which shows how close Fischinger worked with the manipulation of form to express content occurs twice midway in the film. Once when the two men are fighting in front of a sunset background, there appear two black frames on which Fischinger has scratched first a small, then a larger burst of lines as if from an explosion, then he cuts back to the two men in the same positions but in front of a different indoor background. Once when one of the men is sitting down (and his body bends and droops to express his muscular sensations of relaxing) these scratched "explosions" centring in the man's body again accompany a change of context/setting and a repetition of the action. Scratching within the frame is also used to express raw energy or force in the sequence in which the fatter man is kicked out of the house and has a chamber pot dumped on him: the blows issuing from the house-door and even the bumps on the ground are represented by scratched contact points between the man and the object.

All of the metamorphoses of the settings and characters function as expressions of the two men's feelings, or to be more exact, their states of consciousness. Right in the opening sequence, we see the beginning of the argument in the form of a "freak-out" by the one man at being caressed by the other; this moment of intense panic is represented by the insertion of two frames of negative film in which the two men are seen all white against no background, and eight frames of positive film in which the two men are seen as silhouettes again but against a blank background, then back to the previous inn setting. This concretely suggests the momentary loss of sense of context or perspective which characterizes the begin-ning of many fits of temper.

Oskar further uses the sliced-wax imagery as a background in some scenes, which brilliantly suggests the sensation of viscous vagueness that often accompanies severe drunkenness. And this sense of texture is also made concrete late in the film when one man kneels to unlock his door and the surface of the house momentarily shoots out ameboid tendrils.

The general structural editing of the film is also remarkable, containing many repetitions, brief flashes of only a few frames as a premonition or reminder, alternations of positive and negative footage, and other experimental devices.

Despite this, the plot is clear and simple: two men drinking together in a bar become quite drunk, get into an argument, fight, and are finally thrown out, whereupon they stagger off to their houses and fall asleep. This linear reality of a plot is maintained with the simplest and most economic of means: one man faces left, and the other faces right. The perception or consciousness of the two men also vary in texture: one man's world is somewhat fatter and less detailed, while the other's tends toward intricate but always fluctuating images. And finally each of the two men is seen suffering exactly the same vicissitudes, both physical and mental

– moments of rage, moments of tenderness, moments of aggressive mastery and moments of helpless instability – which reinforces the irony of their stupid anger.

The film is a "meditation on violence" and into it Fischinger poured all his loathing of the German penchant for drunkenness and aggression which he had been able to witness first hand since his early childhood at the family brewery-inns. But at the same time he infuses the film with a serene sense (or experience) of consciousness which manifests itself constantly in new guises – now as a slow-motion animation [perhaps, by the way, the first use of this technique] of a man being kicked out of doors; now as a pair of heads that change themselves into everything from a Neanderthal man to the Munich Paulaner-Thomasbrau logo; now as the method of appearance, disappearance and warping of the ordinary furniture of life; now as the intrusion of alligators and ostriches and other impossible exotica; etc. – that finally transmutes the classic clown-pratfalls into a metaphysical instrument of celebration.

In reference to the dating of this film, some of the footage must surely have been made in Munich in 1926 or 1927 since a still photo of Oskar in his Munich studio shows pinned to the wall the charcoal time-drawing of one of the men's heads which appears towards the end of the film. Walter Jerven (op. cit.) also reports having seen Fischinger making silhouette animation with kaolin-wax shapes on a glass plate lit from beneath in Munich in January 1927. How much of this animation was for *Spiritual Constructions*, and whether any of the splendid editing was done at this time, we have no way of knowing. In December 1927, in Berlin, Fischinger wrote someone that he was working on a silhouette film, but gave no details; in 1929 he wrote to a popular author of humourous verse, Joachim Ringelnatz, to ask if he could supply a comic dialogue to accompany a silhouette film about two drunks. On the basis of these last two documents, I appended the date of 1927–29, Berlin, to the titles of the 16mm master of *Spiritual Constructions*, but we must bear in mind that some (and perhaps even all) of the film might have been made earlier in Munich.

The title *Seelische Konstruktionen* was derived from an undated scenario typed on paper Fischinger used during the Munich or very early Berlin period. This scenario clearly describes the opening scene with the two drunks, and also supplies the title, "How strange! As if the world were drunk!".

The only reference to a screening of the silhouette film is in a letter from September 1932, in which Fischinger asks for the return of a print of the film which had been shown successfully in Holland (probably at the Uitkijk in Amsterdam) and was then needed for a performance in Munich, where it would appear on a reel along with other of his silent films. The filmmuseum in Amsterdam has a small nitrate fragment of the opening scene of *Seelische Konstruktionen* in their collection.

The 16mm safety negative of *Seelische Konstruktionen* which I made in 1970 has been the basis for all subsequent rental and video prints, and was coupled with a musical score by Paul Bowles, "Music For a Farce" composed in the late 1930s for Orson Welles. Bowles graciously gave permission to use the score, which fits admirably.

8. *SINFLUT* Special Effects, 1927, 35mm, length unknown

For the feature film *Sintflut* ["Noah's Ark" or The Flood] Fischinger was hired by producer Erdmannsdorffer to prepare special effects sequences amounting to at least 70 metres of film actually used in the final feature (April 1927). The film as a whole was not a great commercial success, and Fischinger appears never to have been paid adequately for his work.

I have not been able to locate a print of the film, but from letters we know Fischinger prepared at least four sequences for the film: a scene in which two pagan idols gloat over the globe of the earth which is spinning in space, the building of the ark, the rains, and the loading of the animals into the ark. Still photos show the first and last of these sequences – the idols and the earth are modelled figures, but the animals loading into the ark are stylized silhouette figures. Notes indicate that the rains were created by dropping water through a sieve on to model landscapes (perhaps those seen in some other stills, maybe including the twisting "wax landscapes"). No surviving notes mention methods for building an ark.

Fischinger received screen credit for his work.

9. *MUNCHEN-BERLIN WANDERUNG*, 1927, b/w, silent, 4 min

In the summer of 1927, Fischinger walked from Munich to Berlin carrying his camera in a back-pack. Along the way he took single-frame images of certain people and landscapes he encountered. The resultant film survives in a single consistent 100 metre negative, of which the last quarter had been cut off by Fischinger himself and placed in one of the cans designated as first priority for transfer to safety film. Fortunately the cut was in the middle of a cluster of similar frames, so I was able to recognize and rejoin the two pieces, and transfer them to a 16mm safety negative.

Occasionally Fischinger took single frame shots with his movie camera in order to use the resultant film as 35mm negative for printing still photos. However, there is no question of that having been the object of the Munich-Berlin film since many of the sequences (e.g. the pea-pickers, the boaters, the sheep, the clouds) involve hundreds of consistent, even exposures calculated to produce a comic or magical time-lapse pixillation of the subjects involved. On the other hand, we have no record of Fischinger having shown the film publicly, so this remarkable achievement may have remained a private joke of Oskar's, albeit one he apparently prized.

Fischinger consciously had chosen a slow, back-road route, so the film provides a valuable documentation of the contemporary life of German peasants in semi-medieval villages with unpaved or cobbled streets and half-timbered houses.

More important, however, is the purely cinematic ambience of the film. The images are separated into clusters by white flash-frames, and each "cluster" consists of varying numbers of images from one single frame to several hundred sequential (stop-motion) frames. The glaring "blanks" between create an atmosphere of high tension in which the humour of the comic scenes seem heightened, and the time-lapse scenes of nature have an uncanny mystical quality.

Furthermore, the comic scenes divide themselves into two levels: those in which the people are working appear genuinely funny in the spontaneous cinematic vein of the best Mack Sennett comedies, while those in which the people are "at leisure" betray a gentle sadness in the subjects' almost grotesque failure to comprehend the new medium in which they are being recorded. The girls, the carousers at the inn, the children, the farmers, even the hoboes all try to pose, twitching rigidly in a pathetic attempt to freeze in a noble stance, almost a parody of the popular idea of still photography, still fatally linked to the Renaissance principles of portrait painting. This tension between the art and life of the past, present and future creates a keen metaphysical sensation of the medium, itself comparable to the best of the recent structural films.

Regardless of whether this film was ever seen publicly, it stands as one of the most important documents of Fischinger's innate genius, and serves to make us regret that he did not more often turn his attention to the manipulation of live photography.

At the time of the "Optical Poetry" Fischinger exhibition in 1993–94 at the Deutsches Filmmuseum in Frankfurt, Walter Schobert planned to have a whole room devoted to the Munich–Berlin trip, and borrowed the 35mm nitrate in order to make frame enlargements which would be mounted on a map on the walls, identifying the names of the sites and villages where Oskar had walked. Unfortunately the enlargement prints proved too costly, and this whole section was eliminated from the exhibition – and the nitrate remained in Frankfurt. Before taking the nitrate to Germany, I had a 35mm safety negative struck as protection. Unfortunately it was not completely even in exposure and no compensation was made frame by frame to guarantee a clear and correctly-lit rendition of each take. In 2000, the Academy Film Archive made a 35mm print from this negative which is adequate, but a few nice scenes are much too dark.

10. *DEIN SCHICKSAL*, 1928, 35mm, other details unknown

Fischinger later spoke proudly of having made a film for the leftist Sozial Demokratische Partei. A print of this film, *Dein Schicksal* [Your Fate], surfaced in an eastern archive only after the breakup of the communist-block hegemony in the early 1990s. I have it only on videotape, but it is clear that Oskar executed all the clever special-effects discussed in his notes and correspondence with Erno Metzner, the director of *Your Fate*, in February 1928. Fischinger Studio receives full screen credit for animated effects, a dozen sequences ranging from simple written texts that move through live-action sequences (a question mark flying out to show the indecision of voters, the word "Lockout" matted in beside workers trudging home), to several animated sequences including for the Communist party an elaborate merry-go-round on which sit various well-known political figures (half Russian, half German) exchanging their mounts and heads as their power and opinions change – and carefully checking their heads with the hat-check girls before entering political chambers. These communists are also seen falling off a cliff because they are blindfolded. Oskar also animated two sequences showing a typical undecided voter with his pipe and dog looking around in dismay and spitting.

The Central Party candidates are also represented by several animated sequences with a target radiating circles, a grinning coin-bodied figure of "Prices" climbing a ladder, "Profits" hitting wages and pensions with a hammer – all bearing the typical Fischinger cartoon face ...

No traces of any of these effects survived among Fischinger own nitrates.

11. UFA and *FRAU IM MOND* Special Effects, 1927–29, 35mm, b/w

Almost immediately upon his arrival in Berlin, Fischinger got some special effect work commissioned by UFA. In October, 1927, he prepared some dragonflies for an educational documentary film *Schopferin Natur* [Mother Nature the Creator], and the next month he prepared some effects for a feature film called *Welt Krieg, Zweiter Teil* [World War, Part 2], probably including a little fragment about 12 frames long showing an animated cannon shooting cyrillic letters, which survived among Oskar's nitrates.

By the middle of the next year, Fischinger was hired by Fritz Lang to help on the spectacular special effects needed for the science-fiction romance *Frau im Mond* [Woman in the Moon], which was released in 1929. Fischinger shared camera credit with Konstantin Tschetwerikoff, Curt Courant and Otto Kanturek; however, it seems that Fischinger may have done all of the "special effects" in the modern sense of animation and model illusions, while Courant and Kanturek filmed the dramatic acting scenes, and Tschetwerikoff created the live action trick scenes such as the boy and mouse floating in weightlessness or the scenes of take-off and landing involving live actors. Fischinger certainly prepared model rockets [a small model attached to a blowtorch to make the exhaust], starscapes made with holes in black velvet, a model of the moon's surface with the Earth rising behind (uncannily correct, as a photo taken by the actual moon landing 40 years later proved) as well as the skywriting of the word "start," the zero-gravity celebration with floating champagne, and the flying lettering of "gold" in the hallucinations of the professor on the moon.

No *Frau im Mond* materials survived among Fischinger's things, as everything would have belonged to UFA.

12. MISCELLANEOUS EARLY BERLIN WORK, 1929–1932

The most striking film fragments from the early Berlin period are a series of time-drawings signed "O.F. Raidon" and dated July 1929. At this time Fischinger was in hospital with a broken ankle, or had just been released and was still relatively incapacitated. These half-dozen time-drawings are charcoal sketches on white paper printed in negative like the black-and-white studies (which Fischinger began to devote himself to full time about then). Each is only about half a minute long, and shows one scene growing in detail. Some are abstract, but one shows the words, "Geld! Geld! GELD!" [gold or money] grow into, or rather get covered over, by a giant "FIEBER!" (cf. Frau im Mond). Another two-part image entitled "Der Unternehmer aus Verstandeskraft" [a difficult phrase to translate: perhaps "He who undertakes with intellectual power"] shows a man whose brain projects out of his eyes a complete range of modern technology – planes, cars, boats, sextant, etc. etc.

A similar effect occurs in a brief sequence in which letters appear spelling out the words, "Quatsch! Du Aas auf der Bassgeige," [colloquial, roughly, "Crap! You ass on the bass viol"] while forming the shape of a bass viol. Because of the movement of the letters, this effect must have been executed with some sort of sequential drawings or cut-outs. It may have been a "special effect" for some commercial film.

Another intriguing fragment is labelled "Studie Transmannfilm" and consists at first of a cluster of tiny rectangles climbing up the screen as they do in *Studie Nr. 6* or *Studie Nr. 8*. Then suddenly looms up from the distance a skeletal face wearing a war helmet, and the date "1914" and the word "KRIEG" [War]. While this sequence might be part of the effects for the 1927 film *World War Part 2*, the use of sophisticated abstract forms points more to 1930 as the date. However, it is hard to imagine how this fits into some other context. Nor am I sure who "Transmann" is.

Among other films we know Fischinger to have worked on during this period are an AAFA film from May 1928, directed by Obal, for which Fischinger designed seven special effects involving a heroine Spaventa and a hero Silvio (traditional commedia dell'arte characters); a film in which a tunnel is built between Europe and America; commercials for Axselrod's and Dr. Spieker's yoghurt; and "dancing stars and moon" for *Die Forster Christl* [Christy the Forester's Daughter] in November 1930.

From 1932, we know he produced a commercial called *Fiesta*, which may be the black-and-white Borg cigarette ad set to samba music, of which only the last minute survives in a nitrate copy. In 1971 I made a 16mm safety negative of this fragment, and in 2000 the Academy Film Archive made a 35mm preservation negative and print. If this is the 1932 *Fiesta*, it would also be Oskar's first cigarette advertising film. Also that same year Oskar made skywriting effects for a musical comedy *Das Blaue vom Himmel* [The Blue of Heaven] with a Billy Wilder script that required the hero (Hermann Thimig) to be forced to tell the heroine (Martha Eggert) that he loves her by skywriting "I Love You, Annie!". As the hit film sold to various foreign countries, Oskar was hired again and again to write the message in different languages.

13. *STUDIE Nr. 1*, 1929?, 35mm, b/w, silent, 4 min

Already in the 1930s when Fischinger gave retrospectives of his work, he would substitute a reel of "early experiments" in the *Studie Nr. 1* slot. Also he referred to *Studie Nr. 5* as *R-5* up into 1930, which might support the idea that *Staffs* and *R-1* (Filmography No. 2 and No. 6 above) were to be counted as *Studie Nr. 1*. However, there survives so much linear charcoal animation material from the late 1920s that it is just as well to consider one of these as the truer *Studie Nr. 1*, beginning of the long series of black-and-white musical-visual partnership.

The most likely candidate for this position is a four-minute film (which I transferred to a 16mm master in 1970) that is prefaced by a few frames of a title reading "Begleitet auf der Wurlitzer Orgel von Hans Albert Mattausch und Gert Thomas" [accompanied on the Wurlitzer Organ by Thomas and Mattausch, who were the house organists at the Kamera Unter den Linden theatre in Berlin where all of Fischinger's films were shown often. I have no notion what the music might have been – whether some well-known tune, or a fresh composition – or indeed if both organists played at the same time or alternately. The objects in this film are all single thin lines without shading. They sometimes group themselves into triads quite effectively. Occasionally they seem to "pop" and "go out" after having performed some graceful swirls and dynamic flows. The action definitely repeats in something like musical phrases. In the centre are two frames of sliced-wax images edited in between the "verses", perhaps at some cymbal crash or the like.

Some of the animation drawings themselves survive. They are on small sheets of un-numbered paper without registration holes, which places them before *Studie Nr. 3* which is already numbered. It is perhaps worth noting that during the 1940s when Fischinger had no access to his papers (which were stored in Germany), he wrote that the drawings for *Studie Nr. 1* had been destroyed.

I made a 16mm safety negative of "*Studie Nr. 1*" in 1970. In 2000, from a surviving nitrate spliced master positive, the Academy Film Archive made a new 35mm duplicate negative and prints.

Also from this earliest group of "studies" is an interesting minute-long fragment in which very long, thin, unshaded lines move about in a special way, entirely bound and contained within the frame line, as if trapped, often bouncing off the sides of the frame at an angle of reflection. Figures and movements similar to this are also seen superimposed over sliced-wax in the *Wax Experiments* (Filmography No. 1). I preserved this on 16mm in 1971.

14. *STUDIE Nr. 2*, ca. 1930, 35mm, b/w, sound (lost), 2 min

This study was synchronized to an Electrola recording No. EG 1663, a Spanish fandango, "Vaya, Veronica". I have been unable to locate a copy of this recording, and would be grateful for any help which might lead to obtaining a tape of this sound that might then be tracked on to the film so that it could be enjoyed in its original form.

One positive print, complete with titles, has been preserved in 35mm at the Cinémathèque Royale de Belgique, and I have transferred to a 16mm master another negative print without titles from Fischinger's own collection. There also survives on film a title giving the information about the "Vaya, Veronica" recording, dated 28 July 1930; however, the film may actually have been made earlier than that, and this title prepared specially for copyright reasons related to the music.

The style of *Studie Nr. 2* is very much like that of *Studie Nr. 1* with all thin-line, unshaded characters, most often in groups of threes, executing many of the "pop-explosions" and also some unique movements like frog hops and flying wedges.

The study is quite short – less than two minutes – and may have been the *Tanzende Linien* (Dancing Lines) film registered at the censor's on 7 August 1930 as No. 26538, a 61 metre film. No charcoal animation drawings survive for this film (cf. *Studie Nr. 1* above). In 2000, from a 35mm nitrate negative, the Academy Film Archive made a safety fine grain, a new duplicate negative, and prints.

15. *DAS HOHELIED DER KRAFT* (*The Hymn of Energy*) Special Effects, 1930, 35mm, other details unknown

In 1930, the Atelier Neuberger engaged Fischinger to prepare some extensive special effects for an hour-long science documentary *Das Hohelied der Kraft* [The Hymn of Energy], produced by Hubert Schonger and released in June 1930. I have not seen a print of this film, but I gather from a publicity brochure among Fischinger's papers that he animated images representative of electricity, including sub-atomic particles and molecules. Oskar's contribution did not receive screen credit, the special effects being listed only for Atelier Neuberger.

16. *STUDIE Nr. 3*, 1930, 35mm, b/w, sound (lost), 4 min

Studie Nr. 3 was synchronized to an Electrola recording No. EG1914, a Hungarian Foxtrot, "Vinka", by Will Coste. I have not been able to find a copy of the disc itself and any help with finding one would be appreciated. The sheet music (for a small jazz combo) survives among Fischinger's papers, and was performed with the film by Maurice Blackburn and other National Film Board musicians on the occasion of a Fischinger painting exhibition and film retrospective in Montreal in the late 1970s. The unique print of the film is preserved as a 35mm positive (and a 35mm safety negative) at the Cinémathèque Royale de Belgique, who kindly gave a 35mm safety positive to Mrs. Fischinger to complete her collection. All of the drawings, however, over 4000 of them, do survive in good condition.

The four-minute-long film seems very good seen silent. For the first time Fischinger uses solid, shaded characters – great fleshy comet-like bodies and flexible crescents, as well as a large mouth-like shape. These thick objects share the screen in complex patterns with the triplets of thin lines and popping explosions familiar from *Studie Nr. 1* and *Studie Nr. 2*. At one point there occurs a glimmering of the atom-splitting motif from *Studie Nr. 6* and *Studie Nr. 8*. This is, by the way, after eight or nine years of filmmaking, the first appearance in Fischinger's films of those sensual shapes reminiscent of Ruttmann's *Opus No. 1* and *Opus No. 2*.

Of the early studies, Fischinger himself was partial to *Studie Nr. 3* and it was always mentioned with praise in the reviews of screenings in Amsterdam, Berlin, etc., 1930–32.

17. *STUDIE Nr. 4* (? lost), 1930, 35mm, b/w, sound (lost), length unknown

Studie Nr. 4 was synchronized to an "English" waltz by Mischa Spoliansky, "Auf Wiedersehen", on Electrola disc No. EG 1714. Although I have never found this exact recording, the song appeared in a 1928 stage revue *Es liegt in der Luft* [It's Something in the Air] starring Marlene Dietrich and Margo Lion, for which a one-disc selection exists including a minute and a half of "Auf Wiedersehen", which appears to be catchy and charming, but quite repetitive: "Goodbye, Goodbye, See you again somewhere in this world, Goodbye, I know we have to meet again, so here till we meet again Goodbye ... etc". So it might be possible to restore the soundtrack from this disc. However, as far as I know, no print of this film survives. A set of about 600 numbered drawings with the title *Ein Spiel in Linien* [A play of lines] might well be the basis of *Studie Nr. 4*, since they contain some heavily shaded horizontal and vertical bars which could fall stylistically between *Studie Nr. 3* and *Studie Nr. 5*. However, in one letter to Ed Pelster of the Uitkijk theatre in Amsterdam dated November 1930, Fischinger lists *Studie Nr. 4* as being 90-100 metres long – like *Studie Nr. 5* and *Studie Nr. 3*. It would require six or seven repetitions of the 600 drawings to make up this length. And I don't think Oskar would have simply repeated the same animation drawings, even though the music is repetitive, but rather would have made some changes each time the refrain came back. It is tempting to think of *Liebesspiel* (Filmography No. 23 below) as possibly being *Studie Nr. 4*, since it definitely has a cyclical repetition pattern – but its use of tempera and large charcoal figures seems more advanced than *Studie Nr. 5* ... But Oskar himself wrote "Studie 4" on the nitrate can containing "Liebesspiel".

A negative of *Studie Nr. 4* should have been in Oskar's Berlin lab, and a print of the film was deposited with the state film archive in Germany in 1936 when the Fischingers left for America. If either survived the war, it would have been temporarily removed to Moscow, then recently returned to the "DDR" film archive, where it may be among the un-catalogued short films in their vast collection.

18. *STUDIE Nr. 5*, 1930, 35mm, b/w, sound, 3:15 min

For the music to this film, Fischinger chose a popular foxtrot, "I've Never Seen a Smile like Yours," that had appeared as a number in an American musical feature, *The Perfect Alibi*. Fischinger transforms the dance into a fantastic abstract ballet, in which two levels of "dancers" flow past and through each other: regular and orderly groups of thin-line, hard-edged figures (unmistakably male and female) which move in patterned configurations reminiscent of Busby Berkeley's later choreography, and extremely fluid, plastic figures which constantly change their consistency and size – fluttering, surging, swirling, melting across the screen like drops of water liberated from the laws of nature.

Studie Nr. 5 was registered with the censor 16 October 1930 as *R.5, Ein Spiel in Linien* [R-5, A Play of Lines], 89 metres long, and was given number 27152.

Studie Nr. 5 has been preserved as a 35mm safety duplicate negative with the help of the Creative Film Society.

19. *STUDIE Nr. 6*, 1930, 35mm, b/w, sound, 2 min

This little gem, next to *Studie Nr. 8* the best of the black-and-white studies, combines a jolly popular air with a clear statement of the profound mystical imagery exploited in Fischinger's later works, especially *Radio Dynamics*.

The music is a fandango, "Los Verderones" [finches] by Jacinto Guerrero, and the figures truly dance to the catchy rhythms. But beyond the barest requirements of choreography, there are two consistent patterns of interwoven imagery – one of flying objects in the warping currents of space (either inner or outer ...), and the second of the eye as a centre of focus – half target, half mandala exuding waves of vibrations. These two images (represented by broad fluid forms sweeping across the frame in fluxuating clusters) are linked by a pattern of dots that split like atoms again and again, sometimes seeming like a dynamic interchange between matter and space, and sometimes like darting points of focus or fragmentation of vision in the cosmic eye.

Studie Nr. 6 was registered as No. 27443, 58 metres long, on 14 November 1930. For the vicissitudes of the music rights and Paul Hindemith's alternate musical score, see the main text. A 35mm safety duplicate negative was made with the help of the Creative Film Society in 1968. The Academy Film Archive used a nitrate composite duplicate negative, probably made from a nitrate print by Oskar himself, to make a safety fine grain, safety duplicate negative and prints.

20. *STUDIE Nr. 7*, 1930–31, 35mm, b/w, sound, 2:30 min

For *Studie Nr. 7*, Fischinger found in Brahms' "Hungarian Dance No. 5" a perfect vehicle for his optical experiments. On one hand, the sharp fast rhythms are an ideal counterpoint for Oskar's first complete exploration of absolute darkness as a space matrix, with hard-edged shapes twisting, flickering and curving through it, rushing past the viewer, razor thin, with astounding illusions of depth. On the other hand, the sensuous gypsy violins are played off against soft but solid shapes that curl about each other with rich geometric languor. Altogether the images are an excellent culmination of the basic visual concepts Fischinger had been working out in the first six studies, wherein the figures gain a modicum of interest in themselves, but function primarily as tracers of complex space constructs. Conceived, charted and executed like the rest of the black-and-white studies with thousands of separate charcoal drawings on paper, the classically simple effects here are no less amazing in their own way than the astounding multiplicity of *Studie Nr. 8*, which was the first Fischinger film to gain wide popular acceptance. It played in first-run German theatres as a short subject with the première of the feature film *Ariane*, starring Elizabeth Bergner and Willi Forster. Already by the summer of 1931, it was playing in America as well.

Studie Nr. 7 was registered with the censor as No. 28290, 73 metres long, on 20 February 1931. Creative Film Society made a 35mm safety duplicate negative of *Studie Nr. 7* in 1969, and the Cinémathèque Québécoise also struck a 35mm preservation negative [together with *Studie Nr. 11* to exceed the laboratory's minimum charge] in the 1970s.

21. *STUDIE Nr. 8*, 1931, 35mm, b/w, sound, 5 min

One of the original German prints of *Studie Nr. 8* ended with a title reading, "Left unfinished, February and March, 1930" [surely a mistake for 1931]. At that time Fischinger did not have enough money to buy the rights for the second half of Dukas' "The Sorcerer's Apprentice". Despite the lack of the finished ending of the music, this study remains the most complex, most stunning, and for Oskar himself the favourite and most important of the black-and-white films.

Fischinger makes no attempt to tell Goethe's story of the magician's helper (Disney was to do that ten years later) but instead he uses the textures and movements of the sounds themselves as the jumping off point for creating an especially rich world in which a multiplicity of forms and movements perform in a deep environment. Rectangles slink across the screen by rippling their contents through their volumes, then slide off into the distance, hovering in space as pure lines, then suddenly swing into action again, pivoting from one corner like fans. Over and over again rectangles split in chain reactions, first as if they were merely being stretched and warped by a distorting mirror, then more positively into twos, then threes, then fours. Amorphous forms describe a series of fluid metamorphoses, one time curling into art nouveau swirls, one time flying apart as straight lines in various directions. Clusters of sharp crescents sweep into the frame from all sides, then suddenly melt into incredibly soft, sensuous swirls.

All of these disparate elements are cleverly balanced on the plane of time so that the action of the film becomes the tension between basic artistic polarities – shape vs. content, random grouping vs. ordered patterns, simple vs. complex structures, etc. – which are seen as mirrors of basic yin-yang polarities in the universe itself. Would the ending of the film have been able to provide a resolution to these tensions? We can never know, but as the film now stands, it is, like Goethe's *Faust*, a mirror of life itself: no resolution, continuous striving.

Fischinger was very proud of the "atom-splitting" sequence, and used to mention it in lectures along with the possible allegorical interpretation of Goethe's tale from the point of view of nuclear fission, a remarkable premonition for 1931, but not unlikely given Oskar's "space" contacts from the Fritz Lang film, and his avid study of scientific journals in Berlin libraries.

Studie Nr. 8 was registered with the censors as No. 29928, 126 metres long, on 17 September 1931. It must have been "finished" several months before, however, probably in March 1931, and Fischinger delayed registering it until he had really lost hope of purchasing the music rights to part two and completing the second half of the film. The film was nonetheless distributed with its "broken-off" ending, and a 35mm safety negative was struck from Oskar's one nitrate print in 1968.

A single nitrate print preserved in the Danish film archive is prefaced by a Dutch-language title card identifying it as a special print meant only for projection at the Uitkijk cinema in Amsterdam, and this copy ends with the final two bars of Dukas' "Sorcerer" music, animated by Oskar, to provide a suitable finish to the film. Ed Pelster apparently paid for the music rights to this brief "finale", and the unique print made its way to Denmark during the war years. Ib Monty of the Danish Film Archive gave Elfriede Fischinger a print from his preservation negative.

22. *STUDIE Nr. 9*, 1931, 35mm, b/w, sound, 3 min

Studie Nr. 9 was registered with the censor as no. 29830, 81 metres long, on 9 September 1931. However, a letter dated in July 1931 says that *Studie Nr. 9* was already finished and available then.

This was the first personal art film of Oskar's which someone else worked on, in this case, his brother Hans. The basic designs for forms and movements were all made by Oskar, and Hans was assigned to complete the sequences, filling in the shadings on the outlined shapes as an apprentice, learning exercise. Hans made a number of changes in Oskar's work method. Oskar had drawn exclusively with charcoal, creating shadings with smudges or light, feathery strokes. Oskar had held the animation papers steady with only a series of nails placed around the edges of the glass plate where the papers were placed during drawing and shooting – doubly remarkable when you consider the incredible steady, smooth flow of the figures in the first eight studies. With more people handling the drawings, it became necessary to punch them with registration holes. Hans also insisted on codifying the shadings (perhaps also a necessity when trying to carry out plans of another artist) by using poster colours and inks which could be mixed in almost endless gradations of grey that could then be numbered and manipulated with great accuracy. The wet-painted shapes, however, tend to look. sharper, clearer, and a bit more stylized than Oskar's charcoal-drawn shapes.

The images in *Studie Nr. 9* are synchronized with Brahms' "Hungarian Dance No. 6", probably in response to the immense success of *Studie Nr. 7*. The graceful figures perform charming choreography which makes *Studie Nr. 9* one of the most pleasing of the series.

The most memorable moment is a sparkling sequence in which dots and rays bounce off a semi-circle, flickering and dividing in conscious interplay with their own after-images, a further extension into pure optics of Oskar's ideas about atom-splitting.

A 35mm safety duplicate negative was prepared in 1969 with the help of the Creative Film Society. No further preservation has been done.

23. *LIEBESSPIEL (Love Games)*, ca. 1934, 35mm, b/w, silent?, 2 min

This film survived in two positive and one negative print, and a series of drawings. All are without titles, but the drawings were labelled in Oskar's handwriting "STUMM!" [silent] in several places, indicating, I assume, that he intended the film to he silent. In one place a label also read, "Oskar stumm wanderung" [Oskar silent journey or meandering] which might indicate an intended title "Wanderung", or that the film was composed while Oskar was on one of his walking trips, or simply that it was an improvisation without a strict musical chart. The currently used title *Liebesspiel* [Love-games] was suggested by Elfriede Fischinger, who said that Oskar sometimes used that word in relationship to love and reproduction, the possible abstract subject of the film.

The drawings are executed primarily with charcoal (there are only a few touches – especially one exquisite overlap of the two principal figures – done with poster colours) on the 9" by 12" paper with registration holes, the same as used for *Studie Nr. 9* and *Studie Nr. 10*, which suggests that it is Oskar's work from 1931 – although nothing in the documents suggests that Oskar undertook such a project then, nor did Elfriede or Trudl recognize it as something they had seen or heard of. Yet Oskar himself [admittedly while aged and in ill health] wrote on the can containing the nitrate print *Studie Nr. 4*. The first 3500 drawings correspond to the film as we see it, but a further 1000 drawings extend the action into another phase (in which squared shapes begin to re-enact the patterns performed by the rounded "comets" in the first part) without, seemingly, any satisfactory conclusion. All three nitrate prints consist only of drawings 1–3536 without much of this "second verse" additional material, so when I prepared the 16mm safety negative, I stopped a few dozen frames before the end of the nitrate copy at a "fade out" point which seems like a logical conclusion, one which I feel Oskar would approve for screenings, which he liked tidy.

Two other possibilities for this footage are *Studie Nr. 4* or *Studie Nr. 13*. Although the paper drawings do not exactly match how those studies might be expected to be rendered, both of the musical scores have a long sequence of sweeping, flowing repetitions, which might correspond to the sensuous meanderings of "Liebesspiel" – but without the exact soundtrack that Oskar used for *No. 4* or *No. 13*, it is hard to check if Oskar's usual tight synch occurs.

In any case, "Liebesspiel" has a classical simplicity unique among Fischinger's work, with a clear sense of phrasing, development and beautiful spatial construction which mark it as his most perfect transcreation in a visual format of the basic musical ideas of melody and harmonies as they might occur in a song or lyrical air. It is significant in this respect that his efforts here were apparently not tied down to a specific piece of music, but rather bent on re-creating in visual terms certain pure concepts, best known otherwise through music. First one, then two, then three similar, comet-like characters (representing the "male principle" in Hindu philosophy) describe an intricate space construct. Then three crescent shapes (representing the "female principle") appear and perform more sensuous clusters of movements, at the climax of which they swallow up the "male" comets. Then one "female" crescent and one "male" comet swirl about until the "male" comet penetrates and melts into the "female" crescent which then grows into a large perfect circle that bursts into a dozen smaller pairs of comets and crescents.

Finally the whole field of action is again swallowed up by a giant circle which appears as if from behind the spectator and is in turn pierced by a flying wedge as it shrinks away in the distance.

The action is frankly and simply erotic, in the way tantric mandalas are often sensuous in expressing the yin-yang, male/female duality principle. The reproductive conclusion is exquisitely beautiful in its balanced form.

I made a 16mm safety negative of *Liebesspiel* (not including the last few feet of "other" footage) in 1970. In 2000, the Academy Film Archive made a 35mm preservation negative of the entire nitrate, including the brief bit of "other" footage at the end.

24. *STUDIE Nr. 10*, 1932, 35mm, b/w, sound, 4:30 min

Oskar had begun working on the ballet music from Verdi's opera *Aida* about the same time as his work on "The Sorcerer's Apprentice" for *Studie Nr. 8*. Family affairs and commercial business interrupted the work late in1930, and the charcoal drawings for the first minute of film lay idle for several months until later in 1931 when Oskar's younger brother Hans was assigned to fill out and execute the rest of the piece. Although following the plans Oskar had already charted, Hans tended to render the shapes with the sharper, more streamlined style he had worked out on *Studie Nr. 9*. Furthermore, he went back over some of Oskar's charcoals and added details with grey tempera. The result is an exciting synthesis of the styles of the two artists: Oskar's loose, flexible and soft images with Hans' tight, hard-edged images. They work especially well together in complex scenes that utilize a full range of grey tones to give the illusion of a deep field of action with several layers of figures interacting, as when "arrows" seem to pierce the black screen and disappear into the distance leaving holes behind, or when thick swaying crescents suddenly turn inside out and wiggle away as thin "eels".

Studie Nr. 10 was registered at 110 metres in October 1932, but we know it was shown already in the spring of 1932, so it seems likely that the censor registration may have been delayed because of problems with the music rights (that were resolved around October) which in this case were confused by the fact that Ricordi, the music publisher, had ceded performance rights for this popular opera to various agents in each country. The film itself may have been finished as early as December 1931.

A 35mm safety duplicate negative of *Studie Nr. 10* was made in 1969 with the help of the Creative Film Society, however the sound quality was somewhat weak, and either another nitrate print or some high-tech sound refurbishing were needed. In the 1970s, the Cinémathèque Québécoise attempted to match a more modern recording to an existent print, which unfortunately contained a splice which was simulated by a brief cut in the music to maintain synch.

25. *STUDIE Nr. 11*, 1932, 35mm, b/w, sound, 4 min

The unusually large selection of sketches and drawings for *Studie Nr. 11* that survive allow us to see concretely some aspects of Fischinger's work methods and theories. Oskar began with several pages of sketches of rococo design – corbels to consoles – which he re-drew, gradually simplifying and abstracting them into pure geometric swirls, curls, etc. (see pp. 68–69). These abstracted forms – linear curling outlines – were then plotted out as the trajectories for the moving figures in the film, rather than as the shapes of the figures themselves. Clearly, then, Fischinger saw the total patterns described by the figures in his films [the choreography] as being of prime importance, and the relationship between the music and visuals (sound and ornamentation, as he was calling his concurrent experiments with drawing synthetic soundtracks) depends more on the pure cinematic values of timing and motion than on the surface qualities of the figures in any one still frame.

The elegant music of the minuet from Mozart's "Eine Kleine Nachtmusik" provides a slow, luxurious, and refined showcase for Oskar's rococo spatial movements which emerge as ribbon-like strips undulating, furling, and uncoiling, less like "dancers" than the figures in some of the other studies, and more like actual manifestations of the music itself (see also *Studie Nr. 12*, and *Spiel in Farben*, numbers 26 and 33 in this Filmography).

I have found no record of the registration of *Studie Nr. 11*. We know it was not yet ready by May 1932 when *Studie Nr. 12* was premièred, and it is not on the programme of the Fischinger retrospective in Munich in October 1932. But Fischinger had been working on it since 1931, and implied in a letter that it was nearly finished in February 1932. Perhaps the interruptions caused by *Coloratura*, and other commission work delayed the completion. And if it were not finished until 1933, most likely the Nazi censors would have denied an official permission to screen this "degenerate" abstraction. In any case, it would hardly have had a chance to be exploited before the craze for colour began.

Studie Nr. 11 was preserved on an excellent 35mm safety duplicate negative with the help of the Creative Film Society. Cinémathèque Québécoise also made a safety preservation negative together with *Studie Nr. 7*.

26. *STUDIE Nr. 12*, 1932, 35mm, b/w, sound, 4:30 min

Studie Nr. 12 is pure Hans Fischinger. As far as we know, he designed and executed it entirely by himself, but the original German title read: "Schule Oskar Fischinger ... Gezeichnet von Hans Fischinger, Leitung Oskar Fischinger" [School of Oskar Fischinger, drawn by Hans Fischinger, directed by O.F.]. Oskar's role of "director" was probably not very great, and Hans felt Oskar unjustly accepted the credit for it. Diebold's lecture for the première at the Kamera theatre in Berlin, in May 1932, was (justifiably) a lecture about Oskar and his achievement – but Hans wanted full, sole credit, and the issue was the key factor in the split between the brothers.

Hans' streamlined, eel-like figures execute slow movements to the "Candle Dance of the Kashmiri Brides" from Anton Rubinstein's opera *Feramors* (also known as *Lalla Rookh*). The leisurely pacing make this an excellent companion-piece to Oskar's *Studie Nr. 11*. A comparison will remind us (among other observations already noted with *Studie Nr. 9* and *Nr. 10*) that Hans tends to treat the screen as a relatively flat area, with the figures moving on a shallow stage or plane surface, whereas Oskar handles the screen as a window opening on deep, dark space with figures moving through it in three dimensions. Two clear examples of this are the movements of Hans' pair of "lovers" as opposed to Oskar's rippling bands (or Oskar's pair of lovers from *Liebesspiel*), and the overlap of Hans' static clusters of rectangles with each preceding group fading out, as opposed to Oskar's falling clusters of rectangles which swirl and intersect, meshing like flurries of leaves. Both styles have their charm, and both sustain an aesthetic integrity, so it is hard not to feel that both *Studie Nr. 11* and *Studie Nr. 12* have about them the expansive feeling of a master come to the ripe end of a series.

Studie Nr. 12 was registered on 4 June 1932 as no. 31663, at 133 metres – the longest of the black-and-white studies. A 35mm safety negative of *Studie Nr. 12* was made with the help of the Creative Film Society in 1969.

27. *KOLORATUREN*, 1932, 35mm, b/w, sound, 2:30 min

Koloraturen (Coloratura) was commissioned by Froelich Film as a trailer to their feature *Gitta Entdeckt ihr Herz* [Gitta Finds Her Heart], starring a popular opera singer who enjoyed a successful career in light comedy film, equivalent, perhaps, to Jeanette McDonald. One hears Gitta singing, but sees only Fischinger's abstract designs, and originally the film ended with a question mark, which was planned to incite the audience to guess the name of the singer, film, etc. After the first run of the film, the full rights reverted to Fischinger, and he removed the question mark.

The film was ordered as a rush job, and had to be delivered in three weeks. Fischinger locked himself in and worked steadily, completing it on time. Yet despite the rush, it shows no lack of care, no signs of haste. It is just as complicated and detailed as the other black-and-white studies, in fact containing the most sensational sequence in the whole series – the whirlpool and wipes that accompany Gitta's final high note. *Coloratura* was ordered, completed, and shown in March 1932.

A 35mm safety negative was made in 1970 with the help of the Creative Film Society, however the sound quality was weak and needed to be re-recorded either from another release print or the original optical track, which also survives in Fischinger's collection. In 2000, the Academy Film Archive made a preservation negative from a composite nitrate print, preserved the track from that print and struck new prints with better sound quality.

28. *ORNAMENT SOUND* EXPERIMENTS, 1932, 35mm, b/w, sound, 4 min

Several reels of sound experiments from 1932 survive in marginal condition, irregularly shrunken, able to be run only once, at which time many of the sprockets will be punched out. At that first time, then, the whole, continuous soundtrack area must be photographed in order to preserve the visual aspect of the ornaments, and I have had no access to a printer without a frame-line. In 1972, however, Fotokem managed to make 16mm safety copies of another sequence of 1932 *Ornament Sound*, which includes some simple tests with different kinds of shapes, as well as a brief fragment of the German folk-song "Fuchs, Du hast die Gans gestohlen" [Fox, you stole the Goose!], which proves that Oskar could also "write out" conventional music with his drawn soundtrack. Fotokem double printed the ornaments so that they appeared directly in the soundtrack area, as Oskar had shot them, but also along the edge of the picture area, suitably adjusted so that you see exactly the shape that is creating the sound you hear at that same moment. This selection seems to give a good overview of Oskar's experiments with ornaments, although a number of shapes that appear in 1932 newspapers are not represented in the bits transfered to safety film.

29. *EINE VIERTELSTUNDE GROSSSTADTSTATISTIK*, 1933, 35mm

Eine Viertelstunde Grossstadtstatistik [A Quarter Hour of City Statistics] was commissioned by Cabinet Film, Toni Attenberger, Munich, in July 1933. Attenberger specialized in producing educational documentaries (for the showing of which theatres received a tax rebate) on the basis of one a month to keep up a constant supply of new ones. This film was so unimaginative and boring, albeit well paid, that Fischinger could not bear to work on it himself, so he hired as a special assistant animator Peter Sachs who had formerly worked for George Pal, who had fled immediately when the Nazis came to power and left his staff suddenly unemployed. Sachs also reports that it was the most tedious job of his life. I have not tried to locate a print of this film.

30. *STUDIE Nr. 14*, ca. 1933, exists only as original animation drawings; Moritz reconstruction, 1996, b/w, silent, 2 min

At the time Hans quarrelled with Oskar and left Berlin to return to Alzenau, he was working on a film synchronized to Brahms' "Hungarian Dance No. 3". He left behind him in Berlin a sequence of 2000 drawings specifically labelled as belonging to "Hungarian Dance No. 3", and a second bundle of 4000 drawings (not numbered consecutively with the first bunch) which is unlabelled but might belong either to "Hungarian Dance No. 3" or to the Brahms' "Hungarian Dance No. 1", which was also a current project in the Fischinger Studio. If the second bundle belongs to the "Dance No. 3" (and some repetition connects it in number to the first bundle) then the drawings for that film must be relatively complete, since the "Dance No. 3" is quite short.

The designs are again pure Hans, containing grids of squares which fade and overlay, as well as a startling image of a dozen blade-like figures interlocked like a roll of barbed-wire in a complex column down the centre of the frame.

I shot some of these drawings on to 16mm film in 1996, but have not experimented with trying to synch them with music.

31. *STUDIE Nr. 13* (Coriolan Fragment), 1933/34, 35mm, b/w, sound, 1 min

In July 1934, Fischinger had an optical soundtrack transferred as the music for *Studie Nr. 13*, which would have been Beethoven's "Coriolan Overture", a pet project which Oskar had been listing for over a year as a work in progress. A half-minute fragment of film and the corresponding animation drawings are considerably shorter than the 120 metres listed as the film's length (and approximately the length of the Beethoven score).

The unfinished segment contains some striking images – a twisting, claw-like cluster of circles/crescents, which swirl out towards the viewer, enveloping the whole screen. This obviously represents the rumbling orchestral clashes at the beginning of the music. A second image shows several grey ovals which contain inside them a small black area that moves somewhat independently of the surrounding mass. We can only regret that Oskar did not complete the "Coriolan" since he seems to be meeting the dramatic, almost flamboyant demands of the romantic music with correspondingly unusual images which remain unique in the Fischinger canon. The lovely repetitive melody for strings that follows this raucous opening might possibly correspond to the swirling comets of "*Liebesspiel*", but this would have to be tested with the exact musical rendition that Oskar intended to use, since he carefully synchronized the imagery to a certain pre-recorded soundtrack, which in the case of *Coriolan* does not seem to have survived.

In 1970, I made a 16mm master of the "Coriolan" fragments, but unfortunately by mistake I ran it after some silent fragments and left the frame alignment fully open so that the soundtrack area (blank black) is visible to one side. In 2000, the Academy Film Archive made a silent 35mm preservation negative of the *Studie Nr. 13* fragment, from a silent nitrate print.

32. *KREISE*, 1933, 35mm, colour, sound, 2 min

Kreise [Circles] was commissioned by the Tolirag advertising agency as a commercial for themselves. Working from the slogan, "Alle Kreise erfasst Tolirag" [Tolirag reaches all circles of society], Fischinger prepared a free-form composition for richly-coloured circles which radiate, fly, flash, interlink and surge past the viewer in triumphant bands. From a purely visual standpoint, it is one of Fischinger's finest achievements. Every one of the 1000 animation paintings is an interesting art work in itself, prefiguring, say, Frank Stella's serial work with coloured circles and arcs.

The first part of the film, synchronized with some of the Venusberg ballet music from Wagner's *Tannhauser* was made with black-and-white images (charcoal and poster paint, like the studies) which were tinted with coloured filters during the printing process. In several cases there are three layers of images, and they overlap in interesting opaque and translucent combinations. The second part, synchronized to the ending of Grieg's "Huldigungs March" from *Sigurd Jorsalfar*, was painted on paper with poster colours. In the original, these circles appeared against a white background, and the letters spelling "Alle Kreise Erfasst Tolirag" were intertwined among the circles during the last few seconds. This version, released in December 1933, caused a sensation, partly because it was probably the first European film made with a three-colour-separation process, and the resultant colours were much more brilliant and varied than those ever seen before. The film was further sold to several more companies in different countries who merely substituted their own firm name for "Tolirag".

In six months, all rights reverted to Fischinger, and he re-photographed the ending with retouched drawings so that the whole film would be purely abstract. In the process, he had the colours printed in negative, or reverse from how they had been in the earlier version, i.e. so that the circles move against a black background. The reversed colours are somewhat more balanced and orthodox than those in the advertisement, so Oskar probably planned ahead on this last reversed version as the definitive artwork. The abstract version was premièred in July 1934, despite the Nazi ban on abstract art, using the censorship approval number of the advertisement.

A 35mm safety negative was made by the Library of Congress in Washington, DC from an old print of the pure abstract version which Fischinger had loaned to Rebay who kept it in her collection, which later passed to the Guggenheim Foundation, then to the American Film Institute then to the Library of Congress.

Only one print of the original Tolirag ending survived among Fischinger's films, and a safety negative from this is currently being used as a master for printing 16mm copies. The Fischinger estate contains several 35mm nitrate prints of the abstract version which were not properly copied until the Academy Film Archive prepared 35mm preservation materials in 2000. The best surviving GasparColor nitrate print was used for preservation of the abstract version. The Tolirag version was preserved by using a nitrate successive exposure negative for the second half, and using part of the abstract version for the first half.

33. *EIN SPIEL IN FARBEN* (*A Play in Colours*), 1934, 35mm, colour, sound, 3 min

In the wake of the brilliant *Circles*, Fischinger attempted as an experiment colouring one of his black-and-white studies, *Studie Nr. 11*, which had been denied a censorship number by the Nazis, and consequently not screened at all. The opportunity was supplied by the AAFA film company, which wanted a vehicle, possibly an advertisement, for a two-colour process that they were trying to exploit. In addition to the animation drawings from *Studie Nr. 11*, Oskar also used some "Staffs" footage and other background materials (including a rather vaginal image) that he had on hand from his older films. The results – quite top-heavy with orange, pastel cerulean blue and lime green – are quite un-rococo, and so dissatisfying to Oskar that he never exploited this colour version, either, beyond its original commitment as an advertising film for the AAFA company. Perhaps to modern eyes, the film does not seem so inadequate, yet to Fischinger a crucial aesthetic question arose. In the black-and-white films, the figures could be used as pure light sources, absolute counters with little importance in themselves as shapes, but rather with meaning in the actions they describe or perform. As soon as colour is introduced, however, the pure abstraction of the figures is compromised; they become objects in a display, characters which must have individual values since they are part of a differentiated light spectrum. This hybrid is simply less satisfactory than his pure black-and-white or his pure colour creations, and Fischinger never attempted such a hybrid again.

Two 35mm nitrate prints of "Studie 11A" material survive among Fischinger's films, one of which has been spliced in the middle to remove a long repetition, and that excised sequence constitutes the second print. Obviously Oskar was so dissatisfied with the film that he tried to shorten it, to make it more bearable. In 1971, a few 16mm prints were struck as direct reductions from each nitrate, but no negative or preservation master was made. In 2000, the Academy Film Archive made a preservation negative of *Studie Nr. 11A* from one of the surviving nitrate prints.

The title *Ein Spiel in Farben* [A Play in Colours] or *Studie Nr. 11a*, was registered as 53 metres, 12 February 1934.

34. *QUADRATE* (Squares), 1934, 35mm, colour, silent, 4 min

Quadrate [Squares] was painted in tempera like the closing section of *Kreise*. Oskar later dated the drawings July 1934, but they may have been made somewhat earlier. The drawings are numbered 1–2505 to 1–2776, indicating perhaps that they were once planned as part of some larger film. In any case, Fischinger had these 271 drawings photographed and loop-printed so that they appeared several times in the same and different colour combinations, positive and negative (which was easily possible by manipulating the filters used to print out the three-colour separation master). Unfortunately the only surviving 35mm nitrate print, a short fragment, has a light leak in one corner.

We have no indication of any sound for this film, or of any public showing. Elfriede Fischinger believes that Oskar hoped to sell it as a commercial (but why, then, not sell it to AAFA instead of the less-satisfactory *Studie Nr. 11A*, or to Farver instead of *Kreise*?). In any case, the serene flow of square shapes in different colours is one of Fischinger's most striking, interesting, and important compositions, prefiguring *Radio Dynamics*. The animation paintings, like those of *Kreise*, are each art works in themselves, prefiguring the balancing squares of Josef Albers.

A 35mm three-colour-separation master, in poor shape, was not preserved in 1970. The defective 35mm nitrate positive print was copied only in 16mm. The animation paintings themselves were rephotographed on 16mm ECO by Bob Konikow in 1972, and the results combined in positive and negative with the 16mm footage from the nitrate to give a vague approximation of Oskar's original intentions of having the loop repeat for some time with various changes of colour. In 2000, the Academy Film Archive made 35mm preservation elements from the nitrate successive exposure negative, and recombined materials to make a 35mm negative and prints with four different combinations of the colour records, creating repetitions to suggest something of the original intentions.

35. *MURATTI GREIFT EIN*, 1934, 35mm, colour, sound, 3 min

Every syllable of extravagant praise which has been lavished on the colour Muratti ad is totally justified by the wonderful film – a creation of absolute delight. Here the pop-classic music – excerpts from Josef Bayer's once popular ballet *Die Puppenfee* [The Dollfairy] – fits appropriately to the mad-cap antics of walking cigarettes.

Fischinger carefully builds up our sense of belief in this impossible world, first by ingeniously reinforcing its "reality" through the use of simulated tracking and boom shots which emphasize the depth and physical presence of the actions, and second by subtly introducing the cigarettes with gradated movements – walking, then marching, then dancing, then ice-skating – each of which is just a little bit more absurd than the last until finally we are willingly exploded into the grand closing image: crowds of cigarettes worshipping the rising sun that radiates their name, Muratti.

As an advertising film it is a supreme masterpiece, thoroughly convincing by being minimally didactic and maximally delightful. The message – the joys of cigarette smoking – are just quietly implicit in the images. And few people who have ever seen the film have forgotten Muratti Cigarettes.

The technique of animating the cigarettes is also one of Fischinger's best ideas. Real cigarettes were used, with a toothpick inserted in one end. The acting surface was a turntable covered with a layer of kaolin-wax which was then sprinkled over with loose tobacco. For each movement every cigarette's toothpick was stuck into the wax to hold it steady, then photographed one frame, then pulled up and reinserted in the wax, then another frame, etc.

This colour *Muratti greift ein* [Muratti Gets in the Act] film was released in April 1934, to thunderous acclaim, and was still playing a year later when *Composition in Blue* premièred.

The best surviving print of this film is in the collection of the Cinémathèque Suisse in Lausanne which received it in the 1970s from the estate of producer Julius Pinschewer. Freddy Buache at the Cinémathèque made a 35mm preservation negative, and gave Elfriede Fischinger a 35mm print for her collection. The Library of Congress has made a safety negative of good quality from one of the Guggenhem–Rebay prints, but the copy I have seen from this negative was missing the tail section, and I have no idea if that was a fault of the print or the original negative. The Fischinger estate contained several good 35mm nitrate prints, from which current rental and sales copies were being struck directly as reductions.

36. *SWISS TRIP [RIVERS AND LANDSCAPES]*, 1934, 35mm, b/w, sound, 11 min

In Spring 1934, after the riotous success of the colour Muratti film, when orders and money began pouring in, Fischinger decided to take a long deserved vacation, and went to Switzerland for a walking tour. He photographed there more than a thousand feet of film, and when he got back, edited them very carefully (with at least fifty splices) into a ten minute film loosely synchronized to Bach's "Brandenburg Concerto No. 3", the exact same musical rendition he later used for his *Motion Painting No. 1*. The scenery shown is predominately rivers and mountains, almost entirely devoid of people and manmade objects other than tilled and terraced fields. The can which contained the positive release print was labelled *Rivers and Landscapes*, so perhaps that was meant as a title for the film. In the second section, some houses and farms are seen (seemingly on the banks of a lake, probably Lac Leman), but only as part of distant landscapes.

The visual style of the film is partially like the Munich-Berlin Walking Trip, containing many short bursts and single-frame material with flash frames included (without a doubt intentionally here, since there are often splices nearby which preserve the flashes). There are, however, also a great many more regular speed shots kept as long takes, which alternate in even, rhythmic patterns with "faster" scenes, according to a rough synchronization with the music.

The ordinary takes are remarkable for their informality and, in many cases, their beauty. The camera is almost always hand held and moves freely about, panning then flashing back to pick up an interesting detail, jiggling with walking and jerking with the motion of a car or train whose window is sometimes visible. Yet the camera can also be static and the image perfectly framed in order to catch a plunging rapids with an immobile shadow falling across it, or to smoothly and imperceptibly single-frame a valley so that a little cloud undulates half way up a mountain side.

As a whole, the *Swiss Trip* film reinforces the impressions suggested by *Munich-Berlin*. At the very base, Fischinger was an experimental filmmaker of the broadest vision; and work of the personal and informal style of *Swiss Rivers and Landscapes* had not been seen before (cf. Ivens' *Rain* or Steiner's *H2O*, or Ruttmann's live-action films, which are slickly professional by comparison) or until at least twenty years later (cf. Anger's *Eaux d'artifice*, or more particularly the work of Baillie and Brakhage, Taylor Mead and Jonas Mekas).

The sense of informality is rendered all the more remarkable by the juxtaposition with the music which, of course he owed to some degree to the influence of music theorist Leonhard Fürst who was his dearest friend at that time, and encouraged him to work with looser and more ambiguous soundtracks. It is hard not to see *Motion Painting* in terms of this film, and this film in terms of *Motion Painting* – for example, the cascading rivers and waterfalls function like the unwinding circular spirals and the distant mountain peaks and terraced fields function somewhat like the overlays of segmented triangles. In this sense we come to appreciate even more how much based in nature (if not "organic") are the shapes and movements of many of the figures in Fischinger's "abstract" films.

Two elements for *Swiss Rivers* survived in Fischinger's films: a 35mm nitrate negative of the complete edited picture, and a 35mm nitrate fragment of a release print, apparently cut out of a print that had begun to suffer nitrate decay so that both the beginning and end had to be destroyed. From this fragment, however, the exact synchronization of the music to the film was apparent. In 1970 I made 16mm safety copies of both the positive and negative prints, and intended to make a full restoration of the soundtrack to the film, but never had the chance. In 2000, the Academy Film Archive made new 35mm preservation materials, and struck the first 35mm prints with the full picture and correct soundtrack. The opening images are silent, then the Bach music begins, plays through to its end, followed by a few moments of silent images. In 35mm, the images and the juxtaposition of the "parallel" music are quite impressive.

37. *MURATTI PRIVAT*, ca. 1935, 35mm, b/w, sound, 3 min

I have found no reference which absolutely identifies or dates the black-and-while film advertising Muratti Privat cigarettes, but one letter dated January 1935, refers to a new black-and-white Muratti commercial, so I have tentatively assigned this film to that date.

However, if the *Muratti Privat* film is later, it is in a way regressive from the famous colour film, in that the cigarettes do not actually simulate walking, but mostly move more simply in clusters or rows, rather like the figures in the Studie. This analogy with the studies is further enforced by the way in which Fischinger uses the patterns of cigarettes to create optical effects such as afterimages, say, when the music produces three bell-like strokes and concentric circles of cigarettes expand, flying out of frame. The soundtrack's pastiche of charming Mozart tunes, including the "Turkish Rondo" provides a nice vehicle for the visuals which range from checkerboard patterns of cigarette packages to a witty scene in which rows of cigarettes, previously standing single and erect, join together in pairs which wave at the audience as if they were the legs of reclining Busby Berkeley girls – the exact reverse of walking!

The only surviving print of this film appears to be an incomplete work copy or a lab error, since two brief scenes near the end are omitted, leaving the screen blank [black] while the music continues. I supplied these missing scenes from other pieces of silent footage, and a title reading, like the colour film, "Muratti Greift Ein" [Muratti Gets in the Act] has been added, though this particular title, in which the letters are formed by rows of cigarettes, may actually have belonged to one of Fischinger's other black-and-white cigarette films. A number of rental and sales prints were struck directly from the 35mm nitrate positive master as reductions, and thus contain the "black" sections of these originals. To restore the two missing scenes, I prepared a "b-roll" and had a new 35mm preservation negative made combining the A and B roles, which then became the source for subsequent prints.

38. Euthymol Ad: *PINK GUARDS ON PARADE*, 1935, 35mm, colour, sound, length unknown; Moritz recreation, 2000, video colour, sound, 3 min

This advertising film for Parke-Davis' pink-coloured Euthymol toothpaste was shot during December 1934, and released in England in January 1935. The soundtrack is an intricate pastiche including fragments of Suppé's *Poet and Peasant* overture, Adam's *Si j'étais Roi* overture, along with bits of jazz and march music that may have been composed for the film or also excerpted from contemporary sources. A 35mm nitrate of the optical soundtrack survived among Fischinger's films, but no substantial remnants of the picture material – except for a few frames and tests for the rising moon and alignments of "toothpaste" which were not labelled and did not obviously belong to *Pink Guards*. Since the Jewish Gaspar brothers had fled to England, Oskar would have had to shoot the footage on three-colour-separation [black-and-white] film in Berlin, then ship the uncut negative to London, where it would have been rendered to GasparColor prints.

I contacted the British Film Institute to see if they had a print of the finished film, which Peter Sachs had told me was a delightful masterpiece of clever advertising art, comparable to the colour Muratti film. Sachs said he had borrowed a release print from the Film Society collection at the BFI several times to show his classes at the Slade art college in the 1950s, but the BFI said they had no materials with this title. They finally, reluctantly admitted that they had "de-accessioned" most of their advertising collection sometime before 1970, and their probably-unique print of the Fischinger film had disappeared by night and fog. However, in the late 1990s, all the original unedited footage for *Pink Guards on Parade* was discovered in the remnants of the "GasparColor collection". Apparently the Gaspar labs had been bombed during the World War II blitz over London, and all the film material that was salvaged was later deposited with the British Film Institute, but it was not catalogued or annotated, so no individual titles showed up on any inventory.

The BFI footage consists of original camera takes, unedited and not particularly in any order. Some of the takes are defective, with a light-leak or glare or a mistake in the animation movement. There is almost twice as much footage as the actual length of the soundtrack (quite normal for a production like this). Some of the scenes are rather obvious, e.g. a sequence showing the toothpaste ascend a staircase towards a "sunburst" labelled Euthymol fits quite exactly to the last minute of the music. Other scenes are less certain and, by the way, none seem to be shot in order, but rather at random, probably dictated by the building and usage of the sets and props. Some shots seem to take place indoors or at a building or arena. Others transpire in an open landscape with rolling hills – and hoops of pink toothpaste go rolling up-hill and down with great charm and panache.

For Fischinger's 100th birthday, I attempted to make a full version of *Pink Guards* on video, and this videotape was screened several times in 2000. It is not by any means perfect, however – a few key images were not fitted in, and I was not sure that some of the musical passages were coupled with the exact footage that Oskar had planned for them. But the pastiche plays very well anyway, and tends to prove that Peter Sachs' high esteem of the film was correct.

39. MISCELLANEOUS LATE BERLIN WORK, 1933–35

During the later Berlin period, Fischinger executed a number of commercial assignments, the most important of which were the two Muratti cigarette commercials listed separately in this filmography. In addition to these two, he also made in October 1934, another black-and-white Muratti commercial synchronized to a Paul Linke march, an ad for Meluka cigarettes, and two commercials for Borg cigarettes, one for the B-3s and one for the regular Borgs. Of these, there survives only assorted trims and a still photo, except for the Borg commercial for which there appears to be extensive if not complete silent work-print that has not been transferred. A few test shots prepared as pilots for the first Muratti film have been copied on 16mm masters: these show cigarettes landing on rooftops from parachutes, marching through the streets of Berlin, through the famous Brandenburg Gate, and finally gathering to watch the sun or moon rise.

Other commercial work from this period includes titles for the Merkur film company of Prague (probably a logo showing Mercury with Jupiter throwing a thunderbolt, pre-figuring a scene in Disney's *Fantasia*), and logos for the Berlin film companies Europa and Rota (December 1934). He also did special effects (probably airplane tricks) for a film called *Annette im Paradies* [Annette in Paradise] (February 1934). He may also have been involved in an abandoned project, to produce a sequel to the famous Golem film, for which his good friend Guido Seeber was in charge of special effects; Fischinger kept a puppet-model of the Golem around his studios until the 1940s.

In October 1933, Fischinger shot a series of colour tests for Gaspar which included some lovely time-paintings, bolts of cloth, some B-3 cigarette packs, a mechanical razor-blade ad, and turning baskets of fruit (in addition to the coloured *Staffs* described above under Filmography No. 6).

Half a dozen other fragments of abstract designs survive on film and as animation drawings in black-and-white. The most striking of these is a sequence which contains some rectangles swinging out through space so that they turn as they approach the viewer and sideways become razor thin (an extension of some scenes in *Studie Nr. 7*), and then a series of circles and rectangles appear and disappear in static positions by fading in and out slowly, producing quiet compositions reminiscent of Malevich or Mondrian paintings.

40. *KOMPOSITION IN BLAU*, 1935, 35mm, colour, sound, 4 min

At the same time that Fischinger worked on cigarette and toothpaste commercials for profit, he worked on *Komposition in Blau* [Composition in Blue] for his own pleasure and delight in experimentation. *Composition in Blue* shares the same jolly atmosphere as the commercials, but whereas each of Fischinger's previous films had utilized only one basic animation technique, *Composition in Blue* bursts forth with half a dozen different new techniques – mostly involving pixillation of three-dimensional forms – for which it was duly recognized by enthusiastic critical praise as well as world-wide popular success.

The basic format of the film centres around solid objects moving about in an imaginary blue room. Fischinger delights in setting up conditions so that the audience makes associations with probable or "real" everyday happenings, and then extending the analogy beyond the limits of possibility, bursting the bubble of the audience's credulity. In the opening scene, Fischinger is careful to show the red cubes entering the "room" through a door, so we will identify with this as a plausible situation. Then he subtly introduces a mirror as the "floor" to the room, again gaining our confidence in this special but logical reality. Then at the climax of the film, a cylinder pounds on the mirror-floor and creates circular ripples as if the floor had suddenly liquified, something that pushes us, with a rush of delight, out of the realm of reality, into a joyous world of sheer, absurd fantasy. The symphonic latitudes of Otto Nicolai's "Merry Wives of Windsor Overture" give Fischinger a further chance to explore a full range of sensations, from the incredible sensuous beauty of a yellow panel merely gliding slowly to the floor, to the startling swift flow of mosaic squares across a field, to the zany whirl of an abstracted weather-vane that always turns in precise rhythmic time, an image later borrowed by Harry Smith in one of his early abstractions.

Beyond the comic facade lies a "serious" discussion of some oriental philosophical issues regarding the yin-yang or male-female polarity principle. The rectangles function as mobile, three-dimensional, but non-regenerative ("male") forms, while the circles are static, flat, but through their radiating, reproductive ("female") forms. The circles gradually draw the rectangles into their creative rhythm, rounding them off in the process, until the phallic column becomes the instrument of new procreation at the climactic moment. This brilliant mixture of the mystic rhythms of concentric circles and the comic pomp of blustering cylinders makes this one of Oskar's most satisfying and memorable creations.

The first answer print of *Komposition in Blau* was accepted in April, 1935, and the film was registered at 108 metres as No. 39267 on 10 May 1935. Several 35 mm nitrate prints survived both in European and American archives. The Fischinger collection had three in excellent condition, from one of which Elfriede struck 35 mm and 16 mm safety internegatives with the help of the Creative Film Society in 1968. New preservation elements were made in 2000 by the Academy Film Archive.

At some of the early performances, *Komposition in Blau* was referred to as *Lichtkonzert Nr. 1* [Light-Concert No. 1].

41. *LICHTKONZERT No. 2*, 1935, exists only as drawings, not filmed by Oskar; recreation filmed by Moritz, 1995, 16mm, colour, silent, ca. 1 min

In December 1935, just a few months before he left Germany for good, Fischinger had transferred to a soundtrack the music for *Lichtkonzert Nr. 2*. We cannot be absolutely certain what this was, but it seems likely – because of the length (115 metres) and the mere survival of that track – that it may have been the "Rakoczy" march from Berlioz's *Damnation of Faust* (rather than the Liszt "Second Hungarian Rhapsody", which was also transferred that month, but which would have been much longer).

There also survives a remarkable sequence of tempera animation paintings – some not filled in with colour – which probably were Fischinger's last Berlin work, so I have assumed they must represent some of the visuals to *Lichtkonzert Nr. 2*. These designs prefigure *Radio Dynamics* to a great degree. About 100 drawings show concentric circles enlarging, radiating and changing colour. They eventually swallow up the whole frame which then becomes solid colours fluctuating in hues for 50 frames. This leads into a sequence in which rectangles become thicker and thinner. Later, in America, Oskar mounted some of these drawings on large boards to use with lectures. The sequence was never completed and never filmed, but must have lingered in Fischinger's subconscious and emerged later as the private experiments of 1940–1942 which produced *Radio Dynamics*.

In 1995, I shot the "*Lichtkonzert Nr. 2*" paintings on to 16mm film and experimented with the Berlioz soundtrack as a parallel accompaniment. They fit neatly to the opening bars of the Berlioz march, which in fact consists of just trumpet fanfares, which are well-serviced by brilliant flickering colours.

42. *ALLEGRETTO*, 1936–1943, 35mm, colour, sound, 2:30 min

One reviewer described the *Allegretto* music – a symphonic jazz number "Radio Dynamics" composed by Paramount studio musician Ralph Rainger, as "a monument to Hollywood vulgarity". This seems an unfortunate, stuffy judgment, for Rainger was a fine composer, with such standard melodies as "Thanks for the Memories" to his credit. His "Radio Dynamics" has the sweeping breadth and dazzle of Gershwin's "Rhapsody in Blue" which preceded it by a mere 10 years. The visual richness of Fischinger's "Allegretto" owes a great deal to the complexity and vibrant texture of the musical score.

There are three different films under the "Allegretto" umbrella. In 1936, Oskar was commissioned by Paramount to create an animation to Rainger's "Radio Dynamics" score as the opening number for their feature *Big Broadcast of 1937*. Since Ernst Lubitsch had specifically mentioned Oskar as the filmmaker of *Composition in Blue* when Paramount telephoned him in Berlin to ask if he would come to Hollywood, Oskar assumed that they wanted him to produce something similar to *Composition in Blue*, and he designed a cel-animation that contained rather primary geometrical shapes, mostly in primary colours. When they informed him that no colour footage had been requisitioned, since the feature itself was all black-and-white, and his three-colour separation negative would just have to be printed in black-and-white, Oskar refused, quite logically, since the dark reds and greens and blues would all become the same black, with no differentiation, and consequently little dramatic tension. As far as we know, this negative was never printed. In 1941, with a grant from the Guggenheim Foundation, Oskar was able to buy it back from Paramount, but he painted a new set of cels and made a completely new film. The original nitrate "Radio Dynamics" three-colour separation masters which had been made at Paramount were printed in 2000 by the Academy Film Archive to create what is now known as the "early version" of *Allegretto*. The print of this first version is quite brilliant, and different from the later better-known version. The animation is simpler, with fewer background textures and elements, and the main figures are pure geometrical shapes, many like the cylinders of *Composition in Blue*, and in primary colours. It is nonetheless impressive, and surely would have been successful if Paramount had printed it in colour as a special episode in the feature.

The second version of "Radio Dynamics" was prepared in just a few weeks to meet the production deadline for the main feature. Oskar used a little bit of the abstract animation from his first version, but all the images are combined on one hand with additional animated patterns (e.g. overlapping concentric circles radiating inwards and outwards) and with special-effects of live-action elements: coffee cans bursting open, champagne bottles blowing their corks and pill bottles recapturing escaped pills through reverse printing, autos and streetcars and neon signs – and walking cigarettes. The result is lively and cute, and would have worked as an introduction to the main live-action comedy of the feature, but apparently it was not finished early enough to be previewed and okayed by key executives, although it was printed, and that black-and-white nitrate among Oskar's films was transfered to a 16mm safety master, synched with the soundtrack, in 1971. The nitrate 35mm materials were preserved and printed by the Academy Film Archive in 2000.

The colour version that Oskar prepared for the Guggenheim grant in 1941, re-named *Allegretto* to please the Baroness Rebay who liked musical references, was largely a new film. Oskar re-painted most of the cels, adding in the concentric-circle textures and other layering of images. Visually, *Allegretto* is very rich indeed. Fischinger's fascination with the new (to him) technique of cel animation led him to experiment with multi-layered see-through constructions which are more diverse and complex on the surface than those in most of his other films. At the same moment, one sees a background pattern of two overlapping concentric radiating circles, comet-like figures, sparkling and stretching diamonds, a row of teeth-like triangles gliding down one side of the frame like a liberated soundtrack, and other sensuous or mechanized motifs, each moving independently. The colours are more diverse, California colours – the pinks and turquoise and browns of desert sky and sand, the orange of poppies and the green of avocados. The figures work themselves up into a brilliant and vigorous conclusion, bursting with "skyscrapers" and kaleidoscopes of stars and diamonds, and Hollywood art-deco of the 1930s. It is a celebration, plain and simple, of the American life style, seen fresh and clean through the exuberant eyes of an immigrant. Perhaps because of the supression of *Allegretto* and its subsequent revelation in 1941, it bears a strong influence on *Radio Dynamics* in form, colour and technique, with, however, a marked advance in structure and clarity in the latter work.

YCM 35mm separation masters and several 35mm nitrate positive release prints survived in Fischinger's collection, along with one 35mm safety release print which had been used as a rental print in Europe in the 1950s. From one of the nitrate release prints a 35mm internegative was struck in 1970. In 2000, from the only surviving nitrate print, a preservation negative and new prints were struck by the Academy Film Archive.

43. *AN OPTICAL POEM*, 1937, 35mm, colour, sound, 7 min

An Optical Poem was executed almost entirely with paper cut-outs which were suspended on sticks and thin wires, and moved around in front of roughly four-foot-square backgrounds on a miniature stage with about an eight-foot-deep acting area – a technique first employed two years earlier for the final sequence of *Composition in Blue* and some effects in *Pink Guards on Parade*. This technique is by no means time – or labour – saving, but it produces some remarkable, almost eerie effects with modulating colour-tones and moving shadows.

Next to *Radio Dynamics* and *Motion Painting*, it is Fischinger's most important and mature statement. He has used the variety of moods or stances suggested by Liszt's "Hungarian Rhapsody No. 2" (music Fischinger had already transferred to an optical track as early as December 1935, but for *An Optical Poem* the track was completely re-recorded by the MGM studio orchestra) to create a microcosm in which the circles, squares and triangles perform a complete range of activities centring around the topic of relationships. They move in irregular clusters like traffic in a market place: they march, they dance, they fly, they orbit each other in twos and threes and fours, they melt into each other, they recoil suddenly away from each other, they expand and contract rhythmically and flicker, alone, together, and across stunning multi-plane perspectives. The "meaning" is for each viewer to contemplate: *An Optical Poem* is an instrument for meditation – microscopic, universal, personal.

This is the only one of Fischinger's films to belong to somebody besides the Fischinger Trust [the legal owner of the Fischinger estate]. MGM, who originally commissioned it and took possession of the negative in April 1937, owned it outright, and those rights have now passed to Warner Brothers.

In 1969, when I first contacted MGM about the possibility of getting new prints from the original Technicolor negative, I was informed that the original had apparently suffered some damage, and had been disposed of, so it would be impossible to strike any further prints. Oskar had received only one 35mm release print from MGM, for his personal use only. He loaned this print to Hilla Rebay who failed to return it, partly out of pique from her dislike of *Motion Painting*. Oskar's 35mm print went from Rebay to the Solomon Guggenheim collection and later was passed on by them to the Library of Congress, who have made a 35mm safety negative in cooperation with the Museum of Modern Art in New York. Louise Beaudet of the Cinémathèque Québécoise also struck a 35mm print from this negative for Elfriede Fischinger.

In 1985, when Laserdisc Corporation was preparing a Pioneer laserdisc devoted to Oskar Fischinger for their Visual Pathfinders series, they contacted MGM to clear the rights to use *An Optical Poem*. They were informed that the original Technicolor negative was in excellent shape, and that MGM would print a new 35 mm print of *An Optical Poem* from which the electronic version could be made. The colour quality and balance on this 35 mm were definitely faulty, with a tendency toward shades of magenta and lime green that do not exist in surviving artwork. There was also a slight scratch in the image during the first few minutes. In 2000, the Academy Film Archive purchased a new 35 mm print from Warner Brothers, which iota used in their KINETICA-2 screenings celebrating Fischinger's 100th birthday. This print, from the same materials as before, was excellent, with a full spectrum of differentiated colours (accurate according to the few surviving artworks).

Oskar had saved a few minutes of faulty YCM negative from the sequence in which bullet-shaped figures flicker to the sound of a zither. In 1970, I made a 16mm copy of this footage, and Elfriede Fischinger screened it several times to stunned audiences dazzled by the extra flickering of the Y, C and M components of each frame.

44. "TOCCATA AND FUGUE" from *FANTASIA*, 1939, 35mm

Enough has been said about *Fantasia* in the main biographical text. Suffice it to reiterate that the Bach sequence was merely adapted by the Disney staff from Fischinger's original designs, and thus at most it is "School of Fischinger". None of Fischinger's own designs were ever executed or filmed exactly as he planned them, though, as I suggested, many of these ideas were formed some years earlier and some were undoubtedly utilized to a certain extent by Fischinger himself in subsquent films like *An American March* and *Radio Dynamics*.

45. *AN AMERICAN MARCH*, 1941, 35mm, colour, sound, 3 min

Fischinger felt very depressed about the Disney Studios, and recalled in a very negative light the factory production methods, prescribed style, hyper-conservative taste and failure to experiment that he had encountered there, a reaction which manifested itself later very charmingly in the series of collages that he made by pasting Mickey Mouse figures cut from Disney comics over Kandinsky and Bauer reproductions (see illustrations, p. 132). Ironically, *An American March*, the first film he completed after his job on *Fantasia*, is the most Disney-like of all his works, with the representational image of the American flag dominating the film. Oskar also used the common Disney style of hard-edged, outlined figures painted on cels, but he carried the technique far beyond Disney's limits and made it an integral part of the meaning of the film. Fischinger has chosen to discuss the idea of America as a melting pot, and he shows this literally by causing the elements in the film – form and colour – to melt. The shapes begin as three clear geometric images (circle, triangle and square) that gradually stretch and warp into a complete range of other shapes (ovals, hexagons, trapezoids, irregular ripples, etc.) each of which also becomes expanded and diffused, its outlines blurred (through using multiple layers of cels). The colours begin as red, white and blue, but also blend through graduated hues (red to maroon to burgundy to mauve, etc.) until they have been a complete rainbow.

The 35mm nitrate print in the Fischinger collection was used in 1970 to make a 35mm and 16mm safety internegative, which made good rental and sales prints. In 2000, the Academy Film Archive made a preservation negative and new prints from a nitrate print which had been cut into pieces. These new prints, which screened with the KINETICA 2 Fischinger 100th anniversary programmes, are very beautiful, with the full impact of the colours' melting very vivid.

46. ORGANIC FRAGMENT, 1941, not filmed by Oskar; reconstruction 1984, 35mm, colour, silent, ca. 1 min

I have given the title *Organic Fragment* to a series of 1000 line animation drawings with periodic colour coding and some completely painted cels, dated 1941. These are exciting drawings, different from any of Fischinger's other films, with warm earth colours, and loose, free-flowing forms that move in sensuous interrelationships. Unless they were meant to be silent like *Radio Dynamics*, the suppleness of these drawings seems to correspond to some sound more flexible than ordinary European classical music – perhaps either a John Cage percussion piece, or Uday Shankar's "Dance Kartikeya", both of which we know were under consideration as projects at that time. However, since some of these drawings are numbered so that they are divided into bars of 78 frames length, they may have been intended for the Bach "Brandenburg Concerto No. 3" which does break itself down into phrases of that length. Like Fischinger's other abandoned productions, we must regret that he did not continue this sequence since it promised to be something very interesting, unique, challenging and satisfying.

In 1984, with a grant from the National Endowment for the Arts, Barbara Fischinger painted all the cels following Oskar's indications, and Amy Halpern, Larry Leichtleiter, myself and Scott Tyget shot it on to film at the Animation School of UCLA, thanks to Dan McLaughlin. Since the *Organic Fragment* was shorter than a small roll of film, we filled up the rest of the roll with a few other very brief fragments or tests that had not been shot.

A number of other fragments of unfinished animation from the 1940s remain unfilmed, including one fascinating item: a film based on whirling yin-yang patterns created with coloured celophane and masks – something that is not easy to shoot in the absence of any instructions about Oskar's intentions for speed, direction, layering, etc.

47. RADIO DYNAMICS, 1942, 35mm, colour, silent, 4 min

I believe this to be Fischinger's best film, the work in which he most perfectly joined his craftsmanship with his spiritual ideas into a meaningful and relatively faultless whole. No music distracts from the visual imagery which moves with sufficient grace and power of its own.

The film has the structure of yoga itself: we see first a series of exercises, only exercises for the eyes or the sense of vision – fluctuating and stretching rectangular objects; then we see a statement of two icons representing meditation, one an image of flight into an infinite vortex defined by finite movement, and the other an image of two eyes' irises opening and expanding/contracting while between them grows a third eye of inner/cosmic consciousness. After a brief introductory exposition of these three themes, each is repeated in a longer, developed version, the exercises working themselves up into complex stroboscopic flickers, and the hypnotic rhythms of the expanding/contracting eyes unite with the motion of the passing rings of the vortex, making the flight become a two-way, inward and outward, flight with the vortex as the eye of the observer as well as the eye of the universe. As I suggested in the main text, the climactic moment expresses through its manipulation of changing colours, sizes, and sense of speed, one aspect of Einstein's relativity theory – the balance between energy, matter and velocity – in clear but emotional, simple but subtle and complex terms, wholly visual terms which happen and can be understood directly with no intervening words.

One 35mm nitrate print – Fischinger's workprint or spliced original – was kept in a can labelled "Radio Dynamics – Orson Welles" along with a title reading "Radio Dynamics" (which was left over from *Allegretto*) and a title reading "No music please – an experiment in colour rhythm", and a set of short pieces from the "exercise" section of the film, spliced together for loop printing, and labelled in Oskar's writing "make loop". In making the 16mm master, Pat O'Neill step-printed the "colour rhythm" title to make it longer, and printed out the "exercise" loop several times. Bob Curtis and I then placed these in front of the "Radio Dynamics" title and the main body of the film, and put a tinted piece of the Fischinger logo (taken from *Muntz TV*) at the end since there was a YCM separation master of a "The End" title in the can as well, but no positive print of it. This was used as the printing master for sales and rental prints. There is no 35mm safety copy of the film. Fischinger had one fragmentary 16mm print which was considerably cut apart and had to be reassembled by Bob Curtis. In 1970, there were also a few tin boxes of original cels for *Radio Dynamics*, which were quite fascinating in that you could see how Fischinger had planned the expanding coloured circles so that they were composed of several layers of cels which showed through each other, some colours being supplied by cels painted one solid colour that was only allowed to be seen through certain rings. Since that time, however, all of these cels have decomposed, since they were made of vulnerable nitrate stock.

In 2000 the Academy of Motion Picture Arts and Sciences made new preservation materials and 35mm prints of *Radio Dynamics* from the surviving nitrate spliced print, including the restoration of the beginning loop according to Oskar's directions.

48. *COLOUR RHYTHM*, ca. 1940, 35mm, colour, silent, 4 min

This was not a film in its own right, since it is primarily the original YCM separation master from which the *Radio Dynamics* footage is drawn, but it does contain one image – of a nebulous, amorphous painting rather like an early Kandinsky – which was not used in the main body of *Radio Dynamics*, though it is seen briefly in the looped section placed as a preface. The can in which the negative was stored contained a note in Fischinger's handwriting saying that he had not had money enough to print this film but he hoped it would be seen someday. At the time of the opening of the Pacific Film Archive in Berkeley, curator Sheldon Renan paid $600 for six prints of early Fischinger films with the understanding that this would help to transfer some materials from nitrate to safety copies. Prints of these six films along with some other newly transferred materials were shown at the opening of the Archive on a programme called "The Private Films of Oskar Fischinger". Only a few weeks were available to prepare the films for that programme, and without having seen it, we selected *Colour Rhythm* and listed it on the programme.

The 35mm first answer print from Technicolor labs, which we showed in Berkeley, was considerably different in colour balance from the *Radio Dynamics* colours (which were verified by Fischinger's 16mm print and the surviving cels), but a second, later printing yielded closer colours.

Even if *Colour Rhythm* is only Fischinger's negative for *Radio Dynamics* unedited, it still represents a rare and fascinating glimpse of a filmmaker at work, since many scenes are backward and almost all are in different order from the way they appear in the edited film. *Colour Rhythm*, then, serves to increase our appreciation and admiration of Fischinger's skill and vision in preparing *Radio Dynamics*.

Colour Rhythm also raises one other question about *Radio Dynamics*. When did Fischinger not have money enough to print out the negative? When did he actually get it printed? And when was it edited? *Colour Rhythm*, the negative, might have been shot as early as 17 September 1940, from which date we have a series of colour tests taken from the flicker section; *Radio Dynamics* might then have been edited during 1941 and 1942 when Fischinger was getting a salary from Orson Welles. On the other hand, *Colour Rhythm* might have been shot during the Orson Welles period, lain unprinted until sometime before approximately 1950 (since the *Radio Dynamics* print is nitrate), and then the final editing, *Radio Dynamics*, could have been done at any time up to 1966. We will probably never know.

49. *MUTOSCOPE REELS*, ca. 1945, 35mm, colour, silent, 2 min

The three mutoscope reels Fischinger designed around the time of Solomon Guggenheim's 86th birthday ought to be considered along with the films, since they are essentially series of animation drawings.

Solomon's actual birthday present now seems to be lost. The Guggenheim Foundation reports that it has no record of the reel (and mutoscope machine, as well) which Fischinger presented to Guggenheim. The Baroness Rebay probably stored it in her barn, where it gradually rotted and rusted away in the severe Connecticut winters – the aged caretaker seemed to remember such a "contraption" when I visited there years later. From a few duplicate cards, we know this reel consisted, at least in part, of oil painted images of coloured circles against a black background, which, in the mutoscope, produces an eerie "ghosting" effect as the cards move by slower and more opaquely than filmed images. Oskar actually filmed the Guggenheim reel on to 35mm film before sending it to New York. Its colour and action is very beautiful, but it does not reproduce the "ghost cone" effect of the actual mutoscope. I transfered this 35mm nitrate to a 16mm safety master in 1971 (this nitrate was not found in 2000). In 2000, the Academy Film Archive prepared 16mm preservation elements and prints from the best surviving element, a Kodachrome print.

The other two mutoscope reels were executed mostly with coloured pencils and crayons. They contain a rich variety of imagery and effects, including one sequence, very much like the *Organic Fragment* film, which is quite frankly erotic [Sara Petty drew a lovely title card for this sequence, reading "Tantra"]. I shot all of the mutoscope cards on to 16mm film, with the help of a framing image of a movie theatre which Oskar himself had prepared, using a colour image of the interior of a cinema cut from a magazine, then the screen area was cut out, and the frame picture pasted to a cardboard which had a corresponding cut-out rectangle where the screen would be. The screen aperture was the exact size of the mutoscope cards, so I assumed that Oskar had actually intended to film at least some of the cards himself, using this framing. The mutoscope sequences proved charming in this filmed version, and have been screened in many Fischinger programmes along with the 16mm version of the Guggenheim reel.

Barbara Fischinger copied both of these mutoscope reels on to duplicate mutoscope cards, so that Oskar's handmade originals could be kept archivally, but the duplicates could be played in mutoscope machines at various Fischinger exhibitions.

Elfriede Fischinger published another nice passage from a mutoscope reel showing star-bursts and swirling comets as a flip-book.

50. *MOTION PAINTING No. 1*, 1947, 35mm, colour, sound, 11 min

The oil-on-plexiglas technique of *Motion Painting No. 1* has been described in the main text. By all odds so delicate and difficult a process for a ten-minute film might well have resulted in a failure or a weak film. At one point Fischinger painted every day for over five months without being able to see how it was coming out on film, since he wanted to keep all the conditions, including film stock, absolutely consistent in order to avoid unexpected variations in quality of image. Thus it is a tribute to Fischinger's skill and artistic vision that *Motion Painting* turned out in fact excellent.

Volumes could be [and undoubtedly will be] written about this film which stands in length and complexity as Fischinger's major work. It is perhaps the only one of his films which is truly and completely (or purely) abstract (or absolute). Its images are actors in a complex being which modulates and transforms itself before our eyes, an object and an experience at the same time, something we must feel and contemplate, and meditate through. It has no specific meanings in a certain important way, and no amount of words could do it justice. What I am going to suggest here are merely some approaches or viewpoints to it.

First of all, it is a painting, and can be appreciated as an exercise in the painter's art. It shows a variety of styles from the soft, muted opening to the bold conclusion through a series of spontaneous changes prepared without any previous planning. All of the figures are drawn free-hand without aid of compasses or rulers or under-sketching, even the incredibly precise triangles of the middle section. It is a remarkable, astonishing document of one creative process – and a genuine document, brushstroke by brushstroke, of a painter at work, for Fischinger habitually painted this way, in multiple layers, the first inner images covered and lost, like a hidden soul, which is what Oskar called the underpainting.

As the title suggests, it is also a painting of or about "motion", and the element of motion is exploited in many forms and variations, from the literal motion of the comet-like bodies in the opening sequence to the motion by addition or concretion at the close. Colour and shape become elements in our sensation of motion, as the variegated spirals unwind themselves with seemingly variable dynamisms or speeds – the motion of music and painting. Even the placement and appearance of static objects becomes an instrument for manipulating the motion of our eyes, which renders all other activity relative – the motion of sculpture, happening, or pageant. And the final dramatic sweeps of the great wedges which form the mandala are rendered more exciting by the relatively static scenes that precede them – theatrical motion of dynamic duration in time.

It is tempting to see symbolic forms in the film, e.g. a human brain as the field of action in the opening sequence, with paths, almost like a road map, leading out of it into a world of architectural designs which grows in magnificence until they become structures of depth and power that collide in the end to form a beautiful, simple, pure mandala.

While this rendition of the film in representational terms is inadequate, unsatisfactory or untenable basically, it lays bare an underlying structure which is appropriate. The opening scene of soft shapes and sensual action is amorphous like the thoughts of a child or an untrained thinker. Out of this develop connections first in the form of slow, logical enlargements of basic kernels, then by the direct connection of the kernels themselves. Then are added large blocks of material to form a new field of action – the process of education – on which logical construction takes place – cogitation and contemplation – which grows very gradually into more and more powerful and beautiful gestures – creativity and transcendental meditation. The film's structure is even richer and more flexible than this suggests, but there are elements of an archetypal pattern – childhood through initiation to maturity – which has a validity on many levels (e.g. the raising of the spiritual energy through the chakras in kundalini yoga) depending on the predisposition of the particular viewer at each time of his meditation/experience with the film.

This crucial and irreplaceable film has given the most trouble in preservation. Fischinger shot the film on a three-colour successive exposure negative. He had six 16mm prints made at the Disney labs, all of which survive in considerably worn condition, including one print with almost all its sprockets ripped out but very few scratches, and the others with many scratches and splices. However, we can see from these prints that the exposure level was consistent, and the colours were both subtle and saturated, representing faithfully the many hues of the original paint [the six plexiglas sheets survive in good condition, now at the Deutsches Film-museum in Frankfurt]. Fischinger's one 35mm positive on Anscocolor stock has little colour range or discrimination (some perhaps from recent fading) so that some sequences – e.g. the cream coloured blocks that build up to the first of the dotted-line structures – are totally washed out so that nothing happens on the screen at all. Mrs. Fischinger innocently had a few 16mm prints struck from this Ansco master, and these copies were distributed by the Museum of Modern Art and the Creative Film Society for some time before the poor quality was noticed and reported. Then Mrs. Fischinger took the three-colour successive exposure negative to Technicolor labs to have a fresh 35mm master made, but three trial printings (each at a cost of more than $500) failed to yield a perfect print, though the best portions of each were spliced together to form an adequate master from which 16mm rental and sales prints were struck. The colours in this version are not exactly true to the original but are in general differentiated, saturated and attractive (an exception being the final sequence in which the farthest, darkest parts of the perspectives of the wedges are muddied over). However, there are several sudden and annoying changes of light level in the middle of consistent sequences, once due to a splice between two prints, but the other times due merely to timing faults.

I prepared a 16mm printing negative by making A-roll and B-roll out of the best sections of the various surviving original Disney 16mm prints, then striking a new interneg from them. This worked better than any of the other attempts, and a number of sales and rental prints were struck, some with a modern soundtrack taken from more recent "high fidelity" recordings.

In the early 1990s, Scott McQueen, the new film archivist at the Disney studios, discovered 35mm nitrate YCM separation masters of *Motion Painting* in the Disney vaults – obviously a printing element from 1947 when Ub Iwerks struck the six 16mm prints. It was in excellent condition, and Scott made a new 35mm print for Elfriede Fischinger before sending the nitrate off to the Library of Congress film storage facility.

In 2000, the Academy Film Archive prepared preservation elements and new 35mm prints of *Motion Painting* from the nitrate camera original that Oskar kept, so it yielded some excellent images and sound. A fine 100th birthday present, after all.

51. *MUNTZ TV COMMERCIAL*, 1952, 35mm, b/w, sound, 1 min

The *Muntz TV* commercial was painted in the same technique as *Motion Painting No. 1* (but consciously limited to shades of black, white and grey), and at its best moments, with the same vigour and brilliance. One can only wish that Fischinger had gone through with his plans to prepare a totally abstract version (as he had done with *Circles* and *Coloratura*) so that we could see the wedges and saturn-like planets in a more serious context. Probably the banal and obsessive music, as well as the colour problem prevented him (see biography text).

A 35mm safety negative was made in 1969 with the help of the Creative Film Society. A 16mm negative was struck later for making rental and sales prints. In 2000, The Academy Film Archive used a composite safety fine grain to make a new duplicate preservation negative and new prints.

52. COMMERCIAL WORK, ca. 1945–55

During the 1940s and 1950s, Fischinger undertook a variety of commercial work, some of which was never used (such as titles for *Jane Eyre* or a dream sequence for Lang's *Secret Behind the Door*). Among advertising films in the 1950s, aside from the *Muntz TV* spot, were commercials for *Oklahoma Gas*, *Pure Oil* and *Sugar Pops Cereal*, all of which were very tightly controlled in terms of subject matter and style. A good 16mm negative for *Oklahoma Gas* has been used for rental and sales prints. No print of *Pure Oil* seems to survive, but some very beautiful artwork with rich jade-green and black designs makes this regretable. Only a few frames of the *Sugar Pops* survive, showing a cereal box riding into town over a bridge like a cowboy.

Oskar also repeated his special-effect rockets from *Woman in the Moon* for some of the popular children's space shows on television, such as *Space Patrol*.

53. *STEREO FILM*, 1952, 35mm, colour, silent, 1 min

The short, half-minute *Stereo Film* pilot was painted some time before August 1952 as the culmination of four years of experiments, through which Fischinger learned to draw and paint three-dimensional pictures in parallel-eye-information panels.

The film shows a beautiful concretion: different coloured brush-stroke rectangles appear one by one (as in *Motion Painting*) until they fill the whole frame, hanging in space at different distances, one series forming a perfect V-shaped alignment with the point at a great distance and the arms coming forward in perfect perspective, up quite close to the viewer. It is a pity Oskar was never able to carry his stereo film work further.

A 35mm successive exposure negative and one 35mm faded Anscocolor print survive. I made a 35mm safety negative and prints. 16mm prints have been made so that Oskar's film could be screened on programmes with other 16mm stereo films by Hy Hirsh, Dwinell Grant, Norman McLaren and Harry Smith – which has happened six times: at the Louvre in Paris, Pacific Film Archive in San Francisco, at museums in Toronto, Ottawa and Montreal, and at Astarte festival in Paris.

In 2003, The Center for Visual Music, thanks to Triage Laboratory and SabuCat Productions, made new 35mm prints for the World 3-D Festival in Hollywood, CA.

54. *SYNTHETIC SOUND*, 1948, 1955, 35mm

Fischinger prepared several reels of synthetic sound in 1948 [used in a court case involving Alexander Laszlo which tried to set standards requiring the presence of live musicians if any music was to be used at all], and several more in 1955. Both were based on a newer principle, different from the 1932 sound experiments. Oskar devised new machinery which held sections of glass masked with black paper cut in patterns simulating variable-area soundtrack. By inserting the glass strips in different slots arranged vertically closer or father away from the camera, one could regulate volume, and by changing the mask/template one could choose different tones and timbres. This makes the production of traditional music quite simple, since the elements are easily codified and learned.

Of the materials prepared with this new system, only two items survived – a 1955 demonstration reel on which Fischinger arranged bits of Khachaturian's "Sabre Dance" and other melodies; and a bit of sound effects which Fischinger made for a banal *Northern Tissue* commercial, involving glissandos and pure noises less like traditional music. These two pieces of sound together were used in 1969 as a soundtrack for a film in which Elfriede Fischinger performed visuals on the Lumigraph. This Lumigraph Film was preserved by The Fischinger Archive in 2002.

55. *MOTION PAINTING No. 2 and No. 3 Fragments*, 1957, ca. 1960, 16mm

The one-minute 1957 fragment is Fischinger's only production originally in 16mm. It shows growing a square-spiral composition of a type common in Fischinger's canvas paintings but otherwise not used in the films. The actual canvas [a small panel, about 8" x 10"] survives, dated 1957, containing the last image on the film. There are also two 35mm pieces from about 1960 which document the painting of two larger canvases (which still exist). In addition, there is a painting of a large bright-red spiral on a bright blue background which was mounted on the motion-painting set-up, so I assume it had been exposed on film, which was then left unprocessed in the camera until it gradually fogged over so that the "motion-painting" was lost. Oskar also made some 35mm footage of a few other of his paintings, moving the camera over the canvas to pick out close-ups of certain details, and one of these paintings no longer exists. In 2000, the Academy Film Archive made new preservation materials for these "motion painting" fragments, and struck new prints for the KINETICA 2 screenings.

56. PERSONAL FILMS

There are a large number of tiny fragments – from three frames to three feet – of film taken of Fischinger and his family over the years. None, as far as I have seen, show him at work painting or filming. The longer scenes include a sequence of Oskar and friends skiing in the mountains near Munich (ca. 1925); Oskar, Hans and Elfriede in Berlin (ca. 1932); and Oskar walking on a street in Hollywood (ca. 1940). Most of these have not been transferred since they are too fragmentary and probably can best be used as still photo materials. One selection, however, of Berlin material (including general street scenes, Oskar's girlfriend Martha, Oskar and Elfriede and Hans in the Friedrichstrasse studio, Elfriede with a baby in the apartment on Rixdorferstrasse, etc.) was copied in 16mm for use in a documentary film which was never finished.

A few home movies on 16mm and 8mm show Fischinger briefly in his later years, mostly on holidays with family members around. From 1953 there is a 4-minute black-and-white 16mm documentary shot by Oskar of a "bon voyage" party when Elfriede and Angie were about to sail to Germany to visit the relatives there. The camera smoothly pans, following some dozen children playing games and eating refreshments on a lawn.

These items have not yet been preserved to archival standard.

Sources for Fischinger films

Some of the films are available for rental from:

Canyon Cinema, 145 Ninth Street, Suite 260, San Francisco, CA 94103, USA. Phone/fax: 415-626-2255; e-mail: films@canyoncinema.com; www.canyoncinema.com

The Museum of Modern Art, Circulating Film Library, 11 West 53rd Street, New York, NY 10019, USA. Phone: 212-708-9530; Fax: 212-708-9531; e-mail: circfilm@moma.org

In Europe: Light Cone, 12 rue des Vignoles, 75020 Paris, France. Phone: 01 46.59.01.53; Fax: 01 46.59.03.12; e-mail: lightcone@club-internet.fr; www.lightcone.org/lightcone/

See The Fischinger Archive website; www.oskarfischinger.org for updated information.

The Fischinger Archive offers rental of a package programme:

A Retrospective featuring many newly restored 35mm prints is available through The Fischinger Archive and The Center for Visual Music. For booking information, contact The Fischinger Archive, 3021 Volk Avenue, Long Beach, CA 90808, USA. Phone/fax: 562-496-1449; e-mail: info@oskarfischinger.org; website: www.oskarfischinger.org

Many of the films are available for sale from:

The Fischinger Archive, 3021 Volk Avenue, Long Beach, CA 90808, USA. Contact Barbara Fischinger. Phone/fax: 562-496-1449; e-mail: sales@oskarfischinger.org; www.oskarfischinger.org

Videotapes:

The Films of Oskar Fischinger on videotape, and on future dvd releases, are available from The Fischinger Archive: www.oskarfischinger.org or The Center for Visual Music, www.centerforvisualmusic.org. Please check the Fischinger Archive web site for updated information.

Paintings and art:

The art dealer for the Fischinger Archive is Jack Rutberg, Fine Arts Inc., 357 North La Brea Avenue, Los Angeles, CA 90036, USA. Phone: 323-938-5222; Fax 323-938-0577. e-mail: jrutberg@jackrutbergfinearts.com; www.jackrutbergfinearts.com

Other materials:

Photographs, documents and other material can be obtained through The Fischinger Archive or The Center for Visual Music.

For all other information, please contact The Fischinger Archive, www.oskarfischinger.org; info@oskarfischinger.org; phone/fax: (562) 496-1449.

Oskar Fischinger
Bibliography

I. Texts written by Oskar Fischinger

1. "Farbe-Tonprobleme des Films. (Zur Vorführung meines synästhetischen Films 'R5' auf dem zweiten Farbe-Tonkongress, 5.10.30, in Hamburg)", 2-page typescript. Fischinger Archive.

2. "Was ich mal sagen möchte...", *Deutsche Allgemeine Zeitung*, Berlin, 23 July 1932.

3. "Klingende Ornamente", *Deutsche Allgemeine Zeitung, Kraft und Stoff* (Sunday supplement), No. 30, 28 July 1932. Syndicated in other papers world-wide.

4. "Der Absolute Tonfilm: Neue Möglichkeiten für den bildenden Künstler", syndicated: *Dortmunder Zeitung*, 1 January 1933; *Schwäbischer Merkur*, 3 January 1933, etc.

5. "My Statements are in my Work", in *Art in Cinema*, ed. Frank Stauffacher. San Francisco Museum of Art, 1947. pp. 35–37.

6. "Véritable création", in *Le Cinéma à Knokke-le-Zoute*, 1950, pp. 35–37.

7. "My Paintings/My Films" (brochure) Frank Perls Gallery (Beverly Hills), October 1951.

8. "Bildmusik: Meine Filmstudien", *Der Film Kreis* (Munich) No. 1, Jan/Feb 1955, pp. 42–43 (text largely translated from *Art in Cinema*, #5 above).

9. "Painting – and Painters Today" (brochure) Pasadena Art Museum, 1956.

   Further texts (including #9 above), letters and documents by Oskar Fischinger are reproduced in William Moritz articles (below).

II. Selected publications about Oskar Fischinger

10. Rudolph Schneider, "Formspiel durch Kino", *Frankfurter Zeitung*, 12 July 1926.

11. Walter Jerven, "Bei Fischinger in München", *Film-Kurier*, 15 January 1927.

12. Hans Böhm, "Zeichenfilme nach Wachsbildungen", *Die Kinotechnik*, Vol. IX, No. 21, 5 November 1927, pp. 571–572.

13. Rudolph Schneider-Schelde, "Geist im Film", *Die Zeitlupe*, Vol. I, No. 5, 1 December 1927.

14. Fritz Böhme, "Der Tanz der Linien", *Deutsche Allgemeine Zeitung*, 16 August 1930.

15. "Berlin acclaiming new series of short sound films", *Close-Up*, Vol. 7, no. 6, December 1930, p. 393.

16. Simon Koster, "Een Gesprek met Oskar Fischinger", *Nieuwe Rotterdamsche Courant*, 17 January 1931.

17. de Graf, "Oskar Fischinger over Filmkunst", *Allgemeen Handelsblad*, 24 January 1931.

18. "Dansende lijnen", *Haagsche Courent*, 27 January 1931.

19. Lou Lichtfeld, "Fischingers muzikale Films", *De Groene Amsterdammer* (no. 2800) 31 January 1931, p. 17.

20. —, "Oskar Fischinger, zijn werk en zijn ontwikkeling" *Weekblad Cinema* 15 (1931), pp. 6–7.

21. Paul Hatschek, "Die Filme Oskar Fischingers", *Filmtechnik*, Vol. VII, No. 5, 7 March 1931.

22. Fritz Böhme, "Die Kunst des lebenden Lichts", *Deutsche Allgemeine Zeitung*, 11 July 1931.

23. Emile Vuillermoz, "La Motoculture intellectuelle: la musique radiographiée", *Excelsior* [Paris], 29 October 1931.

24. Caroline A. Lejeune, "A New Break in Movies: The Fischinger Films", *Observer* [London], 20 December 1931.

25. Walther Behn, "Abstrakte Filmstudie Nr. 5 von Oskar Fischinger (Synästhetischer Film)", in *Farbe-Ton-forschungen*, ed. Georg Anschütz, Vol. III (Hamburg: Meissner, 1931), pp. 367–369.

26. Dr. Menno Ter Braak, *De Absolute Film* (Rotterdam: Brusse, 1931), p. 47.

27. Philippe Roland, "Le Cinéma: Etude 8", *Journal Des Débats* [Paris], 31 January 1932.

28. Jean Vidal, "Miracles", *L'intransigeant* [Paris], 6 February 1932.

29. Karel Mengelberg, "Oskar Fischingers Latest Film", May 1932.

30. Bernhard Diebold, "Über Fischingerfilme: das ästhetische Wunder", *Lichtbild-bühne*, 1 June 1932.

31. Lotte H. Eisner, "Lichtertanz", *Film-Kurier*, 1 June 1932.

32. Fritz Böhme, "Lineare Filmkunst", *Film-Kurier*, 4 June 1932.

33. F.T.G., "Bernhard Diebold vor dem Mikrophon", *Frankfurter Zeitung*, 18 June 1932.

34. Lou Lichtfeld, "Een gesprek met Oskar Fischinger", *Nieuwe Rotterdamsche Courant*, 27 July 1932.

35. Fritz Böhme, "Verborgene Musik im Lindenblatt: Die Bedeutung von Fischingers Entdeckung für den Tonfilm", *Deutsche Allgemeine Zeitung*, 30 July 1932.

36. —, "Tönende Ornamente: Aus Oskar Fischingers neuer Arbeit", *Film-Kurier*, 30 July 1932.

37. Dr. M. Epstein, "Elektrische Musik", *Berliner Tageblatt*, 24 August 1932.

38. "'Studie 8', A new film by Oskar Fischinger", *Close Up* [London] Vol. IX, No. 3, September 1932, pp. 171–173.

39. Luc. Willink, "Film als zichtbare Musiek: De tooverkunsten van Fischinger", *Het Vaderland* [Den Haag], 10 September 1932.

40. Dr. Adolf Raskin, "Klingende Ornamente – Gezeichnete Musik", *Kasseler Neueste Nachrichten*, 24 September 1932.

41. Dr. Albert Neuberger, "Ornamente musizieren", *Deutsche Musiker Zeitung*, No. 42, 15 October 1932, pp. 495–496.

42. Margot Epstein, "Gezeichnete Musik", *Allgemeine Musikzeitung* [Berlin], 25 November 1932.

43. Jean-Pierre Chabloz, "Ce que découvrent les 'antennes' du cinéma", *Le Mondain* [Geneva], 7 January 1933.

44. Fritz Böhme, "Gezeichnete Musik – Betrachtungen zur Entdeckung Oskar Fischingers (mit einem Nachwort von Agnes Gerlach)", *Deutsche Frauenkultur*, Vol. XXXVI, No. 2, February 1933, pp. 31–33.

45. Janusz Marja Brzeske, "Film absolutny: Abstrakcyine obrazy i grajace ornamenty Oskara Fischingera", *Kuryer Filmowy* [Krakow/Warsow], 28 March 1933.

46. Max Fischer, "Gezeichnete Musik", *Giessener Anzeiger*, 3 May 1933.

47. ***** *Cinema Quarterly*, Spring 1933, p. 153.

48. W. Fiedler, "Der gefärbte Film verschwindet – der Farbfilm ist da!: der Farb-Ton-film", *Deutsche Allgemeine Zeitung*, 8 July 1933.

49. Ettore Margadonna, "Cineritmica", *L'Illustrazione Italiana*, 10 September 1933.

50. Hans Schuhmacher, "Fischinger", *Film-Kurier*, 1 October 1934.

51. ***** *Lichtbildbühne*, 18 October 1934.
[*Intercine*, January 1935, p. 36]

52. Fritz Böhme, "Zum Internationalen Filmkongress: Beiprogramm ist keine Neben-sache! Gespräche mit Lotte Reiniger und Oskar Fischinger", *Deutsche Allgemeine Zeitung*, 27 April 1935.

53. Alman, "Der absolute Film: Oskar Fischingers Arbeiten", *Filmwelt* (Sunday supplement of *Film-Kurier*), 16 June 1935.

54. Fritz Böhme, "Geschaute Musik: Kompositionen in Farben", *Deutsche Allgemeine Zeitung*, 29 July 1935.

55. Ettore Margadonna, "Filme ohne Schauspieler und Abenteuer", *Hamburger Tageblatt*, 29 July 1935 [partly translated from No. 42 above]

56. Jiri Lehovec, "III. mezinárodní filmový festival b Benátkách", *Narodni Osvobozeni* [Prague], 17 August 1935.

57. Dr. Leonhard Fürst, "Film als Ausdrucksform", *Film-Kurier*, 11 November 1935.

58. L.J. Jordan, "The Last of the Mohicans", *Filmliga* [Amsterdam], 15 November 1935.

59. Menno ter Braak, "Film en Kleur: 'Symphonie in Blau' van Oskar Fischinger", *Het Vaderland*, 2 December 1935.

60. Roger Spottiswoode, *A Grammar of the Film* (1935), p.110

61. —, "Fischinger's 'Cirkels' Reclame-film voor Van Houten", *Dagblad Van Rotterdam*, 19 December 1936.

62. Victor Schamoni, *Das Lichtspiel, Möglichkeiten Des Absoluten Films* (Münster: Doctoral Dissertation, 1936).

63. Paul Rotha, *Movie Parade* (London: Studio, 1936) p. 138.

64. Kay Proctor, "Abstract Harmony, Cinema's Newborn", *Evening News* [Los Angeles] 9 January 1937, p. 3.

65. Harry Mines, "Raves and Raps", *Daily News* [Los Angeles], January 1937, p. 10.

66. Gordon Fawcett, "Screen Oddities" [Bell Syndicate], 1 December 1937.

67. Hans L. Stoltenberg, *Reine Farbkunst In Raum Und Zeit Und Ihr Verhältnis Zur Tonkunst, Eine Einführung In Das Filmtonbuntspiel*, (Berlin: Unesma, 1937), pp. 36–40.

68. Fritz Aeckerle, "Avantgarde tut not!", *Deutsche Allgemeine Zeitung*, 12 February 1938.

69. "Novel Color Short", *Hollywood Reporter*, 25 February 1938.

70. Louella Parsons, "Movie-Go-Round", *Examiner*, 6 March 1938, p. 46?.

71. Frederick C. Othman, "Officials in Dreamy Mood", *Hollywood Citizen News*, 12 March 1938.

72. Ed Sullivan, "Looking Glass", *Hollywood Citizen News*, 29 March 1938.

73. R.V.D. Johnson, "Animating Music", *Minicam*, Vol. II, No. 5, January 1939, pp. 101–104.

74. Arthur Rosenheimer Jr. [Arthur Knight], "The Small Screen", *Theatre Arts*, Vol. XXXI, No. 5, May 1947, pp. 1, 9–10.

75. Lewis Jacobs, "Experimental Cinema in America (Part 1: 1921–1941)", *Hollywood Quarterly*, Vol. III, No. 2, Winter 1947, p. 124. Lewis Jacobs, "Experimental Cinema in America (Part 2: The Postwar Revival), *Hollywood Quarterly*, Vol III, No. 3, Spring 1948, pp. 283–284.

76. Giuseppe Lo Duca, *Le Dessin Animé* (Paris: Prisma, 1948), pp. 29, 55–56, 138–139, 143, 165.

77. Lou Jacobs Jr., "Master of Motion", *International Photographer*, Vol. XXI, No. 10, October 1949, pp. 5 + 10.

78. Roger Manvell, ed., *Experiment in the Film* (London: Grey Walls Press, 1949), pp. 131, 140, 198, 229–230, 233 [includes reprint of No. 59 above].

79. Ty Cotta, "Oskar Fischinger: Abstract Movie Master", *Modern Photography*, Vol. XVI, No. 7, July 1952, pp. 74–75, 82–84.

80. Will Seringhaus, "Höhepunkt der Göttinger Filmtage: Die Arbeit des 'Film-Malers' Oskar Fischinger", *Frankfurter Neue Presse*, 14 July 1953.

81. Arthur Millier, "Fischinger Still Paintings on Exhibit at Pasadena", *Los Angeles Times*, 30 December 1956.

82. Walter Alberti, *Il Cinema di Animazione* 1832–1956 (Turin: Radio Italiana, 1957), pp. 71–73.

83. "Oskar Fischinger", *Cultural Echo* [Los Angeles], 1962, No. 2 (Summer), pp. 50–51 + colour cover.

84. Jules Langsner, "Los Angeles Letter", *Art International*, Vol. VII, No. 3, 25 March 1963, pp. 76–77.

85. Sheldon Renan, *An Introduction to the American Underground Film* (New York: Dutton, 1967), pp. 51, 59, 79, 81–82, 93–95, 116.

86. Mike Weaver, "The Concrete Films of Oskar Fischinger", *Art and Artists*, Vol. IV, No. 2, May 1969, pp. 30–33.

87. William Moritz, "Oskar Fischinger: *Fantasia*'s Forerunner", *Coast FM & Fine Arts*, Vol. XI, No. 6, June 1970, pp. 44–45.

88. Birgit Hein, *Film Im Underground* (Frankfurt: Ullstein, 1971), pp. 27, 32, 38–39, 50, 52, 55, 62, 68, 111, 178.

89. David Curtis, *Experimental Cinema: A Fifty-Year Evolution* (London: Studio Vista, 1971), pp. 30, 53–61, 131, 134.

90. Max Tessier, "Oskar Fischinger et la crème de l'animation", *Ecran 73*, January 1973, pp. 29–32.

91. William Moritz, "The Films of Oskar Fischinger", *Film Culture* No. 58–60, 1974, pp. 37–188 + plates.

92. Hans Scheugl and Ernst Schmidt Jr., *Eine Subgeschichte Des Films: Lexicon Des Avantgarde-, Experimental- und Undergroundfilms* (Frankfurt: Suhrkamp, 1974), pp. 280–288 of first volume.

93. Retrospective Oskar Fischinger, The Working Process (Programme booklet), International Animated Film Festival, Ottawa, 1976. Includes: William Moritz, "The Importance of Being Fischinger", pp. 1–6, and André Martin, "Pourquoi il faut voir, revoir et revoir encore les films de Oskar Fischinger", pp. 7–16.

94. Cecile Starr and Robert Russett, *Experimental Animation* (New York: Van Nostrand Reinhold, 1976) pp. 8, 11, 33-34, 41, 57–64, 84, 100–101, 163–164, 181 [reprinted 1988 by Da Capo Press].

95. William Moritz, "Fischinger at Disney – or Oskar in the Mousetrap", *Millimeter*, Vol. V, No. 2, February 1977, pp. 25–28, 65–67.

96. Georges Daumelas, "Oskar Fischinger", *Filmer*, No. 1, Summer 1978, pp. 15–19.

97. John Canemaker, "Elfriede! On the Road with Mrs. Oskar Fischinger", *Funnyworld*, No. 18 (Summer 1978), pp. 4–14.

98. *Film Als Film, 1910 Bis Heute*, ed. Birgit Hein and Wulf Herzogenrath. Kölnischer Kunstverein, 1978. pp. 74–78, passim. English-language version: *Film as Film: Formal Experiment in Film, 1910–1975*, Hayward Gallery/Arts Council of Great Britain, 1979.

99. Herman Weinberg, "Oskar Fischinger Remembered", *Films in Review*, June/July 1980, pp. 369–370?

100. Elfriede Fischinger, "Remembrances", Fischinger, a Retrospective of Paintings and Films (catalogue), Gallery 609 [Denver], 1980.

101. William Moritz, "You Can't Get Then from Now", *Los Angeles Institute of Contemporary Arts Journal*, No. 29, Summer 1981. pp. 26–40, 70–72.

102. John Canemaker, "The Abstract Films of Oskar Fischinger", *Print*, March/April 1983, pp. 66–72.

103. Ingrid Westbrock, "Zur Spezifik der Produktions- und Distributions-modalitäten im Werbefilm am Beispiel Oskar Fischingers"'m in *Der Werbefilm* (Hildesheim/Zurich/New York: Olms, 1983), pp. 92–101.

104. Joan Lukach, *Hilla Rebay: In Search of the Spirit in Art* (New York: George Braziller, 1983).

105. William Moritz, "Critical Essay on Oskar Fischinger", *Cinegraph, Lexicon Zum Deutschsprachigen Film*, ed. Hans-Michael Bock (Munich: Edition Text + Kritik, 1984).

106. Elfriede Fischinger, "Writing Light", *The Relay* [Visual Music Alliance, Los Angeles], Vol. III, No. 2, May 1984, pp. 4–7.

107. William Moritz, "The Spirals of Oskar", *Spiral* [Pasadena], No. 2, January 1985, pp. 50–59 + cover.

108. William Moritz, "Towards a Visual Music", *Cantrills Filmnotes* [Melbourne], Nos. 47/48, August 1985, pp. 35–42.

109. William Moritz, "The Private World of Oskar Fischinger", in *The World of Oskar Fischinger*, Pioneer Laserdisc SS098-6015, 1985. Contains 14 Fischinger films, 100 still photos of paintings, and a biographical booklet.

110. William Moritz, "Abstract Film and Color Music", in *The Spiritual in Art: Abstract Painting 1890–1985* [catalogue of exhibition, Los Angeles 1986, The Hague 1987], (New York: Abbeville, 1986), pp. 296–311.

Italian version: "La Drammaturgia Cromatica", *Teatro Contemporaneo*, Vol. VI, No. 11–12, May 1986, pp. 167–186.
Dutch edition: William Moritz, *Het Mysterie In De Abstracte Film* (Amsterdam: Nederlands Filmmuseum, 1987), 48 pp.
German edition: "Abstrakter Film und Farbmusik", *Das Geistige In Der Kunst: Abstrakte Malerei 1890–1985* (Stuttgart: Urachhaus, 1988), pp. 296–311.

111. William Moritz, "Towards an Aesthetics of Visual Music", *ASIFA Canada Bulletin*, Vol. XIV, No. 3, December 1986, pp. 1–3.

112. William Moritz, "Der Traum von der Farbmusik", *Clip, Klapp, Bum* (Cologne: DuMont, 1987), pp. 17-160.

113. Susan Ehrlich, "Oskar Fischinger", *Turning the Tide; Early Los Angeles Modernists, 1920–1956*, Santa Barbara Museum of Art, 1990, pp. 63–67 + booklet and colour plates.

114. William Moritz, "Film Censorship During the Nazi Era", *Degenerate Art; The Fate of the Avant-garde in Nazi Germany* (New York: Abrams, 1991), pp. 184–191.

German version: "Filmzensur während der Nazi-Zeit", *'entartete Kunst' – Das Schicksal Der Avantgarde Im Nazi-deutschland* (Munich: Hirmer, 1992), pp. 184–191.

115. Marianne Lorenz, "Oskar Fischinger", *Theme and Improvisation: Kandinsky and the American Avant-garde* (Dayton Art Institute, 1992), pp. 159–162 + plates.

116. William Moritz, "Oskar Fischinger: Leben und Werk", *Optische Poesie* (Frankfurt: Deutsches Filmmuseum, 1993), pp. 7–90.

117. William Moritz, "Oskar Fischinger: artiste de ce siècle", *L'Armateur* [Paris], No. 12, July/August/September 1994, pp. 29-33.

118. Giannalberto Bendazzi, "Oskar Fischinger", in *Cartoons: One Hundred Years of Cinema Animation* (London: John Libbey & Co. Ltd, 1995), pp 120–125.

119. Martina Dillmann, *Oskar Fischinger (1900–1967), Das Malerische Werk* (Frankfurt: Goethe Universität, 1996). Dissertation.

120. William Moritz, "Oskar Fischinger in America", in *Articulated Light* (Boston: Harvard Film Archive/Anthology Film Archive, 1995).

121. William Moritz, "Oskar Fischinger" in *L'Art du Movement*, ed. Jean-Michel Bouhours (Paris: Centre Pompidou, 1996), pp. 154–158.

122. William Moritz, "In Passing ... Elfriede Fischinger" (Los Angeles: Animation World Magazine, 1999). Online archives at www.awn.com

123. William Moritz, "Oskar Fischinger: Artist of the Century", in KINETICA-2 catalog (Los Angeles: iotaCenter, 2000).

124. John Canemaker, "The Original Laureate of an Abstract Poetry", *New York Times* (New York, 2000).

Please visit The Fischinger Archive website at www.oskarfischinger.org for updated information.

Index of Illustrations